SUPPORTED EMPLOYMENT

SUPPORTED EMPLOYMENT

Providing Integrated Employment Opportunities for Persons with Disabilities

Thomas H. Powell

Eastern Montana College

Ernest L. Pancsofar

Institute for Human Resource Development
Glastonbury, Connecticut

Daniel E. Steere

Institute for Human Resource Development
Glastonbury, Connecticut

John Butterworth

Boston College

Judy S. Itzkowitz

Institute for Human Resource Development
Glastonbury, Connecticut

Beverly Rainforth

University Center at Binghamton State University of New York

Longman
New York & London

Supported Employment: Providing Integrated Employment Opportunities for Persons with Disabilities

Longman, 95 Church Street, White Plains, N.Y. 10601

Associated companies:
Longman Group Ltd., London
Longman Cheshire Pty., Melbourne
Longman Paul Pty., Auckland
Copp Clark Pitman, Toronto

Executive editor: Raymond T. O'Connell
Production editor: Ann P. Kearns
Text design: Betty L. Sokol
Cover design: Betty L. Sokol
Text art: Fine Line Inc.
Production supervisor: Joanne Jay

Library of Congress Cataloging-in-Publication Data

Supported employment: providing integrated employment opportunities for persons with disabilities.
p. cm.
Includes bibliographical references.
1. Handicapped—Employment—United States. 2. Vocational rehabilitation—United States. I. Longman (Firm)
HD7256.U5S877 1990
362.4'0484—dc20 90-30857
ISBN 0-8013-0504-7 CIP

ABCDEFGHIJ-MU-99 98 97 96 95 94 93 92 91 90

We dedicate our work to:

Quincy Abbot
Peg Dignoti
Terry Edelstein
Charlie Galloway
Baruch Gould
Ed Preneta
Rita Schilling

Whose belief in supported employment and tenacity to make a system change has made integrated employment a reality for many persons with severe disabilities.

If something good happens to people because of human service programs, then the task before us is to create the employment and support services that demonstrate that independence, productivity and social integration are not elusive concepts, but have value for developmentally disabled adults. Goethe expressed this concept well when he purported to have said, "If you treat an individual as he is he will stay as he is, but if you treat him as if he were what he ought to be and could be, he will become what he ought to be and could be."

R.L. Schalock and M.L. Hill, "Evaluating Employment Services"

CONTENTS

Preface xiii

CHAPTER 1 **An Overview of Supported Employment 1**

What Is Supported Employment? 2 / Supported Employment Is a Concept 5 / Supported Employment Is *Not* an Outcome! 8 / Phases of Supported Employment 8 / Supported Employment Models 9 / Who Benefits from Supported Employment? 11 / The Employment Specialist 11

CHAPTER 2 **Searching for Excellence through Guiding Principles 13**

Why Have Guiding Principles? 14 / Developing a Supported Employment Creed 14

CHAPTER 3 **Career Planning for Persons with Severe Disabilities 19**

Goals of Career Planning 20 / Who Should Be Involved? 21 / Steps in the Career Planning Process 21 / Summary 28 / Action Options 28

CHAPTER 4 **Compatibility Analysis 29**

Introduction 30 / Breaking the Myths 30 / Developing a Compatibility Analysis 31 / Summary 39 / Action Options 39

CHAPTER 5 A Team Approach 40

Implementing the Transdisciplinary Team Model 42 / Identifying the Supported Employment Team 44 / Action Options 45

CHAPTER 6 Instructional Tactics 47

Instructional Strategies: What Are the Options? 48 / Antecedent Changes 48 / Consequent Changes 54 / Modification of the Task 56 / Summary 58 / Action Options 58

CHAPTER 7 Assessment Strategies in Supported Employment 59

Natural Cues 61 / Task Analysis 61 / Conducting Baseline Assessment 64 / Formative and Summative Assessment Strategies 66 / Graphing Data 75 / Action Options 80

CHAPTER 8 Helping Employees with Behavioral Challenges 81

Introduction 82 / Help Is Possible 83 / Guiding Principles Associated with Behavior Change 83 / The Behavioral Intervention Process 86 / Select Interventions 91 / Closing Remarks on Behavioral Intervention in Community-based Employment 97 / Action Options 98

CHAPTER 9 Ongoing Supports 99

Introduction 100 / Listing of Supports 100 / Range of Activities 101 / Activity by Level of Intensity 102 / Monthly Profile 103 / Weighing the Benefits and Challenges 103 / Action Options 103

CHAPTER 10 Goal Setting 105

Introduction 106 / Goal-setting Steps 106 / Goal-setting Example 108 / Summary 114 / Action Options 115

CHAPTER 11 Coworkers and Supervisors 116

The Critical Role of an Employment Specialist 118 / Roles and Functions of the Coworker 119 / Coworkers as Friends or Advocates 119 / The Coworker as Observer: Social Validation Strategies 122 / The Coworker as an Instructor: Overt Support Strategies 123 / The Coworker as Partner: Direct Participation Strategies 125 / Summary 125 / Action Options 126

CHAPTER 12 Assisting Families 127

The Family System 128 / Needs of Families 130 / What Families Need to Know about Supported Employment 131 / Benefits of Supported Employment 133 / Families as Key Team Members 134 / What Families Are Looking For 134 / What Employment Specialists Can Do 135 / What to Do When Problems Occur 136 / Action Options 137

CHAPTER 13 Generalization of Work and Work-related Behavior 138

Planning for Generalization 139 / The Generalization Map 140 / General Case Programming 142 / Implementing General Case Programming 144 / Summary 145 / Action Options 145

CHAPTER 14 Assisting Employees with Special Medical and Physical Needs 146

Medical Conditions 147 / Medications 147 / Employee Safety 152 / Assisting Employees with Physical Disabilities 153 / Action Options 164

CHAPTER 15 Creative Problem Solving 165

"There Are No Gurus" 166 / A Simple Strategy 166 / Steps for Creative Problem Solving 166 / Action Options 172

CHAPTER **16** **Transition from School to Supported Employment 173**

The Process of Transition **175** / Transition Principles **175** / The Role of Family **176** / School Preparation **176** / Individualized Transition Planning **178** / Adult Services **178** / Conclusion **179** / Action Options **179**

CHAPTER **17** **Effective Management for Supported Employment 180**

Employment Specialist Roles and Functions **181** / Developing the Position **183** / Training and Orientation **183** / Career Development **184** / Sources of Employment Specialist Support **184** / Action Options **187**

CHAPTER **18** **Governmental and Regulatory Issues 189**

Issue: SSI **190** / Issue: SSDI **191** / Issue: PASS **192** / Issue: Volunteering **192** / Issue: Subminimum Wage **193** / Issue: Incentives for Employers **194** / Summary **195** / Action Options **195**

Bibliography 196

Appendix A *Forms for Program Implementation 203*

Appendix B *Quick Reference for Emergency First Aid Procedures 273*

Appendix C *Checklist to Use to Determine Whether Buildings Are Accessible to People with Physical Disabilities 281*

Index 287

PREFACE

Just a few years ago many of us did not know the term *supported employment,* much less how to provide it. In the past few years professionals, consumers, family members, and employers have recognized the value of supported employment in assisting individuals with disabilities in their quest to become full, participating members of their communities. In this brief time period, supported employment has become a major vocational service option for persons experiencing severe handicaps.

Since the advent of vocational rehabilitation, people with severe disabilities were not considered truly employable and were either not provided vocational services or were relegated to segregated programs. The typical vocational program for persons with severe handicaps was characterized by no activity, no pay, and no escape. Many of these people remained in work activity day programs for life with no real outcomes other than a place to go. It became clear that people served in these programs were not realizing the promise of an improved quality of life.

Discontented with the status quo and the obvious failure of traditional vocational programs, professionals and parents began experimenting with new ways to provide meaningful vocational services. As a result of these efforts *supported employment* emerged. Bolstered by numerous research studies and demonstration projects that illustrated the efficacy of the new approach, supported employment has become an accepted and viable alternative to the restrictive, segregated vocational programs of the past.

Since 1984, public laws, regulations, and funding have helped to make supported employment available to individuals experiencing severe handicaps. Through special grants from the U.S. Department of Education, many states are developing comprehensive supported employment services. Over the next decade we should see a proliferation of these services so every person with a disability can have the option of supported employment.

Providing supported employment services is the *right* thing for us to do. Properly implemented, these services lead to tangible outcomes for the consumer—outcomes such as relationships with others, greater community participation, higher wages, meaningful contributions, and opportunities to exercise greater levels of choice and freedom. Providing supported employment is also the *smart* thing to do. Through supported employment services people with disabilities pay taxes and contribute to the commonwealth of society and become less dependent on social services. Supported employment services help improve the quality of life experienced by persons with disabilities.

Supported employment programs provide opportunities for excitement and joy as well as challenge and frustration. Implementing supported employment will require not only knowledge and skill but also a strong set of values.

However viable supported employment may be, it will not serve people with severe disabilities unless those providing the service are competent and committed to the values inherent in the concept. This book attempts to provide a foundation for those professionals who will directly implement supported employment services. Written especially for employment specialists (also known as job coaches), the book can also be used by program supervisors and vocational rehabilitation counselors. Parents, social workers, and those funding supported employment can use the book to learn about minimum standards for program implementation. The eighteen chapters cover essential ingredients for comprehensive supported employment services. The chapters have been arranged in a sequential order with precise learning objectives to assist the employment specialist with mastery of the content. The intent is also to serve as a regular reference for the employment specialist. The content, procedures, and forms should be referred to as one develops the skills to address new supported employment challenges.

So how should one proceed?

First, employment specialists must have a *sense of urgency*. Too many citizens with disabilities are without aggressive vocational programs. Too many people are sitting in segregated settings waiting for competent, caring professionals to act. More supported employment programs are needed today.

Second, employment specialists must approach service provision with a *questioning attitude*. Is the service improving an individual's life? Is the individual establishing real relationships? Does the service lead to a career? Are the services geared to teaching new skills? Are the services as aggressive as they can be?

Third, employment specialists must be committed to *integrity* in terms of professional skills. Implementing supported employment services will require continual refinement of knowledge and skills. Individuals with disabilities rely on employment specialists to use state-of-the-art procedures. Employment specialists have been entrusted with the provision of critical services to people who are vulnerable. This trust cannot be taken lightly.

Fourth, a spirit of *collaboration* must be adopted by all who provide supported employment services. Employment specialists must cooperate with other professionals, family members, and the business community. Without a team spirit, the best intended services will fail.

Fifth, employment specialists must be *advocates* for persons with disabilities. They need to champion the right to community services. They must confront barriers to full community participation and be vigilant in pursuit of full citizenship for persons with disabilities.

Finally, employment specialists need to be committed to *outcomes* rather than the *process* of supported employment. Improving a person's quality of life is the essential element of supported employment. The process of supported employment may vary as new methods are discovered; thus, the employment specialist must remain flexible, focusing on the outcomes rather than specific models. Employment specialists should remain firm in their commitment to improve the lives of people with disabilities.

To all those employment specialists willing to take the challenge of learning to provide the best possible supported employment services, I hope you find this book valuable in your practice.

ACKNOWLEDGMENTS

Throughout the production of this book we were fortunate to receive the advice and assistance of many colleagues, consumers, and friends. We would like to thank Tom Calo, Hope Costa, Linda Goodman, Paul Harvey, Beth McArthur, Tony Hecimovic, Jan McNabb, Linda Rammler, and Robin Wood for their substantial contributions, which enhanced the quality of our work; Loreli Jenkins, Noreen Jones, Theresa Mahoney, Greg Gerard, Jerry Fisher, Pat Reiners, Myrene Peterson, Jean Monahan, Judy Schopfer, R. N., and Cindy Dell for their assistance with the technical aspects of earlier versions of the book; Bill McLellan for keeping us honest in our work; Ron Rucker for his vision; and our families for providing us with time, encouragement, and support.

Finally we wish to thank all the employment specialists and their supervisors who used the first drafts of this book to help establish supported employment programs. It has been because of their commitment to quality integrated employment that many persons are receiving supported employment services.

Thomas H. Powell

CHAPTER 1

An Overview of Supported Employment

The need for expanded training and employment opportunities for developmentally disabled adults is obviously created to increase economic self-sufficiency and social assimilation. Without that opportunity, the productive contributions of over a million of our citizens are needlessly limited.

W. E. Kiernan and R. H. Bruininks, "Demographic Characteristics"

Learning Outcomes

After reading this chapter you will be able to

- Describe the rationale for supported employment.
- List the four major goals of human service programs.
- List ten vocational needs of persons with disabilities.
- Describe the concept of supported employment and describe its six critical characteristics.
- Describe the four phases of supported employment.
- List six major goals or outcomes of supported employment programs.
- Describe five models of supported employment.
- List the job duties and characteristics of employment specialists.

WHAT IS SUPPORTED EMPLOYMENT?

Stedman gets up every day at 6:30. He takes a shower, puts on his work uniform, has breakfast, and waits for his ride to work at a local restaurant. When he arrives, he punches in on the time clock, puts on his apron, and begins his daily tasks working in the kitchen. After two hours he takes a coffee break with one or two other employees. At lunch time he orders from the menu of the restaurant. Around 2:00 he punches out and waits for his ride home. Like all the employees in the restaurant, Stedman participates in company parties, social events, and the other work activities. Stedman has been employed for three years and has received a number of raises, putting his hourly wage well above minimum wage. Stedman has severe mental retardation as well as hearing and visual impairments, yet he is a successful employee. He earns wages, completes critical work, has friends, participates in his community, learns new skills, and contributes to society. Stedman has realized the outcomes of supported employment.

Who Is Served by Supported Employment

Supported employment has been intended to serve individuals with severe disabilities who have not benefited from traditional vocational programs. These persons were either excluded from community services, were institutionalized, or were in segregated vocational programs for long periods of time. Supported employment has been proven to be an effective vocational option for numerous individuals with disabilities.

Supported employment has been successful for:

Persons with prolonged mental illness
Persons with cerebral palsy
Persons with mental retardation
Persons with traumatic brain injury
Persons with spinal cord injuries
Persons with sensory impairments
Persons with critical health problems
Persons with severe epilepsy
Persons with neurofibromatosis

Persons with Down's syndrome
Persons with spina bifida
Persons with tuberous sclerosis

as well as other developmental and acquired disabilities.

The Goals of Human Service Programs

Human service programs serving persons with disabilities must be dedicated to four major goals.

1. To help individuals develop a sense of self and their own values
2. To help individuals develop relationships with other people
3. To help individuals perform life skills as independently as possible
4. To help individuals make contributions to society

These four goals direct the nature and scope of human services. These goals are presented in a priority order; that is, developing a sense of self is paramount to developing life skills. Likewise, learning independent life skills is more important than making a contribution to society. It is essential for all human service workers to know these goals and their priority order.

All human services must be designed around accomplishing these four goals. Typically, human service programs develop numerous objectives to address each goal. These objectives include skills to be taught as well as services to be provided. No objective or service should be provided that impedes one of these goals.

The Vocational Needs of Persons with Disabilities

People with disabilities have the same needs in regard to employment as other people. These needs include:

A Career. Individuals should have specific careers that lead to various job experiences.

Paid Employment. Members of society earn wages to provide for their needs and enjoyment.

Opportunities for Career Advancement. Many workers seek to increase job responsibilities and duties as they advance.

Benefits. Through job-provided benefits individuals are able to take care of health needs and enjoy periodic paid vacations from their work.

Security. Most workers prefer situations in which they know that their jobs will continue in the future.

Training Opportunities. Employees are often given in-service training to advance skills as well as to ensure opportunities for career advancement.

Fair Bosses. All employees seek supervisors who will be fair and treat them with dignity and respect.

Friendly Coworkers. Workers wish to be associated with a group of colleagues who are friendly and helpful. Work is enhanced by the interactions of the people who work together.

Safe Work Conditions. No employee should jeopardize health or safety as the result of work performed. Well-lighted, well-ventilated locations as well as safe machinery and tools are needed by all workers.

A Reasonable Commute. Most employees work in the vicinity of their residence. While reasonable commuting distance varies, many workers prefer no more than a one-hour commute to work.

Along with common needs many people with disabilities have special vocational needs. These special needs include:

Competent Helpers. People with disabilities require the assistance of skilled professionals who practice state-of-the-art procedures.

Advocates. People with disabilities often require the assistance of individuals who will help them learn their rights and entitlements in terms of vocational services. Advocates can help provide access to the maze of service options.

On-the-Job Support Services. People with disabilities typically require special assistance to complete job assignments. This special support varies and is detailed throughout this manual.

Work-Related Support Services. People with disabilities sometimes require assistance with aspects of their life that are indirectly related to employment. Living arrangements, after work recreation and medical needs all influence work performance.

Any comprehensive vocational service will systematically address these fourteen needs of persons experiencing disabilities.

Defining Supported Employment

It is sometimes helpful to consider how the term *supported employment* is defined in official language of laws and regulations. Supported employment was first introduced into federal legislation with the Developmental Disabilities Act of 1984, (Public Law 98–527). This act (*Federal Register,* 1984) defined supported employment as:

Paid employment which

- Is for persons with developmental disabilities for whom competitive employment is unlikely and who, because of their disabilities, need on-going support to perform in a work setting;
- Is conducted in a variety of settings, particularly work sites in which persons without disabilities are employed;
- Is supported by any activity needed to sustain paid work by persons with disabilities including supervision, training, and transportation.

Later, the 1986 Rehabilitation Act-Amendments (Public Law 99–506) also presented a definition of *supported employment* to guide the development of these new services. This act (Federal Register, 1987) defined supported employment as

(i) Competitive work in an integrated work setting with ongoing services for individuals with severe handicaps for whom competitive employment—
 (A) Has not traditionally occurred, or
 (B) Has been interrupted or intermittent as a result of severe handicaps, or
(ii) Transitional employment for individuals with chronic mental illness.

As used in the definition of *supported employment:*

(i) "Competitive work" means work that is performed on a full time basis or on a part time basis, averaging at least 20 hours per week for each pay period and for which an individual is compensated in accordance with the Fair Labor Standards Act,
(ii) "Integrated work setting" means job sites where—
 (A) (1) Most coworkers are not handicapped; and
  (2) Individuals with handicaps are not part of a work group of other individuals with handicaps; or

(B) (1) Most coworkers are not handicapped; and
(2) If a job site described in paragraph (A)(2) of this definition is not possible, individuals with handicaps are part of a small work group of not more than eight individuals with handicaps; or

(C) If there are no coworkers or the only coworkers are members of a small work group of not more than eight individuals, all of whom have handicaps, individuals with handicaps have regular contact with non-handicapped individuals, other than personnel providing support services, in the immediate work setting;

(iii) "Ongoing support services" means continuous or periodic job skill training services provided at least twice monthly at the work site throughout the term of employment to enable the individual to perform the work. The term also includes other support services provided at or away from the work site, such as transportation, personal care services, and counseling to family members, if skills training services are also needed by, and provided to, that individual at the work site;

(iv) "Transitional employment for individuals with chronic mental illness" means competitive work in an integrated work setting for individuals with chronic mental illness who may need support services (but not necessarily job skill training services) provided either at the work site or away from the work site to perform the work. The job placement may not necessarily be a permanent employment outcome for the individual; and

(v) "Traditionally time-limited post-employment services" means services that are—
(A) Needed to support and maintain an individual with severe handicaps in employment;
(B) Based on an assessment by the State of the individual's needs as specified in an individualized, written rehabilitation program; and
(C) Provided for a period not to exceed 18 months before transition is made to extended services provided under a cooperative agreement pursuant to Section 363.50.

SUPPORTED EMPLOYMENT IS A CONCEPT

The best way to consider supported employment is as a concept that has a number of critical attributes or characteristics. Each of these characteristics must be met in order for a service to be considered supported employment. Every supported employment program must contain seven critical characteristics.

Critical Characteristic 1—*Integration*

Perhaps the most essential of all characteristics of supported employment is the opportunity for persons with disabilities to work alongside others who do not have disabilities. Unlike other vocational options for persons with disabilities, supported employment makes a commitment to foster true integration among people with and without disabilities. Integration must occur at all levels of employment including production, coffee and lunch breaks, use of facilities, transportation, and after-work activities. The level of integration is one measure of the success of supported employment services.

In supported employment programs, workers with disabilities are fully integrated into the general production of the business. Work is not brought to a special area; nor do workers with disabilities congregate in a special location within the business. Special facilities are *not* used by workers with disabilities.

Naturally, some jobs provide greater opportunities for integration.

However, in any job one way to foster greater integration is to limit the number of persons with disabilities at a particular job site. *No more than six workers or 5 percent of the work force* (whichever is *less*) should be at any employment site.

Integration does not mean mere physical presence. It does mean full participation in all activities in which other employees participate. True integration provides opportunities for relationships and friendships among all employees. It is incumbent upon the supported employment service to support integration of workers with disabilities.

Critical Characteristic 2—*Wages and Benefits*

Every person served by supported employment must be paid for work completed. Like other employees, their wages should be directly related to job titles and work performed. Workers with disabilities need to receive wages as well as benefits that are similar to those of their coworkers. They should receive sick leave, vacation, health benefits, bonuses, training opportunities, and other similar benefits received by other employees. The goal of all supported employment programs must be to start workers with disabilities at no less than minimum wage. Where less than minimum wage is needed, as the result of the severity of a person's disabilities, a special work certificate is required (See Chapter 18). To enhance an individual's economic self-sufficiency, supported employment programs must provide at least an average of twenty hours of paid employment per week. Most of society needs to work full time to enjoy the freedoms associated with economic security. Persons with disabilities are no different.

Critical Characteristic 3—*Placement First*

Unlike traditional vocational programs, supported employment places a person on the job and provides training and support that is directly related to the job. More traditional programs provide readiness and preparation training. Unfortunately, much of the readiness and other training activities do not lead to paid, community employment. "Place first; train second" is the essence of supported employment.

Many persons with severe disabilities have problems generalizing the skills they learn in readiness programs to actual work situations. Supported employment services adhere to the concept that the most appropriate training is job specific and can be accomplished in the real work environment. Supported employment programs do not have *pre*supported employment training programs.

Critical Characteristic 4—*Zero Reject*

Supported employment was designed especially for those individuals who have severe handicaps. Supported employment is a service for persons who have not benefited from traditional vocational services or who were excluded from vocational training programs. In other words, a person cannot have too severe a handicap to be served by supported employment programs.

It should be noted that supported employment services can benefit many groups of persons, from those experiencing mild to those experiencing severe handicaps. Individuals with prolonged mental illness, mental retardation, physical disabilities, or sensory impairments can benefit from supported employment. No one should be denied access to supported employment services because of the severity of disability.

Critical Characteristic 5—*Flexible Support*

The aim of supported employment is to deliver a wide range of necessary services that will allow individuals with disabilities to be productive employees. Since the type of support that is delivered must be individually determined, the supported employment program will need to offer a variety of services. The program should not limit its support to just a few options. The fewer the support services, the fewer number of persons will benefit from the program. Support services can include any program that helps the individual to be successfully employed. These may include (but are not limited to):

After-hours job club
Assistance with banking and wages
Coworker training and support
Career development
Extra job supervision
Family services
Job evaluation
Job modification
Job securement
On-the-job training
Personal care services
Transporation

Along with delivery of support, flexibility must be maintained as to who will deliver the support. In some cases the human service provider will deliver support along with family members. In other cases, the employer and coworkers may provide some support. In still other situations, the vocational rehabilitation counselor may provide direct support services. Throughout supported employment services flexibility must be maintained.

Critical Characteristic 6—*Life-long Support*

People with severe disabilities have lifelong needs. Like other aspects of their lives, employment needs will be constant. Supported employment services must allow for ongoing supports to allow the individuals to maintain employment. Like most of society, persons with severe disabilities will hold numerous jobs as part of a career. As a person moves from one job to another the need for support will intensify. If critical support is not provided it is not likely that the person will succeed. It is the responsibility of those funding as well as those providing supported employment to ensure the provision of lifelong support.

Critical Characteristic 7—*Choices*

Supported employment services enhance the person's ability to make choices about his or her life. Instead of telling the person where he or she will work, supported employment allows the individual to develop a number of reasonable options and make a choice about where and under what conditions he or she will work. Choice begins with the development of career preferences and continues with the type of job, the time of work, and the location of employment. Like all workers, the employee with a disability may wish to change jobs or to seek an advanced position. The supported employment service will provide the support to enable the individual to exercise choice.

SUPPORTED EMPLOYMENT IS *NOT* AN OUTCOME!

Some people mistakenly think that supported employment is an acceptable outcome for persons with a disability. Just placing an individual in a job and providing support is *not* a measure of the program's success. Supported employment is *not* an outcome; as noted in the previous section, it is a *concept*.

Acceptable outcomes as the result of supported employment are

Self-esteem
Relationships with other people
Exercise of choice
Development of new skills
Community participation
Improved quality of life
Wages and economic self-sufficiency

Supported employment programs must be designed to achieve these outcomes for the people they serve.

PHASES OF SUPPORTED EMPLOYMENT

Supported employment has four phases. Initially, each phase is developed in a sequential manner. However, after proceeding through this process any of the components may become the principle focus, depending on the unique circumstances of each worker.

Phase 1—Career Planning

Career planning involves the identification of desired outcomes of employment that will enhance the quality of life for individual workers. For instance, developing relationships, earning money, or increasing one's self-esteem are all possible outcomes of employment. Not all people work for the same outcomes. Therefore, the outcomes identified during the career planning phase should be individually developed. A team of people who are committed to improving the quality of life for the worker should participate in the career planning process.

Phase 2—Job Development

Once desired outcomes of employment have been identified for the individual worker, the team should critically analyze several potential jobs to determine the one that will best meet the needs of the individual. During this phase a process called *compatibility analysis* is used to identify good versus poor matches between the worker and specific jobs on factors such as likes/dislikes, scheduling, and strength requirements. In general, workers will have a greater probability of success in jobs that are more closely matched to their abilities and needs. Most importantly, workers should be able to obtain the outcomes that were identified in the career planning phase. If not, the probability is low that employment will have a positive effect on the person's quality of life.

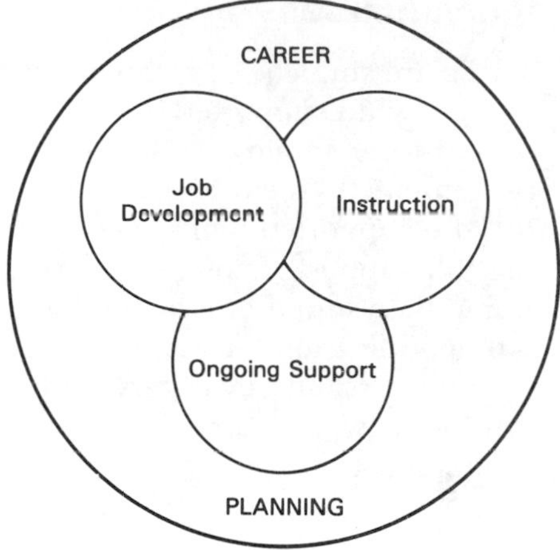

Figure 1.1 Career Planning

Phase 3—Instruction

After a specific employment site has been identified, the worker is placed in the job and receives instruction. During this phase the worker learns the critical work and work-related skills that are necessary at the employment site. Instruction is arranged in a specific sequence for each worker and varies in intensity based on the worker's progress.

Phase 4—Ongoing Support

Supported employment is based on the premise that workers will receive support for as long as it takes. This means that many workers will receive ongoing, lifelong support to continue a successful work experience. In most cases, the intensity of support will decrease over time as workers become more independent.

While it may be easy to consider these phases as rather separate, the fact is that each phase interacts with the others. *Career planning* is the overall phase that is continually addressed throughout every phase. *Job development, instruction,* and *ongoing support* processes will all influence aspects of supported employment services. It may be helpful to consider these phases using Figure 1.1.

SUPPORTED EMPLOYMENT MODELS

Over the past few years, a number of unique models have emerged that enhance the likelihood of achieving the supported employment outcomes mentioned previously. While several models have been described and used, it is important to know that any model that adheres to the critical characteristics mentioned earlier (pp. 5–7) can be considered supported employment. So, there are many possible models for supported employment services. Professionals need to be creative and flexible to investigate all possibilities related to supported employment. The type of supported employment service should be determined by the needs of the individual consumer.

Five major models are typically used to deliver supported employment services.

Individual Jobs

These are single jobs within a business. The individual is employed by the business and supported by the human service agency. These are either full or part-time employment. Ongoing support is provided throughout the job placement. As the individual with a disability learns the job and is successful, the supported employment professional spends less time in actual on-the-job support. Typically, managers and coworkers learn how to provide immediate support to the worker. Ongoing support may include retraining, job modifications, extra supervision, transportation, and meetings with supervisors and coworkers. Typically, these placements provide at least minimum wage, but wages can vary according to Department of Labor regulations.

Apprenticeships

In this model, a person with a disability serves as an apprentice or helper to a tradesperson. The person may be employed in a plumbing business, as a carpentry helper, metal shop helper, delivery helper, or in similar trades. The unique feature is that the individual typically works for one or two skilled individuals and assists in the performance of a particular trade. The person is given on-the-job training by the skilled tradesperson. The human service agency arranges special support such as transportation, supervision assistance, training to the tradesperson, financial incentives, and special equipment. Wages are usually no less than minimum wage and the individual is employed by the business.

Small Enterprise

In this model, a small business is established. Within the small business, a number of workers have disabilities, but no more than individuals without disabilities and never more than six persons with disabilities. The small business operates like any business, generating work and paying employees from revenues received. The small enterprise is located within the community to enhance opportunities for integration. Successful small businesses encourage integration within its workforce as well as with other merchants and businesses. Several successful small business models include restaurants, bakeries, stationery stores, hardware stores, and gift shops.

Mobile Work Crews

This is a special type of small business in which a small group of persons with disabilities (never more than four) performs work for customers at the customer's workplace. These often include janitorial, housekeeping, or groundskeeping services. A supported employment specialist is assigned the duties of supporting the crew via transportation, contract procurement, supervision, and training. Better work crews are set up like a small business and control work to meet the varying needs of the employees. Employees are paid by the supported employment program and wages vary according to the crew members' ability and hours worked. To enhance integration, the crew usually works in places where contact with nondisabled peers is likely. Additionally, emphasis is placed on using community resources such as restaurants, stores, and community services.

Enclaves in Industry

In this model, a small group of persons with disabilities (no more than six) is employed in an industry and receives continual support by the supported employment specialist. Creative enclave models do not cluster the persons with disabilities together, but rather facilitate placement of individuals throughout the work plant. Support is typically more intense in this model. Support is also more systematic, continuous, and reliable. Workers are either paid by the business at a rate of at least minimum wage or as approved by the Department of Labor. Integration is achieved by facilitating interactions among employees at break times, lunch times, before and after work, and through work-related interactions.

WHO BENEFITS FROM SUPPORTED EMPLOYMENT?

Supported employment is a service option that provides benefits to a number of persons.

The person with a disability receives an opportunity for paid employment that leads to relationships, community participation, skill development, economic self-sufficiency, the exercise of choice, and dignity and respect.

Family members have the opportunity to see their loved one as a productive, contributing member of society. Additionally, they may have increased freedom to pursue their own activities.

Business benefits from increased labor resources. Persons with disabilities have a reputation for reliable work production with low absenteeism and low accident rates.

Society benefits because more persons are actively engaged in commerce and the production of goods and services. Persons with disabilities, through their activities and greater economic self-sufficiency, make contributions to society and are less dependent on government resources.

THE EMPLOYMENT SPECIALIST

A unique aspect of supported employment services is the use of a professional called an *employment specialist*. Sometimes this position is referred to as a job coach or employment training specialist. The employment specialist is a key ingredient in the delivery of supported employment services. Employment specialists perform numerous tasks to support the individual on the job. While specific job descriptions vary from agency to agency, these professionals typically provide

- On-the-job training
- Supervision
- Career development
- Assistance locating jobs
- Assistance with job application
- Transportation
- Liaison between business and the human service agency
- Communication with family members
- Analysis of job performance
- Information to other professional team members

Employment specialists need specific competencies in dealing with the various needs of persons with disabilities. They need additional skills to understand and appreciate the needs of businesses in which people with disabilities will be employed. Ideally, the employment specialist will have experience in a relevant human service field, with advanced training in vocational rehabilitation. However, the lack of formal training should *not* be a barrier to performing as an employment specialist. Specific competencies should be the measure of employability for these professionals.

As critical as specific skills, the employment specialist must possess a number of attributes. These include:

Caring. The employment specialist must show true concern for the individual with a disability.

Respect. The employment specialist must be respectful of the person with a disability.

Attentiveness. The employment specialist must listen to the consumer and strive to accommodate the vocational desires of the individual.

Knowledge. The employment specialist must be aware of the vocational options and alternatives available to the individual.

Connected to the community. The employment specialist must know community resources and value community participation.

Sensitivity. The employment specialist must be sensitive to the individual's needs, especially for privacy, dignity, and productive employment.

Zeal. The employment specialist must have a sense of urgency about the employment needs of persons with disabilities.

Advocacy. The employment specialist must be willing to advocate for the rights of persons with disabilities and help ensure that no one abridges or impedes the exercise of those rights.

Employment specialists perform many critical tasks to make supported employment a reality for persons with disabilities. They are teachers, counselors, advocates, and champions. Employment specialists build bridges between the persons they serve, business, and the human service agency and community. Without them, supported employment would remain a dream. Thanks to these professionals, it is a reality.

CHAPTER 2

Searching for Excellence through Guiding Principles

You have to know where you're going, to be able to state it clearly and concisely—and you have to care about it passionately.

T. Peters and N. Austin, A Passion for Excellence

"Developing supported employment alternatives is anything but easy," lamented Jim, an executive director of a small, private human service organization. Just yesterday, several of his board members suggested that people with severe handicaps would be better served in a sheltered workshop. The board members went on to propose the development of a special work facility for persons with severe disabilities. And he thought his resistance to supported employment was going to come from outside his new organization! Well, it might be easy to quote experts and research reports, but Jim took wiser action. At the next board meeting he led a discussion on the organization's values and the principles that must guide the development of new initiatives. He asked the board to reaffirm its values and guiding principles. After the discussion, the proposal for a facility was never raised again. Jim has been encouraged by this board to develop integrated employment options for all his consumers.

Learning Outcomes

After reading this chapter you will be able to

- Develop a set of guiding principles for supported employment programs
- State the legal rights of persons with disabilities

Sarah challenges the best of us. Sarah is 32 years old and has lived most of her life in a nursing home. Sarah does not talk and ambulates with a great deal of assistance. She occasionally hits her face and screams. She requires assistance to complete many life skills. Sarah was fortunate to receive a personal advocate from the Office of Protection and Advocacy. At the recent team meeting the new advocate urged the professionals to develop a supported employment program for Sarah. Although the team members were polite, their amazement at this suggestion was evident. A few finally spoke up. "Is this right for Sarah?" "Will this meet her needs?" "I don't think she belongs in the community, much less in a work environment." "How do we know supported employment is the right type of program?" What followed was a discussion about differing values. Many team members just sat there wondering to themselves, "What do I think?" "What do I value?" "On what principles should I base my decision?" And there was no resolve. No action. No referral to a supported employment program.

WHY HAVE GUIDING PRINCIPLES?

All the challenges inherent in establishing supported employment programs have not been encountered. As more programs are established and more persons served, the number of challenges related to supported employment will increase. And for each challenge, professionals will seek answers. Some answers will be evident, others will not. Some challenges have been carefully researched to determine the best solutions. However, most have not. Professionals will be on their own to consider the best solutions.

What will guide the search for solutions? The best we can hope for is that professionals will be guided by a clear set of values and principles that will focus their search on methods that enhance dignity and opportunity for persons with disabilities. Without a clear set of values and principles the search for solutions will be haphazard and may lead to actions that compete with essential beliefs of the professional, the organization, and the consumer.

Guiding principles help

- Direct the nature of the service delivery
- Clarify to consumers, families, and advocates the rationale and intention of supported employment services
- Guide the development of new programs
- Provide a base to consider options and solutions as they relate to supported employment

DEVELOPING A SUPPORTED EMPLOYMENT CREED

Every day each of us faces new challenges in the development of integrated employment options. There are no easy solutions, no thorough guidebooks, no magic, and no "gurus" to help us face these challenges. We need to turn to clear statements of our beliefs that will serve as a foundation for solutions to challenges.

In periods of rapid growth, turmoil, and confusion it helps to have an anchor. It helps to have some constant that will provide perspective as well as direction. Most human service agencies develop a concise mission statement to provide that perspective and direction.

Given the newness and variability of supported employment endeavors, all agencies implementing supported employment should develop a *creed* concerning their services. These statements will help staff, administrators, board members, and consumers move toward a consensus regarding the aims of supported employment services. As new services are developed the goals and outcomes inherent in supported employment must be clarified for consumers, advocates, families, and the general public.

A creed specific to supported employment programs should

1. Establish the fact that supported employment programs are a new option different from the more traditional services provided by the agency.
2. Clarify the underlying principles upon which the service program is based. A creed provides an essential set of beliefs that say, "This is what we believe and to these statements we will be true."
3. Establish an overall yardstick to measure the program's success. Once the statement is established, evaluation can occur to see if staff and board members behave in ways that support the creed.
4. Provide direction for the continued growth and development of the supported employment programs.
5. Establish a perspective from which to solve problems related to these new vocational options.

Developing a supported employment creed will require time and careful attention. Like all effective statements it should be brief and preferably contained on one piece of paper. The actual development of the creed should involve staff and board members in an interactive process of discussion and debate. Instead of having a creed mandated for them, those who will follow it must be vested in its development. A starting point is to simply ask staff and board members to develop their own personal creeds, which are then shared with the group. From these individual statements comes an overall agency creed. Involving all agency personnel and directors helps ensure that the creed will be practiced.

Naturally creeds evolve as new information and experience enhance understandings of supported employment. Continual reassessment of beliefs and operating principles is very much a part of the creed development process. Devoting time at the first staff meeting and the first board meeting to analyze the agency creed and how it is carried out sets the stage for a renewal of beliefs and commitment.

Agencies and professionals implementing supported employment owe it to themselves and their consumers to develop a creed for supported employment.

One Set of Guiding Principles

As you begin to consider your guiding principles and values it may be helpful to review those held by others. Agencies wishing to clarify their organizational values may find it useful to consider other statements of principles that have been adopted by other organizations. While it is not suggested that you simply adopt the guiding principles of other organizations, statements adopted by other agencies can serve as a benchmark to begin the development of your own creed.

The Institute for Human Resource Development in Connecticut has articulated a number of principles that guide the development of services and support programs.

People with Disabilities Are Entitled to Full Participation in All Aspects of Life within Their Communities. Persons experiencing disabilities have the same legal and human rights as all other persons. They are full members of society and have the right to fully participate in community life. This participation includes, but is not limited to

Attending civic meetings
Community employment
Eating in restaurants
Joining a church or synagogue of choice
Joining clubs and organizations
Living where they choose
Purchasing a home
Shopping
Using community health facilities
Using public transportation
Using recreational facilities
Voting

All supported employment programs must enhance the value that individuals with disabilities are entitled to full community participation.

Integrated Employment Allows Persons with Disabilities to Continue to Develop to Their Fullest Potential. Supported employment programs help individuals with disabilities by giving them opportunities to develop new skills, especially social skills and specific work competencies. Employment provides a natural motivation for learning new skills and developing one's potential.

Integrated Employment Assists Individuals in Becoming Contributing Members of Their Communities. Too often society does not view people with disabilities as contributors to society's commonwealth. Supported employment assists persons with disabilities with an opportunity to contribute to their society. Contributions focus on the product or service the person produces. Secondary contributions include taxes paid, goods purchased, relationships established, and service to others. Supported employment programs reassert that people with disabilities can enhance the quality of community life via their contributions.

People with Disabilities are Capable of Being Integrated into Local Work Settings. Most community employment opportunities can meet the employment needs of persons with disabilities. Most jobs can be adapted or modified to allow the person with a disability to be a successful, productive employee. The role of the supported employment program must be to identify and provide the right level of assistance to ensure that the community employment situation will be successful for the worker as well as the supervisor.

Valued Work Provides Opportunities for Building Respect, Dignity, and Self-Esteem. People with disabilities must be afforded opportunities to perform valued work for their communities. Through work, one not only develops skills and new relationships, but more importantly develops self-esteem. As coworkers and the general public witness the completion of valued work, the dignity and respect given to the individual will increase.

Persons with Disabilities Should Be Afforded Opportunities to Make Choices in Pursuit of a Personal Future. All persons should have choices in regard to their lives. Supported employment programs must provide choices in terms of career, types of jobs within career areas, hours of employment, and how wages are spent. Naturally, choices are often influenced by the necessities of life; however, within that reality persons with disabilities must be given choices as to how they want to work, where, and under what conditions.

Persons with Disabilities Must Be Paid a Fair Wage for Work Completed. It is illegal to have persons with disabilities perform work without paying them. Unfortunately, many people with disabilities perform work for subminimum wages. Supported employment programs must strive to secure employment that will pay at or above minimum wage. It is impossible to realize the outcomes of supported employment if the individual does not make the necessary wages to enjoy an improved quality of life. Volunteer or charity work is not acceptable for supported employment programs.

Employment Specialists, Employers, and Coworkers Are Powerful Allies in Facilitating the Entry of People with Disabilities into Valued Roles of Society. Persons developing and implementing supported employment programs have a unique role in assisting people with disabilities. Likewise, employers and coworkers are instrumental in helping people with disabilities become full, contributing members of society. Supported employment programs must recognize the unique role these individuals play and must actively support them.

Family Members Must Be Actively Involved in the Supported Employment Process. Family members should be encouraged to become team participants in the delivery of supported employment programs. Parents, siblings, aunts, uncles, and grandparents often have unique perspectives about the person with a disability. Family members can help ensure that supported employment programs truly meet the needs of individuals. Family members should also be encouraged to evaluate supported employment programs and meet regularly with habilitation teams.

Employment Is Only One Part of the Range of Experiences and Relationships That Contribute to an Individual's Happiness and Success. While work is a critical aspect of most lives, other aspects of life are equally, if not more, important. Certainly someone's family and friends are paramount to one's work. Home life, recreation, spiritual endeavors, and hobbies greatly contribute to a person's sense of self and quality of life. Supported employment programs must recognize and foster the value of experiences other than employment of persons experiencing disabilities.

No Person Should Be Denied Access to Supported Employment because of the Severity of That Person's Disability, Behavioral Deficits, or Behavioral Excesses. As discussed in Chapter 1, supported employment was initially designed for those individuals who were denied access to traditional vocational programs. If support is flexible and intense, every person can benefit from supported employment opportunities.

The Value of Supported Employment Programs Should Be Judged in Terms of the Outcomes Provided to Persons with Disabilities. The bottom line for all supported employment programs is the quality of life experienced by the individual with a disability. Supported employment must lead to tangible outcomes that improve the quality of life.

These twelve guiding principles are easy to write, easy to read, and easy to adopt. They are much more difficult to implement and live. Supported employment programs and professionals must articulate a set of guiding principles that will provide direction to staff, consumers, families, employers, and advocates. Once a core set of principles is adopted, these principles can be used to judge the effectiveness of the program.

CHAPTER 3

Career Planning for Persons with Severe Disabilities

None of us makes our life alone. We rely on a variety of formal and informal resources to create better life experiences.

— *J. O'Brien, "A Guide to Life-Style Planning"*

Mary works at a large firm that manufactures small parts for industrial machinery. At work she has the opportunity to interact with her coworkers, both those with and without disabilities. She earns enough money to purchase a new coat that she has desired for some time. Since she left the workshop she has felt increasingly proud of her abilities at work, especially as she increases her speed with her work assignments (and increases her pay!). Her parents often brag to their friends about their daughter's success. Mary is happiest about her job because it is the one that she chose, not one that was selected for her. Clearly Mary's new job has had a positive impact on many aspects of her life.

Learning Outcomes

After reading this chapter you will be able to

- Describe a process for determining desired quality of life outcomes for participants in supported employment
- Complete an outcome compatibility analysis for a particular worker and job
- Evaluate the placement of a worker in terms of the outcomes that were specified by a career planning team

For all individuals, employment should be a vehicle for attaining an improved quality of life. Most of us work at our present jobs for a variety of reasons, including the opportunity to develop relationships, improve our skills, make money, and gain the respect of our colleagues, friends, and family members. In addition, most of us have held several jobs that have given us access to these desired outcomes of employment, and we may change jobs because we feel that a new position will allow us to obtain a better quality of life. For many workers, then, career goals are a guiding force in the choice of employment activities and environments.

Workers who experience significant disabilities also desire a better quality of life and consequently their career goals should be a driving force in the development of employment opportunities within integrated community environments. Too often, workers with severe disabilities are placed in jobs that are available without consideration of the potential of these employment sites to contribute to the overall quality of their lives. In addition, initial placements for persons with disabilities are often thought of as permanent, with no opportunities to move to other desired jobs. In this chapter, a career planning process is described that can be used to assist workers with disabilities to obtain employment based on individual quality of life factors. The approach that is described is a *lifelong process* that is based on the assumption that, like many nondisabled individuals, persons with severe disabilities may hold many jobs throughout their lives in order to best attain an improved quality of life.

GOALS OF CAREER PLANNING

As described in Chapter 1, supported employment consists of four phases or components: career planning, job development, instruction, and ongoing supports. These phases are considered to be ongoing and overlapping. In particular, career planning is a process that continues throughout a worker's employment and does *not* end after the attainment of a particular job. The recommendations that are made in this chapter should be considered within the framework of these four phases of supported employment.

The process of career planning that is described here is based in part on the work of O'Brien (1987a) and on the work of the staff of the Positive Futures Project in Connecticut, notably Beth Mount and Joe Patterson. It is based on the assumption that work has a broad impact on the quality of life of individuals. Variables that affect personal job satisfaction at work are probably similar to those that affect the job satisfaction of any worker. Moseley (1988) suggests that attention be given to such variables as autonomy and control over the task, the social culture of the workplace, wages, and task complexity. More importantly, career planning suggests that there are variables that are unique to each individual that define whether a job will have a positive impact on that individual's quality of life (O'Brien, 1987a). Major goals of the career planning process include

- To assist the worker to describe his or her vision of a desirable personal future
- To define the individual standards that a job must meet in order to support realization of that vision and to enhance quality of life
- To plan and organize resources to support employment in a job that meets individual quality of life standards
- To establish an ongoing process that emphasizes a lifelong approach to career planning and recognizes that personal priorities change as each person develops

WHO SHOULD BE INVOLVED?

It is clear that significant others play an important role in how effectively people find and maintain jobs. In Vermont a full 83 percent of recent graduates of special education found jobs on their own or through family or friends (Hasazi, Gordon, & Roe, 1985). Family and friends also provide critical support that affects whether workers keep their jobs over time (Brickey, Browning & Campbell, 1982; Turnbull & Turnbull, 1988). Career planning emphasizes a team process that involves those individuals who play the most significant role in the worker's day-to-day life, and should represent all of the major environments that the individual participates in: home, school, work, social, and recreational.

STEPS IN THE CAREER PLANNING PROCESS

Suggested steps for the process of career planning for workers in supported employment follow:

1. Orientation
   Establish the career planning team.
2. Develop a Personal Profile
3. Identify Individual Quality of Life Outcomes
   A. Brainstorm quality of life outcomes that describe an optimal employment situation for the identified worker.
   B. Prioritize the top outcomes.
   C. Specify standards for each outcome.
4. Compatibility Analysis
   Compare the specific quality of life standards identified in step 3 to specific job-opportunities.
5. Analysis of Challenges to Optimal Employment
   A. Identify potential/real challenges.
   B. Brainstorm solutions to these challenges.
   C. Prioritize five solutions to each challenge.
6. Action Plans
   Develop an action plan.

Recommendations for the completion of each of these steps are detailed throughout this chapter.

Step 1: Orientation

The first activity is to identify those perons who will serve on the career planning team and to orient them to the career planning process. The members will assist the worker to develop a personal profile and to define those personal quality of life outcomes that they want to achieve through work. Team members will also be the individuals who are most critical to the implementation of supports for the worker. Team members should include persons who work or live with the worker on a day-to-day basis and who know him or her as a friend as well as on a professional basis. The worker should help determine who will participate in the career planning process and should be encouraged to invite friends. A team leader is designated to coordinate the group process.

The active career planning team should be a small working group of no more than six to eight people in most cases. Figure 3.1 illustrates the career planning team for Chris. Chris is the central participant in the career plan-

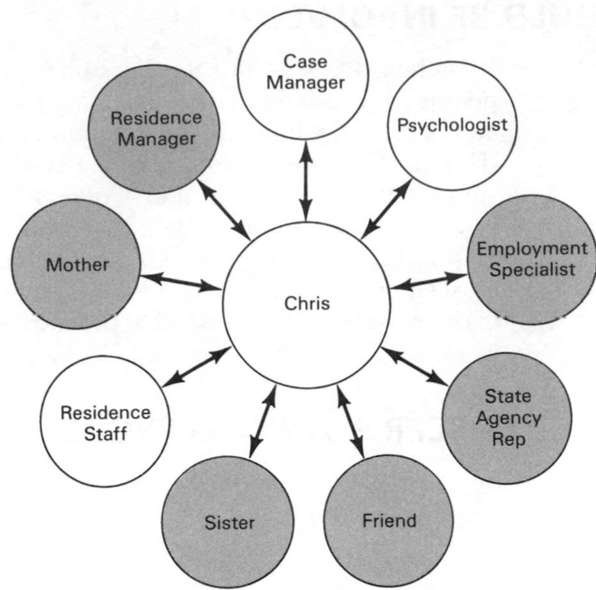

Figure 3.1 Career Planning Team for Chris

ning process and occupies the center of the diagram. Participants include the following:

Shaded Circles: The Career Planning Team

Significant others who are active members of the career planning team.

These members have a commitment to identify valued quality of life outcomes and to implement and support job opportunities that achieve these outcomes.

Open Circles: Other Interested Persons

Interested persons who need to be kept informed about career planning activities but who should not be involved in week-to-week meetings about the worker.

These persons are typically not day-to-day participants in the person's life but have some interest in or responsibility for the services the person receives. In Chris's team the case manager, while not someone who has daily contact with Chris, has been included in the active career planning team as a liaison to some of these resources and to the formal interdisciplinary team that reviews Chris's individual service plan.

The team should be convened in a place that is comfortable and relaxed for each member. Often the worker's own living room or kitchen is the best location. Once the career planning team has been convened, it is helpful to orient the members to the major steps that will be followed. A typed agenda is a useful tool for reviewing the steps and for focusing the meeting. The team should also make sure that no one has been left out of the process who should be involved, and that each of the members present is comfortable, and willing and able to participate in the team process.

Step 2: Develop a Personal Profile

A profile of the individual needs to be developed by team members. Excellent strategies for developing these profiles have been initiated through Positive Futures Planning conferences (cf., O'Brien, 1987a). The profile should focus on personal preferences and interests rather than strengths and weaknesses. Using an easel or large sheets of paper taped to the wall, the leader should lead the team through an exhaustive review of the person's

Personal work history, including paid and unpaid jobs and chores
Likes and preferences
Dislikes
Special interests or activities
Personal choices

The team should review these categories for each of the environments the worker spends time in, including home, school, work, and social or leisure activities. Because many workers do not have extensive work experience, other areas of his or her life may provide important clues to the characteristics of an ideal job.

The personal profile provides the foundation for the remainder of the career planning process. Sufficient time, typically as much as two to three hours, should be spent on this step. This step also is a positive experience for both the workers and others who often have limited participation in service planning meetings, such as family. The focus on information that these participants know best and the emphasis on *positives* rather than weaknesses or needs play an important role in setting the groundwork for later steps and ensuring full participation by all team members.

A portion of the personal profile for Chris is included in Figure 3.2. Notice that both home and work have been reviewed in detail.

Step 3: Identify Individual Quality of Life Outcomes

A. Brainstorm Quality of Life Outcomes. Once the profile has been developed the team leader initiates a brainstorming session to generate a list of possible quality of life outcomes of employment. These outcomes are identified by organizing and interpreting the information in the personal profile and reflect quality of life dimensions that are desired by the individual and that may be attained as a direct result of employment. Example outcomes may include self-esteem, friendships, recreational opportunities, financial security, integration, and choices.

Team members should first concentrate on attempting to draw from the worker his or her perception of desired outcomes. The team leader should list possible outcomes on large sheets of paper as members suggest them. The member who suggests an outcome should also give a brief definition that identifies the individual's perception and intent of the outcome. The outcomes listed by Chris's team are shown in Figure 3.3.

B. Prioritize the Outcomes. In this step the planning team needs to narrow the outcomes that were suggested and listed in the previous step. Group consensus should be reached on whether each outcome is equally important to the worker, and if necessary the list of outcomes is narrowed to the top four to six. For example four outcomes were clearly identified as equally important for Chris in Figure 3.3, but for Randy a large number of outcomes were initially identified. Randy's outcomes are listed in Figure 3.4. They were narrowed down to two that were considered most important and three additional ones that were slightly less important to Randy.

Personal Profile

Chris

Work

Resume	Likes	Dislikes
Pembroke Gardens	Work with crew	Changes
MTS Gift Shop	Plants and flowers	Pembroke after crew left
Light assembly	Machines	Down time
	Liked all jobs	Dirt

Home

Likes	Dislikes
Magazines	Nothing to do
Chores	Staying home
Libraries/books	Being in group if others have disabilities
Typewriter	Unfamiliar people
Staying busy	

Choices

Goes to work even when sick
Not socializing with other residents from house

Figure 3.2 Personal Profile for Chris

C. Specify Descriptors for Each Outcome. Each of the outcomes that has been identified by the initial planning team is now looked at more closely. Specifically, examples of descriptors that serve as standards for each outcome are listed through a similar process as the brainstorming for the original outcomes. For example, if integration was the outcome under discussion, sample descriptors might include (a) developing a friendship with a coworker who has no identifiable disability, or (b) that the proportion of disabled to nondisabled workers is no more than 1 to 10.

Each outcome for Chris and Randy has from one to several descriptors listed that make it possible to clearly identify whether a job opportunity does or does not meet the requirements for that outcome. Members of the team may also want to take selected outcomes and arrange a sequence of acceptability for each descriptor from minimally acceptable to the ideal situation.

Outcomes

Chris

Pride in accomplishment

- A clear completed product

Work for work's sake

- Keeping busy
- Minimal down time
- Steady work

Structure and routine

- Routine
- Consistency
    - Supervisors
    - Coworkers
    - Schedule

''Normal'' work environment

- Nonhandicapped coworkers

Figure 3.3 Quality of Life Outcomes for Chris

Step 4: Initial Compatibility Analysis

The career planning team now integrates the information on outcomes for the person and begins the process of matching the outcomes with possible current and future employment opportunities. A modified compatibility analysis is used to compare the worker's outcomes and corresponding descriptors with the conditions of existing or known job options (see Figure 3.5). This outcome compatibility match provides an initial screening of compatibility prior to investigating jobs in more detail, and should be used concurrently with more skill-based compatibility matching techniques (cf. Moon, Goodall, Barcus, & Brooks, 1986).

For example Chris can be compared to two possible jobs, one planting ivy and pachysandra at Pembroke Nursery and one doing packaging and

Outcomes

Randy

High Priority

People

- Opportunity for friends
- A work group or team

Choices

- Flexible schedule
- Variety
- Able to choose order of tasks

Medium Priority

Active

- On your feet
- Outdoors and/or space

Full Day of Work

- Day shift
- 4 to 6 hour day

Money

Figure 3.4 Prioritized Outcomes for Randy

assembly for the Packit Corporation. Both jobs meet the standards of pride in accomplishment and a normal work environment. Clearly, work in a seasonal job at Pembroke Nursery does not provide a good match on work for work's sake because of down time in the off season, and for stable structure and routine for the same reason. Much of the workforce is seasonal

STANDARD	PEMBROKE'S	PACKIT
Accomplishment	+	+
Work	−	+
Routine	−	+
Environment	+	+

Figure 3.5 Compatibility Analysis

and many changes in routine and coworkers occur in the fall and winter. Work at Packit does a better job of meeting Chris's outcomes, providing a steady supply of work year round, a clear routine, and membership in a stable team of coworkers.

Step 5: Analysis of Challenges to Optimal Employment

A. Identify Potential/Real Challenges. As employment types (i.e., work crew, enclaves, individual placements, small businesses) or specific jobs are considered, the career planning team lists all the potential barriers or challenges that impede movement from a current placement to the work option that matches outcome descriptors most closely (Figure 3.6). All challenges are listed on a worksheet for additional consideration. Examples of challenges include staffing and funding issues, transportation problems, and interfering behaviors.

B. Brainstorm Solutions to These Challenges. Each challenge from the previous step is addressed separately through a brainstorming process. Career planning team members brainstorm potential solutions to each identified challenge. All solutions are initially recorded by the team leader from the lists established by each member. These solutions are written as a list on a board or easel for all team members to view. All possible solutions are accepted, and creative ideas are encouraged. In order for this step to be effective, an attitude must be adopted by the team that is based on the belief that a creative solution exists for each challenge and that all possible solutions are worthy of consideration.

C. Prioritize Five Solutions to Each Challenge. Potential solutions that were identified for each challenge in the previous step need to be analyzed to determine their feasibility. A Likert scale may be used to prioritize the solutions from which action plans will be developed. The team members rate each solution on a 1 to 5 scale of feasibility and a discussion begins about their ranking. Team members can adjust their ranking, and the team leader develops an average ranking and lists the top five solutions for each barrier.

Step 6: Action Plans

Develop an Action Plan. Action plans are developed to address the solutions for each challenge. The action plan specifies the activities, responsible persons, timelines, and follow-up activities that are necessary to ensure that activities are accomplished (see Figure 3.7). These action plans form the framework within which the challenges will be overcome.

Following the completion of the action plans, the members of the career planning team should continue to meet on a follow-up basis to monitor the

1. Placement resources not available for 3–6 months
2. Public transportation not available: Rural area
3. Behavioral challenges (stealing, object destruction)

Figure 3.6 Barriers to Work Outcomes

1. Identify short-term work placement
   who: Work Program Manager
   Case Manager
2. Resolve transportation for short-term placement
   who: Residence
   Case Manager
3. Begin job development
   who: Work
4. Problem-solve regarding long-term transportation planning and behavioral challenges
   who: Team

Figure 3.7 Action Plan

completion of team activities. The steps of the career planning process should lead smoothly to the activities in the job development phase, as described in Chapter 4.

SUMMARY

Career planning for persons with severe disabilities is a critical activity in the development of quality supported employment programs. The process that was described in this chapter provides a mechanism for establishing priority career goals that are geared toward the improvement of the quality of life for each worker. Although the process that has been recommended may be modified to meet the needs of specific agencies or individuals, the basic premise of focusing on the desired outcomes of employment is critical. The selection of employment opportunities for persons with severe disabilities should therefore be guided primarily by the contribution of employment to the quality of the lives of workers and not merely by the availability of jobs.

Action Options

- Participate on a career planning team for a worker in your agency.
- Make a list of 10 preferences for one person you support.
- Make your own list of quality of life outcomes that you consider essential.

CHAPTER 4

Compatibility Analysis

Finding a job for a person is not the problem; job openings are available almost daily. The real challenge is to find the job that is right for the individual.

M. Barcus, Personal Communication, 1985

John is successfully working for a company that publishes an advertising circular. His duties include making telephone contacts to delinquent accounts to encourage prompt payment. Since John's appointment, delinquent accounts of over three months have dropped by half. John secured this employment after a job development specialist obtained information about his desires, aspirations, skills, special needs, and critical factors that contribute to successful long-term employment for an individual with cerebral palsy. As the job developer was searching for employment, she compared John's profile with similar factors in several work opportunities. After comparing the pros and cons of each critical factor, the marketing company appeared to offer John conditions best matched to his personalized outcomes. Through this compatibility matching process, John and all persons with disabilities have a brighter future and higher probability of success at employment options as they advance in their selected professions.

Learning Outcomes

After reading this chapter you will be able to

- List three myths that hinder people with disabilities in securing employment
- Describe the rationale and process of a compatibility analysis
- List factors that could contribute to workers with disabilities leaving or remaining at future employment sites
- Describe the process of contacting employers and beginning the initial job development activities
- Describe the matching process and provide a rationale for determining an excellent, good, or poor match for two sample factors within a compatibility analysis

INTRODUCTION

Compatibility analysis is the process of comparing the requirements of a work environment with the current assets and needs of a prospective worker. This process involves a careful analysis of all factors that are presumed to influence the long-term success of the worker. After completing this thorough analysis adequate supports can be planned and implemented. The percentages are now in the favor of the worker and there is an increased probability for success. This chapter begins with a discussion of traditionally held views regarding employment readiness and continues with a detailed explanation of the process of conducting a compatibility analysis.

BREAKING THE MYTHS

There are several long-held beliefs about the development of employment skills for persons with severe disabilities. Many of these beliefs are myths that need to be dispelled, since they place unnecessary restrictions on individuals who are targeted as "not work ready."

Myth: Prerequisite Skills

The myth that specific prerequisite skills need to be mastered before advancing to more involved activities originates from a developmental model of instructional sequencing for students who acquire skills in structured education settings.

For example, in order to tell time from a regular clock face, the prerequisite skills might involve recognizing the numbers 1 through 12, distinguishing the hour hand from the minute hand, recognizing the hour, half-hour, and quarter-hour positions of the hands, and so on. Instructors conduct sessions of building skills that eventually lead to the ability of the individual to correctly tell time from a clock. However, telling time may not be an essential skill for a worker to possess. Rather, managing one's time using the natural cues within the environment may be much more essential and more easily mastered than progressing through 15 steps to learn to tell time. The concept of prerequisite skills is an idea of the past when addressing the needs of adolescents and adults who are entering employment. There are many creative ways to generate alternative solutions to presumed deficits. These deficits should not hinder the opportunities for individuals to experience the world of work as soon as possible.

Myth: Continuum Approach

There has been a long-held belief that individuals need time in a variety of work environments before community employment is secured. History does not support this premise. For example, in the continuum approach individuals with severe handicaps would begin in a work activity center and when they mastered some designated exit criteria would advance to a sheltered workshop. In the sheltered workshop there are different levels of advancement. Each level contains its own exit criteria that may eventually lead to employment in the community. Even when community employment becomes a reality, there typically exists a continuum of restrictiveness from enclaves and work crews toward advancement to an individual placement.

The premise appears at first to be a sound one. Unfortunately, it is an unnecessary set of criteria that is not supported by research to verify its value. On the contrary, there is ample evidence to support the concept of identifying the best community placement that is based on a matching of employee and work factors. From this analysis the immediate supports are determined that enable the optimal placement to occur *now* instead of waiting for the potential employee to exit from several previous stages of employment readiness. The entire concept of supported employment is based on identifying the supports, providing those supports for as long as it takes, and fading assistance in a gradual, steady manner while monitoring the worker's progress.

Myth: Traditional Vocational Assessment

Traditional vocational assessment instruments are based on norms established by peer groups whereby scores can be established relative to the standing of the individual to those norms. In their favor, these devices assist in identifying individuals who should be eligible for services that are targeted for persons with severe handicaps. The misuse occurs when these same assessment tools to get people into a system of services are used to make predictions about their future potential for succeeding in employment. This is a gross misuse of these tests and they should be avoided when making decisions about matching individuals with employment opportunities within the local community. Some useful information can be obtained from traditional assessment batteries (e.g., medical information, sociological background, likes and dislikes). However, they should take a backseat when making decisions about the future supports that can be established to enable an individual to access community employment.

DEVELOPING A COMPATIBILITY ANALYSIS

The remaining sections of this chapter highlight the *steps* of a compatibility analysis and include

1. Proactive planning
2. Job retention
3. Employment observation
4. Participant observation
5. Developing matches
6. Initial screening
7. Single factor analysis
8. Decision making

Step 1: Proactive Planning

A major assumption for requiring a compatibility analysis is that planning supports for anticipated challenges to employment increases the probability of future success in community employment. A visual that illustrates this need to be proactive was first observed on a billboard for a local bank (see Figure 4.1).

This same advice holds true for an initial placement of a worker in the community. If the steps outlined in this chapter are not adhered to, the employment specialist and supervisor will be reacting to crisis after crisis and end up blaming the worker for failing. Instead, careful planning and developing of good matches between employee and work environments is essential to *plan ahead* and not be caught short.

Figure 4.1 You Need to Be Proactive

The initial work of a compatibility analysis follows from the quality of life outcomes that were developed in the career planning process (see Chapter 3). Team members need to quantify each outcome and be prepared to distribute this list of standards to the personnel who are responsible for completing the compatibility analysis. The placement of an individual into community employment is founded upon the premise that access to work allows for attainment of that person's quality of life outcomes.

Step 2: Job Retention

There were many reasons why we chose to remain at or leave previous jobs that enabled us to advance to our current occupation. This is a good place to begin to understand the factors that are included in a compatibility analysis. Reasons for remaining at jobs may have included a financial bonus, valued friendships, flexibility of time, location from home, educational requirements, personal fulfillment, etc. Alternatively, many of us left jobs due to low pay, conflict with supervisors, moving to a new locale, it wasn't what we thought it would be, etc. If you had known more about the job and how it matched your needs, would that job have still been selected?

Factors to Consider. Just as we select new jobs based on our needs, competencies, reinforcers, and experiences at previous jobs, individuals with disabilities have these same experiences with some additional challenges. Wehman (Wehman and Moon, 1988) and his colleagues developed an initial list of factors that contributed to individuals leaving their employment in the community. This initial list included factors associated with employment sites:

Appearance
Attention to task
Availability of reinforcement
Behavior acceptance
Changes in routine
Communication
Discrimination skills
Employer attitude
Employer's financial needs
Endurance
Initiation of work
Interactions
Mobility
Orientation
Rate

Schedule
Strength
Task sequencing
Time management
Travel location

This list is an excellent place to begin to identify factors for a compatibility analysis. However, it is just a beginning and the following suggestions need to be heeded to develop a format that is unique to the specific needs of your agency:

Survey past participants in community employment and list the reasons these workers failed to maintain their employment.
Include unique aspects of local participants.
Include unique aspects of the local economy.
Include outcome analysis factors from career planning as described in Chapter 3.

For example, accessibility is a factor of need for individuals who use wheelchairs for mobility. The hazards of specific machines are necessary factors for school-age students below the age of 16.

Thus, the first step in developing a compatibility analysis that specifically addresses the needs of your agency is to develop a list of factors to investigate the present challenges for individuals with disabilities with whom you work.

Analysis of Key Factors. After identifying the factors that will be included in the compatibility analysis from your agency, descriptions for each factor need to be established. For example the factor *availability* could have a range of descriptions, including

Day shift
Weekend
Split shifts
9:00 A.M. to 4:00 P.M. only
Not available for *x* hours each week

After developing a series of descriptions for each factor, an agency develops a master form to be used for its workers and employment sites. These two forms parallel each other so that a comparison of the worker characteristics relative to each factor can be compared to the existing conditions at a prospective employment site. Forms 04 and 23 (Appendix A) were developed for agencies to use as master compatibility analysis forms. They are sample forms for factors that have been identified at an adult service agency for describing a worker's adherence to the descriptions of each factor. In the same manner, a corresponding form is developed from which to evaluate potential employment sites on the same factors that are included on the worker characteristic form. These sample forms are generic for agencies to begin the development of their own forms. Sample formats from three sources are found in Figure 4.2.

Step 3: Employment Observation

After an agency adopts its version of the forms for identifying the compatibility factors for both an employment site and the individuals with whom that agency has contact, the process of collecting the information on the

Agency A's Form:

Endurance:	[ ] Easy [ ] Many breaks	[ ] Demanding [ ] Few Breaks

Comments:

____

____

____

Agency's B's Form:

Endurance:	Short Day Many Breaks	Full Day Many Breaks	Short Day Few Breaks	Full Day Few Breaks
	________	________	________	________

Specifics/Comments:

Agency C's Form:

ENDURANCE

Full Time ________ **Part Time** ________

Breaks	No Breaks	Few Breaks	Many Breaks
________	________	________	________

Comments:

Figure 4.2 Modifications on Job Analysis Form for Endurance

forms begins. The following steps are recommended for completing an employment compatibility form:

Schedule a one-hour block of time with the job site supervisor.
Obtain responses to the items on the form.
Observe currently employed workers.
Summarize the information.

Scheduling Time for an Interview. Before scheduling an hour meeting with the employment supervisor, visit that person and introduce yourself on an informal basis and mention that you will be calling to set up a more detailed information-sharing session in the near future. If the person operates a restaurant, buy a breakfast or at least a cup of coffee. If the person is part of a large chain of operation, find something to compliment the representative about in reference to the company. Leave pertinent information from your agency that describes the critical elements of supported employment, your calling card, and a positive marketing kit. Ask the person to suggest a convenient time to call to set up an appointment and schedule that appointment to meet at the convenience of the company supervisor. Human service professionals need to adopt more flexibile work hours when meeting with business representatives.

Obtain Responses for the Compatibility Form. Don't begin the meeting by presenting the compatibility form and developing a question-and-answer format for the hour. Instead, begin by emphasizing the need to match the needs of the company with the capabilities and needs of the applicants you represent. The better the match, the greater the probability of long-term success.

The interviewer should know the key factors identified for the workers by heart and not have to read all the descriptions from each one. Six factors can be equally spaced on a blank sheet of paper and the job developer can ask general questions about the factor.

For example, if schedule is the first factor, lead questions would include, "What are the typical hours employees in your company work?" "Is there flexibility in the hours?" "Do you have both full and part-time work?" As the supervisor responds to the questions, write key words that quickly summarize what was said. The interviewer needs to have a list of 10 to 12 quality of life outcomes that are being sought by individuals with disabilities from the agency. As the conversation progresses, questions can be asked that provide indications of acceptance on each outcome. For example, one potential worker might be seeking opportunities for developing friendships and might want to converse with coworkers while completing activities. Accordingly, the interviewer can obtain information about work space and the opportunities to converse while working.

Don't try completing the final employment compatibility form at this interview. It will be completed from your notes later. Also, you are bound to be interrupted during your interview. Be patient. If all the information that you need is not obtained at this meeting, schedule a second one as soon as possible. Schedule a time when you are able to observe currently employed workers at the job(s) under consideration.

Observe Currently Employed Workers. Schedule a three- to four-hour block of time to observe currently employed workers at the job(s) under consideration. This observation should be as unobtrusive as possible. If the situation allows, find some validation for what the supervisor related about critical factors that you know will affect the work of individuals who you represent. For example, what did the supervisor tell you about the required rate of work? Is this verified by the worker? Do this in as informal a manner as possible. Remember, your intent is not to conduct a detailed job skill inventory but to obtain additional information about the factors on the compatibility analysis employment form. (See Forms 04 and 23 in Appendix A).

Summarize the Information. Complete a Job Analysis Form (See Form 23 in Appendix A) based on the information that has been obtained from the interview with the supervisor and the observations at the work site. Have your scoring and comments typed and obtain a clean copy. Mail the copy to the supervisor with whom you previously met and request that he or she review it for accuracy and additions. Typically, the supervisor has not seen an analysis completed in as much detail as the one he or she is reading. Send a letter and the completed form to the supervisor's boss expressing your appreciation for the time he or she took to meet with you and to complete the compatibility form.

Call the supervisor three days later and find out if the information is accurate and if you can now proceed to screen prospective applicants for positions that match their needs and abilities.

Step 4: Participant Observation

Each prospective worker at the agency who is being considered for supported employment needs to have a current participant compatibility analysis form in their files. Some agencies employ job developers who typically do not know the proper responses to the factors; therefore, they need to identify the key persons to obtain the information. This can be achieved either in one-to-one interviews or by chairing a general planning meeting where the responses to each factor can be obtained through a consensus of the opinions of the significant members who are present. The job developer presents each factor and asks for the most critical concerns that need to be addressed and considered in an employment site relative to each factor. Regardless of the method used, it is critically important to receive verification and validation that the ratings are shared by a majority of people who know the participant and are not the biased opinions of one or two people.

As discussed in Chapter 3, the most critical factors to initially consider are the outcomes that are expected to be achieved through employment. These outcomes will be the driving force for determining the weights of the factors. Following these meetings, the job developer completes a draft of the participant form and sends it to the participating team members for verification. The job developer then calls each member for final comments within three days.

Step 5: Developing Matches

Based on the observations and information from the two compatibility analysis forms, an initial decision is made about the type of match that occurs. A recommended process is to view each pair of factors as an excellent, good, or poor match. If sufficient information is lacking, mark it as undecided.

Excellent Match. An excellent match occurs when the needs and accommodations of the employer contain many similarities to the needs and abilities of a prospective worker. An excellent match requires little intervention by the employment specialist to address this factor. Using the example of endurance, we see that an excellent match could be decided if the circumstance represented in Figure 4.3 occurred.

Good Match. When circumstances are observed that generally favor the worker's job compatibility, a good match is made. There may be aspects of the job or needs of the worker that will require some attention, but there is a reasonable expectation of success. The example in Figure 4.4 with the "Endurance" factor would receive a good rating.

Poor Match. When there is a clearly negative difference between the information on the job form and that on the participant form, a poor match occurs.

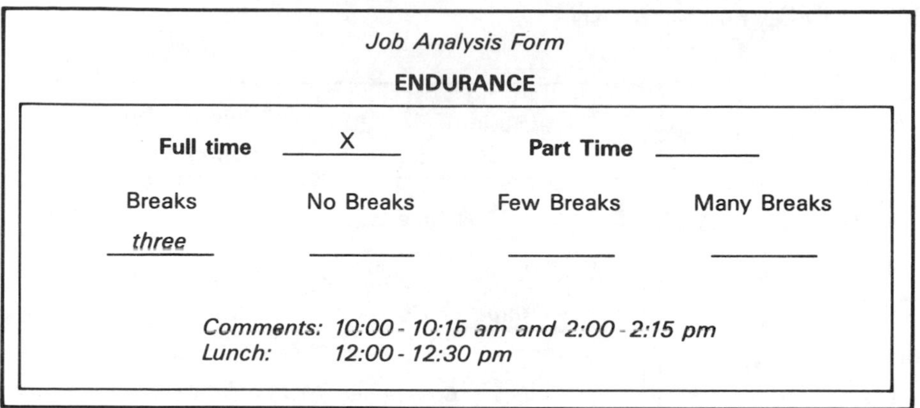

Job Analysis Form

ENDURANCE

Full time X **Part Time** ________

Breaks	No Breaks	Few Breaks	Many Breaks
three			

Comments: 10:00 - 10:15 am and 2:00 - 2:15 pm
Lunch: 12:00 - 12:30 pm

Participant Analysis Form

ENDURANCE

Length of Time Working/Playing Before Needing a Break	Typical Number of Breaks Throughout the Day
2 hours	*4*

Comments: excellent stamina; doesn't tire easily; in good physical health

Figure 4.3 An Excellent Match on Endurance

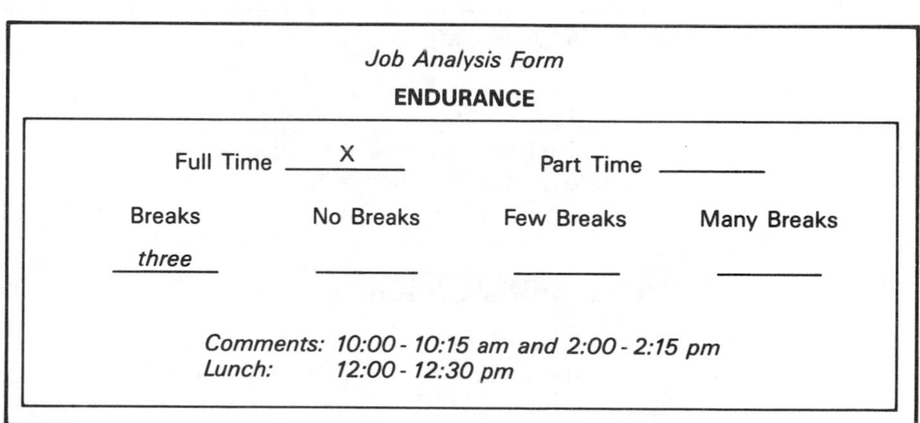

Job Analysis Form

ENDURANCE

Full Time X Part Time ________

Breaks	No Breaks	Few Breaks	Many Breaks
three			

Comments: 10:00 - 10:15 am and 2:00 - 2:15 pm
Lunch: 12:00 - 12:30 pm

Participant Analysis Form

ENDURANCE

Length of Time Working/Playing Before Needing a Break	Typical Number of Breaks Throughout the Day
approx. 1/2 hour	*6-8*

Comments: has only had part time jobs; good physical health

Figure 4.4 A Good Match on Endurance

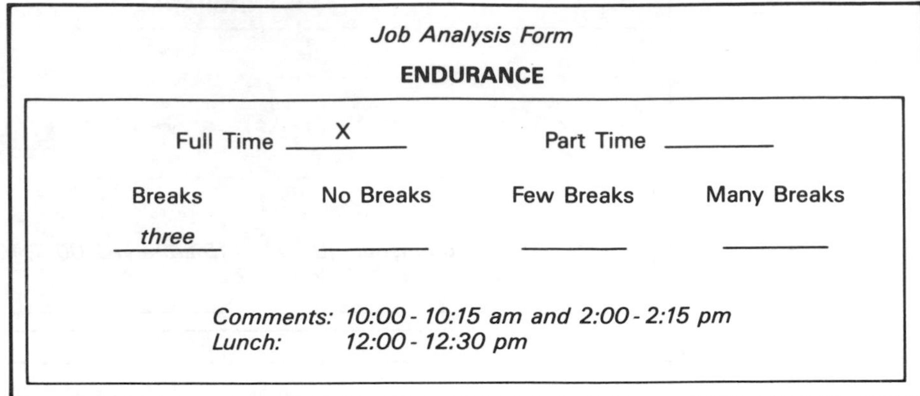
Job Analysis Form

ENDURANCE

Full Time X Part Time ______

Breaks	No Breaks	Few Breaks	Many Breaks
three			

Comments: 10:00 - 10:15 am and 2:00 - 2:15 pm
Lunch: 12:00 - 12:30 pm

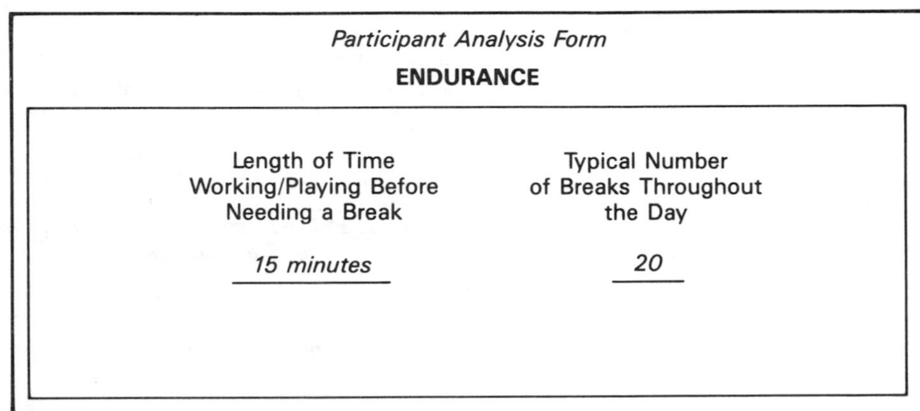
Participant Analysis Form

ENDURANCE

Length of Time Working/Playing Before Needing a Break	Typical Number of Breaks Throughout the Day
15 minutes	*20*

Figure 4.5 A Poor Match on Endurance

Extraordinary effort would need to occur to bridge this gap. This doesn't preclude the job from being investigated further; it just indicates that on this factor, endurance, a poor match currently exists (see Figure 4.5).

Step 6: Initial Screening

A job analysis form is completed for each prospective employment opportunity in the community. Additionally, a corresponding participant employment screening form is completed or is on file for each prospective candidate for available community employment. A review team meets and compares the responses on each factor and develops a consensus based on the currently available information from both forms. If members of the group agree, the designated match (excellent, good, poor) is entered on the participant's summary page. An "undecided" description is obtained when team members disagree on a match or if insufficient information is available from which a definitive match can be made. A blank copy of the summary page is located in Appendix A. (See Form 06).

Step 7: Single Factor Analysis

A single factor analysis form is used when an undecided initial match occurs. More information needs to be obtained from both the participant and employment perspective. The factor under consideration is written at the top of the form. In the right column a more in-depth description about the work site is included. In a similar way, more complete information about the participant is included in the left column. A decision about the type of match is then agreed upon only after this more in-depth discussion about the factor with the additional information supporting the decision. A copy of this form is located in Appendix A. (See Form 05).

Step 8: Decision Making

There are no formal computer-generated answers for determining the ultimate feasibility of obtaining the best matches between participants and community employment sites. At best, a consensus occurs among team members to pursue a decision that makes the most sense with the amount of information available. Team members weigh the pros and cons of each potential match and decide where to proceed from there. It is advisable to isolate the employment/participant factors that should receive more weight as being extremely critical to the long-term success of each participant. Initial planning of acquisition and ongoing supports can be predicted based on the number of excellent, good, and poor matches that exist.

SUMMARY

The steps of a compatibility analysis outlined in this chapter contain the features for each agency/school to develop a unique process. Team members who follow this sequence increase the probability that the best match can occur between workers and their future employment. An agency that adopts a compatibility analysis approach to job development contributes to the long-term success of workers with disabilities.

Action Options

- Develop a list of critical factors within your agency that can be incorporated into the compatibility process.
- Construct a generic participant screening form and a matching job analysis form as an initial assessment form for all consumers within your agency.
- As part of an individual's yearly plan, incorporate the compatibility analysis as a principle assessment process.
- Participate in the compatibility analysis matching process for an individual with a disability.

CHAPTER 5

A Team Approach

Moreover, future professionals must learn to function as educational synthesizers by coordinating a comprehensive transdisciplinary team of professionals, para-professionals and family members. Ultimately, educators must help to train the community-at-large to accept handicapped persons as individuals with an equal right to and stake in the benefits of the normal environment.

N. Haring and F. F. Billingsley, "System Change Strategies to Ensure the Future of Integration"

Learning Outcomes

After reading this chapter you will be able to

- Define a transdisciplinary team
- Describe the transdisciplinary team process and its relationship to supported employment programs
- Describe the roles of various team members, including
  - The person with the disability
  - Employment specialists

- Family members
- Occupational therapists
- Physical therapists
- Physicians
- Psychologists
- Social workers
- Speech and language pathologists
- Vocational rehabilitation counselors

Sarah has multiple handicaps. She has profound mental retardation, visual and hearing handicaps, mobility problems, and tends to have a continual cold. Sarah's family and teachers want her to receive the benefits of supported employment. Sarah's needs are so many and so complex that the talents of a team of caring professionals will be needed.

Employees with disabilities have diverse needs that require the attention of team members from many different disciplines. Traditionally, the members of habilitation teams have recognized the importance of other disciplines, and have made referrals to one another, but in other respects they have worked independently of one another. Although this may have seemed efficient, the result was services that were isolated and fragmented. As shortcomings of the *multidisciplinary* team approach were recognized, habilitation teams adopted the *interdisciplinary* model, in which team members met to discuss evaluation results, discuss needs, and establish a plan of service delivery. A case coordinator was usually assigned to oversee the plan, but services were still delivered as independent entities. The result was a fragmented program, with interventions that were isolated, sometimes overlapping, and sometimes even conflicting (Hart, 1977). An employee with emotional or behavior problems might have simultaneously received medication from a physician, counseling from a psychologist or social worker, and a behavioral intervention from the employment specialist, with little or no communication or coordination among the team members. In an effort to improve service delivery systems, the *transdisciplinary* approach was developed (Hutchinson, 1978).

The transdisciplinary model is based on disciplinary collaboration. Team members are expected to be knowledgeable and skillful and to keep abreast of new developments in their disciplines. From this foundation, each team member systematically engages in the process of "role release" (Lyon & Lyon, 1980), which occurs at three levels:

1. Providing other team members with *general information* about basic procedures and practices
2. Teaching team members to use *specific information* to make treatment decisions
3. Training team members to *implement specific program procedures*

For example, the physical therapist might

1. Provide the other team members with general information about physical disabilities
2. Teach them principles of good posture and general rules for positioning people with physical disabilities

3. Teach the team members to position an employee so the employee can successfully complete tasks in a particular job

The final level of role release clearly involves a high degree of skill by other team members. Without attempting this level of role release, however, the team will most likely use methods of instructing or managing the employee that are ineffective if not detrimental. In contrast, when team members have engaged in all three levels of role release as both teachers and learners, the result is a comprehensive habilitation program into which all services are thoroughly and consistently integrated.

As suggested earlier, the implementation of a transdisciplinary team approach requires a cooperative commitment from all team members. They must not only demonstrate competence in their own discipline, but must also develop skills in a variety of new areas. While most staff enjoy this opportunity for professional growth, the primary benefits of the transdisciplinary team approach are received by consumers (Albano, 1983).

Many people with severe disabilities acquire new skills slowly, generalize across persons and situations poorly, and maintain skills only when there are frequent opportunities for practice (Peterson, 1980). These characteristics are counterbalanced somewhat when a transdisciplinary approach is used. This approach allows the employee to receive instruction on important skills daily or many times per day, rather than periodically. Instruction is also delivered in ways that develop functional clusters of motor, language, social, and work skills, rather than numerous isolated skills that the employee must somehow integrate (Guess & Helmsletter, 1986). There are built-in opportunities for generalization across persons since each team member has similar expectations of the employee. The generalization of skills to new situations is also facilitated since management and instruction procedures are implemented more consistently across the day. The emphasis on clusters of functional skills increases the opportunity to use natural cues and correction procedures that will enhance the maintenance of learning (Peterson, 1980; Sternat, Messina, Nietupski, Lyon, & Brown, 1977). The employee who might have spent only a small portion of the week learning to move or learning to communicate would then learn to use these and other functional skills in a variety of meaningful situations throughout each day.

The transdisciplinary team approach has applications in every aspect of an employee's life, at work, at home, and while learning to use community services. In the context of supported employment training, the employment specialist has primary responsibility for providing instruction to the employee, and therefore becomes a central figure in adopting the transdisciplinary model. The employment specialist will be the focus of most training, the person who synthesizes information and skills from other disciplines, and the primary communicator of information about the employee's job performance and program effectiveness. Every member of the team continues to be a program designer and implementor, a data manager, an observer, a problem-solver, and both teacher and learner. Throughout the process, each team member also continues to be accountable for the practices associated with his or her own discipline (Hutchinson, 1978).

IMPLEMENTING THE TRANSDISCIPLINARY TEAM MODEL

The exact manner in which the transdisciplinary team model is implemented will vary across teams, employees, and employment sites, depending on employee needs and team members' schedules. The following guidelines will assist each team to develop the model that is efficient and effective for its own situation.

Staffing the Transdisciplinary Team

To ensure the transdisciplinary approach can be implemented adequately, the case manager must arrange for services from all the disciplines needed by the employee. When contracting with community service providers, it is important that potential service providers understand that they will be expected to participate in a transdisciplinary team approach. Contracts should include provisions for the direct services that may be needed, as well as time for consultation, team program development, and training/supervision of program implementors. Without arrangements for indirect services, team effectiveness will be limited. Furthermore, the team may find that some employee needs can be met better through indirect services, and direct services may be reduced.

When assembling a team, it is also important to realize that there is variation and overlap in the skills possessed by professionals from different disciplines. The case manager should confirm with potential team members that they can actually provide the types of services needed by the employee. While recognizing this precaution, there are roles that are traditionally associated with different disciplines.

Employment specialists are the primary instructors of employees, and therefore the team members who most often solicit and synthesize information from other disciplines. Employment specialists offer expertise in job development, training, identification of vocational needs, working with employers and coworkers, transportation, and motivation.

Educators who have worked with the employee can offer assistance in terms of vocational programs provided in school settings. They provide a vital source of information on teaching tactics that have proven successful, as well as the employee's past interests and skills.

Vocational rehabilitation counselors are typically responsible for helping to arrange and coordinate an array of service options to facilitate the delivery of supported employment. Like the case manager, the vocational rehabilitation counselor may assemble the team, arrange for funding, and evaluate the outcomes of the service provided.

Physical therapists offer expertise in positioning, handling, and teaching gross motor skills such as walking. They also help select and teach people to use adapted equipment including wheelchairs, walkers, braces, and artificial limbs. Many states require physical therapists to have a physician referral before they can develop programs to provide services.

Occupational therapists offer expertise in fine motor and perceptual motor skills, oral motor skills, and activities of daily living (e.g., self-care, homemaking). They also select or develop adapted equipment, especially to increase independence in work or daily living activities. Some occupational therapists have expertise related to supported employment and vocational rehabilitation.

Speech/language pathologists are knowledgeable about communication skills as well as oral motor skills related to eating and speaking. They offer expertise in selection and instruction on a variety of communication modes (e.g., speech, sign language, picture communication boards). They may also perform analysis of communicative functions and interaction patterns.

Psychologists often have a primary function of performing standardized assessments. They can become more active members of the team, however, bringing expertise in counseling and applied behavior analysis, which are important in programs to reduce inappropriate behavior and concurrently teach more appropriate behavior or problem-solving strategies.

Physicians are involved in all aspects of health care, including health maintenance and treatment of acute and chronic medical conditions. Physicians often engage in role release at the level of information sharing and decision making, but procedures such as dispensing medication, providing a prescribed diet, or performing intermittent catheterization are usually released. Although physicians may be unable to participate in all activities of the habilitation team, it is essential that the entire team knows when an employee is receiving medical treatment, the desired effects, and the possible side effects of such treatment. The team should also establish a regular schedule and procedure for medical status reports that incorporate feedback from all team members serving the employee.

Social workers often fill the role of case coordinator locating services needed by an employee, seeking access to funding, and serving as liaison between the direct service providers and agencies that provide support services. In these activities, social workers usually engage in role release at the levels of sharing information and making decisions, rather than in sharing procedures.

Family members are important members of the habilitation team. When an adult lives with family members, they have important information to share about life-style, preferences, abilities, and needs. Even when an adult lives independently or in a supported living arrangement, family members have relevant information and concerns that other team members need to recognize and respect. In some cases, a family member is the legal guardian for an adult with a disability, giving this person a legal as well as personal concern for the employee. If an adult with a disability has lost contact with natural family members, he may have a legal advocate or friend who assumes the role of surrogate family member. In either event, it is appropriate to recognize this person as part of the employee's team. While family members should be encouraged to participate in the transdisciplinary team process, "professional" team members must also understand demands upon the family that may limit their involvement (see Chapter 12).

As suggested by these descriptions, the different team members may assume different roles. Employment specialists, therapists, and psychologists might all be involved in training employees, while vocational rehabilitation counselors, social workers, and physicians would provide various types of support services.

IDENTIFYING THE SUPPORTED EMPLOYMENT TEAM

The supported employment team develops, implements, and evaluates programs that help the employee initiate and sustain integrated employment. In the interest of using resources well, there is no set composition for a supported employment team. Rather, the team for each employee is composed of the members required to meet individual needs. Therefore, one employee's team may consist of only an employment specialist and a psychologist, while another employee needs the addition of an occupational therapist, a physical therapist, and a speech/language pathologist. Because the transdisciplinary team is needs-based, team members should also be selected on the basis of the skills each person can bring to the team, rather than on the basis of professional titles (Campbell, 1983).

Once the supported employment team is identified, team effectiveness can be enhanced through efficient scheduling for service delivery. Previously an employee might have been sent to a rehabilitation center after work, or sent to another area at the worksite to receive services such as physical therapy. Rather than provide the employee with an hour of direct therapy service twice a week in a separate location, it is preferable that part or all of that time be spent with the employee and the employment specialist at the worksite. This allows team members to observe, work with, and train the employment specialist to use effective methods with the employee during all employment activities. If several team members will provide these indirect services at the worksite it is usually most manageable to schedule team members for different days and/or times.

Facilitating Communication among Transdisciplinary Team Members

If the supported employment team is to be effective, one area that is crucial for team members to address is that of communication. Peterson (1980) asserts that most teams have haphazard and informal communication, however.

Each team must develop mechanisms to assure that communication occurs and that it occurs in a timely and efficient manner. The following strategies may assist in achieving this end:

1. **Need:** Notify responsible team members of questions and concerns about employment.
   Strategy: Write down questions and concerns when they arise, and file in a designated location to be checked regularly.
2. **Need:** Monitor employee performance on many programs.
   Strategy: Record, plot, and analyze data at least weekly.
3. **Need:** Develop solutions to instructional problems.
   Strategy: Engage in group problem solving at team meetings.
4. **Need:** Notify all relevant staff of program revisions.
   Strategy: Discuss program revisions at weekly team meetings; write revision on Instructional Planning Sheet promptly.
5. **Need:** Monitor general employee progress.
   Strategy: Formally review each employee program monthly at a team meeting.

A team meeting can be an important mechanism to facilitate regular communication while providing a forum for staff development. One team member, perhaps the case manager, assumes responsibility for planning an agenda to include program review, problem solving, and training. In addition, the team process can be discussed and problems addressed as they arise, assisting in the development of a smoothly operating, integrated approach to service delivery.

Action Options

- If you are an employment specialist, write down the special needs of your workers. Based on these needs, who should be on the supported employment team for each individual employee?
- Each month, meet with a colleague who represents a different discipline. Find out more about their profession and how it relates to supported employment.

- Facilitating good team communications requires mutual respect and understanding. Next time you meet with a team member, send a follow-up thank-you note, mentioning how their special expertise has helped the person with a disability to be more successful on the job. The follow-up note will go a long way to facilitating future communications and services.

CHAPTER 6

Instructional Tactics

And if that doesn't work, what do you do next . . . ? . . . and next . . . ? . . . and next . . . ?

M. Gold, Did I Say That?

Finally! Theresa has become more independent on her work task. Her employment specialist Bill was beginning to think that nothing he did was going to help Theresa learn, but he never gave up looking for a different approach that might work. Despite his (and Theresa's) previous frustration, Bill feels elated to have discovered one more effective teaching procedure with Theresa and to witness her progress. Although it's a small step, and there will be other difficulties, Bill realizes that his skills as an instructor have had an important impact on Theresa's life.

Learning Outcomes

After reading this chapter you will be able to

- Describe the difference between natural cues and artificial cues (prompts)
- List five natural cues in a work environment
- Determine reinforcers for a worker with severe disabilities
- Develop a prompt sequence for a particular worker
- Teach a complex task using a backward or forward chaining procedure
- Describe a time delay procedure for fading prompts

Workers experiencing severe disabilities present complex challenges to employment specialists. In the past, many professionals have characterized these individuals as too disabled to learn. These professionals blamed the worker for failing when they should have focused their energies on their own lack of teaching skills. In recent years, researchers have documented that individuals with severe disabilities can acquire work and work-related skills if employment specialists employ effective and systematic instructional strategies (Rusch, 1986; Wehman, 1981). The training power that employment specialists possess is directly related to their skill with systematic instructional procedures and creative problem solving (Gold, 1981).

An important consideration about instructional strategies such as prompting, reinforcement, and other procedures that will be discussed in this chapter is that many of these procedures are artificial. That is, these procedures are ones that employment specialists introduce into the work environment and are not ones that would naturally occur in the workplace if the employment specialist was not there. In general, it is preferable for a worker to respond to natural cues and reinforcers in the work environment.

Examples of natural cues in a work environment include

The sound of the work bell
The movements and actions of coworkers
The physical features of the machinery in the workplace

Natural cues are conditions that would occur in the work environment if the employment specialist or worker were absent. Natural reinforcers also occur in work environments, including

Lunch or coffee break
A compliment from the supervisor
A paycheck

Employment specialists should always try to pair artificial prompts and reinforcers with natural cues and reinforcers. The more that workers can respond to natural cues and reinforcers, the greater their independence will be in the work environment.

In this chapter, we will review several critical instructional strategies that, when used effectively, can help increase the employment specialist's power and contribute to more successful outcomes for persons experiencing significant disabilities.

INSTRUCTIONAL STRATEGIES: WHAT ARE THE OPTIONS?

Employment specialists should be skilled in using several effective instructional strategies. Effective employment specialists need to know not only how to use these specific procedures, but also when, under what conditions, and in what combination to use them. Coupled with experience in teaching people with severe disabilities, these strategies enhance the longevity of employment for workers.

As suggested by Pancsofar and Blackwell (1986), the instructional strategies described in this chapter will be organized into three categories:

Antecedent changes
Consequent changes
Modification of the task

ANTECEDENT CHANGES

The first group of training strategies is referred to as antecedent changes. Antecedent changes refer to the employment specialist's intervention before the worker's response. In this section there are examples of antecedent prompting procedures, including specific types of prompts and prompt sequences.

For purposes of our discussion of antecedent changes, we will refer to the activity of operating a commercial dishwashing machine. A task analysis of this activity is shown in the list below.

Task Analysis of Operation of Commercial Dishwashing Machine

1. Press switch to on position
2. Turn lever to open position
3. Watch drain until water stops flowing
4. Turn drain lever to shut position
5. Open door of dishwashing machine
6. Inspect strainer for debris
7. Remove strainer trays
8. Rinse debris into sink
9. Replace strainer trays
10. Close door of dishwashing machine
11. Turn hot water faucet in clockwise direction
12. Watch drain until water flows
13. Turn hot water faucet in counterclockwise direction
14. Open dishwashing machine door
15. Press switch to off position

Prompts: A Definition

Prompts are a form of information that the employment specialist provides the worker before he or she responds to help the worker complete an activity correctly. For example, the employment specialist may point to a particular material to help the worker locate it. A different employment specialist could physically guide the worker's hand or arm to allow the worker to use the correct motion in washing and wiping a table. In both of these examples, the employment specialist provides the worker with extra information to help the worker respond correctly. In the next section we will examine specific types of prompts that may be used by employment specialists.

Type of Prompts

We will now describe eight specific types of prompts that may be used by employment specialists.

Nonspecific Verbal Prompts. Nonspecific verbal prompts are general statements from employment specialists to help the worker perform the correct response. For example, in teaching a worker to operate a commercial dishwashing machine, the employment specialist could use one of the following prompts:

"What do you do next?"
"What is the next step?"
"What's next?"
"Now what will you do?"
"What else do you need to do?"

Nonspecific verbal prompts are usually the least intensive type of prompts, that is, prompts provide workers with the least amount of information to enable them to respond correctly. Nonspecific verbal prompts are also relatively easy to fade as the worker learns to respond independently.

With all prompts, employment specialists should always think about how they will fade prompts so that workers can be more independent in performing their jobs.

Pacing Prompts. A pacing prompt is a type of nonspecific verbal prompt that an employment specialist provides to maintain the pace or rate of a worker's activity. For example, the prompt "Keep working" serves to prompt the worker to continue the present activity. Bellamy, Horner, and Inman (1979) suggest three guidelines for the use of pacing prompts (pp. 156–157):

1. Provide pacing prompts only for those steps on which pauses seem likely;
2. Deliver a pacing prompt just as the worker correctly finishes a step; and
3. Use pacing prompts together with reinforcement for independent initiation of a step

Pacing prompts are thus a special type of verbal prompt that serves to maintain the rate or pace of a worker who might otherwise slow down or pause too long between steps.

Specific Verbal Prompts. Specific verbal prompts provide workers with more information than nonspecific verbal prompts. In using specific verbal prompts, an employment specialist should specifically state the next behavior or response that the worker should demonstrate. For example, in teaching an individual to operate a dishwashing machine, a specific verbal prompt that might be used is: "Next, you need to push the 'on' button."

This prompt tells the worker specifically what the next step is in the operation of the machine. Other examples of specific verbal prompts include

"Pick up the box of detergent."
"Push the dish rack into the dishwashing machine."
"The red light went off. It's time to take out the clean dishes."

Notice that specific verbal prompts are usually given as statements, while nonspecific verbal prompts are often given in question form.

Pictorial Prompts. Pictorial prompts are diagrams that are presented before the worker responds, to give the worker additional information to enhance correct responding. Prior to each step in the operation of the dishwashing machine, for example, the worker could look at the corresponding picture or a picture sequence to determine the next step. The main advantage of this type of prompt is that the employment specialist may not have to be present for the worker to use it. However, picture booklets or cards may be cumbersome in job situations. In addition, many workers need to have an employment specialist present in order to use pictorial prompts correctly. If possible, the employment specialist should always attempt to fade out all extra prompts, including pictorial prompts, in order to increase the worker's independence. If permanent pictures are being planned, the employment specialist must obtain feedback from the employment supervisor about the acceptance of these adaptations to the work environment.

Gestural Prompts. Gestural prompts are motions that the employment specialist makes that direct the worker's attention toward specific materials, or an area of the work environment. For example, pointing to the "on" button on the dishwashing machine is an example of a gestural prompt. Gestural prompts may also take the form of a partial demonstration of the behavior to be performed. For example, the employment specialist could demonstrate the motion of turning on the water in the sink or of wiping the counter tops around the dishwashing machine, without actually touching any of the materials. Thus, gestural prompts are any pointing or motioning by the employment specialist to draw the worker's attention to the important aspect of the task.

Modeling. Modeling is another type of prompt that provides the worker with additional information about the task. During modeling, the employment specialist performs the tasks with the appropriate materials to demonstrate to the worker exactly what should be done next. For instance, in teaching the worker to operate the commercial dishwashing machine, the employment specialist might actually push the dish rack full of dirty dishes into the machine. In order to demonstrate the correct method of prompting, modeling involves the actual use of the materials to be used by the worker. A word of caution about modeling: Once the employment specialist pushes the rack of dishes into the machine and then removes it for the worker to do, the worker may think that putting the rack in and immediately taking it back out is part of the activity.

Partial Physical Prompts. In using partial physical prompting, the employment specialist provides a slight touch to part of the worker's body. For example, the employment specialist might lightly touch the worker's elbow to direct the worker's motion toward the "on" button on the dishwashing machine. This type of prompting is also called partial physical guidance, because the employment specialist is actually guiding the worker's body with a light touch.

Full Physical Prompts. Full physical prompts, like partial physical prompts, involve physical guidance of the worker. However, *full physical guidance,* as the term implies, usually takes the form of firm, complete grasp of the worker's hand, wrist, or elbow. Full physical prompting is the most intensive type of prompting and may be difficult to fade so that the worker is able to work more independently.

The preceding prompts are some of the primary strategies that employment specialists use in training persons with significant disabilities within supported employment settings. In the next section the use of prompts in combination by pairing and by using them in prompt sequence will be described.

Prompt Sequences

A prompt sequence refers to the arrangement of different levels of prompts into a hierarchy or ordered sequence. The purpose of arranging prompts in such a sequence is to systematically provide assistance to workers and to allow for subsequent fading of prompts.

An example of a prompt sequence is as follows:

1. Nonspecific prompt, such as "What do you do next?"
   (Wait three seconds)

2. A combination of a specific verbal prompt plus a gestural prompt. For example: "Push the dish rack into the machine," while pointing to the dishwashing machine.

   (Wait three seconds)

3. A combination of a verbal prompt plus a physical prompt. For example: "Push the dish rack into the machine," while guiding the worker's movement with hand-over-hand assistance.

Notice that in this example the employment specialist starts with the least intensive prompt (the prompt that provides the worker with the least amount of information), then uses a prompt that is somewhat more intensive, and then ends the sequence with the most intensive prompt. This type of prompt sequence is referred to as a *least prompting sequence* (Wehman, Renzaglia, & Bates, 1985). Not all least prompting sequences use these particular three steps. Different prompts may be used and the sequence may be made up of two levels of prompts. A second example of a least prompting hierarchy is as follows:

1. Picture prompt. For example, a picture/photograph of a designated step in the use of a dishwashing machine, such as pushing the correct button to start the wash cycle.

   (Wait five seconds)

2. Combination of a picture prompt plus a nonspecific verbal prompt. For example: "What do you do next?" while pointing to the picture of the step for turning on the wash cycle.

   (Wait five seconds)

3. Combination of a picture prompt plus a specific verbal prompt. For example: "Push the on button," while pointing to the picture prompt.

In this example the employment specialist waits for a count of five seconds between prompts. Prompt sequences should be based on the unique needs of specific workers. Each worker should have a prompt sequence that is specific to that person and is based on the learning history of the worker. In order to be effective, employment specialists need to determine each worker's optimum prompt sequence. One worker's prompt sequence should not be applied to another worker without considering the unique needs of the second worker.

A second point to remember about prompt sequences is that the least intensive prompt used in the first step of prompt sequence can be repeated along with the more intensive prompts in the next steps. For instance, in the first example given earlier, the verbal prompt used as the first step is repeated and paired with the second and third steps (the gestural and physical prompts). The purpose of this pairing of the less intensive prompt with the more intensive prompts is to help the worker to consistently respond to the less intensive prompt. That is, it would be better if the worker in the first example could respond to a verbal prompt alone than if he or she required a full physical prompt to complete the work task.

Time Delay Procedures. A powerful strategy, when used consistently, is to steadily increase the interval of time between the availability of a natural cue and the introduction of artificial prompts. Using the dishwashing machine example, an instructor may initially provide a gesture (pointing to the red button) and a verbal prompt ("Push the botton") at the same time as the worker sees the button (natural cue). As the worker responds correctly with the gesture and verbal prompt over successive attempts, the instructor can delay the prompts by one full second from the time he or she ordinarily delivered the prompt. At this time the instructor can, through facial expression, indicate that something needs to be done next, but the prompts are delayed. After one second has elapsed, the instructor delivers the gesture and verbal prompt. After successive days of responding correctly to a one-second delay, the instructor delays these prompts by two full seconds and again has a look of expectancy that something should be occurring. This technique, if provided in steady incremental delays, can result in the worker responding correctly in the absence of the artificial prompts before the delay reaches five or six seconds. The experienced instructor, after working with a person, will adjust the number and length of delays that work best for that person.

An inexperienced employment specialist should begin by using a set schedule as follows:

Simultaneously present the natural cues and prompts.
After the worker successfully responds two or three times, delay the prompts by one full second.
After the worker successfully responds two or three times, delay the prompts by two full seconds.
Repeat this process until the delay reaches five full seconds.

If, following a five-second delay, the worker is not responding by correctly completing the activity, an instructor should proceed to a more powerful instructional strategy. Also, some activities that only occur once or twice a day may progress more slowly than activities that have multiple occurrences per day.

A second variation of the time delay strategy is the fading of combinations of artificial prompts in the presence of the natural cue. For example, if the previous combination of a gesture and verbal prompt was successfully providing information to the worker about what to do next, the instructor may begin a delay in the following sequence:

Simultaneously present the natural cue (red button) and the gestural and verbal prompts.
After the worker responds two or three times, the verbal prompt is provided but the gestural prompt is delayed one full second.
After the worker responds two or three times, the verbal prompt is provided but the gestural prompt is delayed two full seconds.
This process is repeated until the delay between the verbal and gestural prompt reaches five full seconds.

As the worker completes the activity with only a verbal prompt, the delay procedures that were outlined at the beginning of this section between the verbal prompt and the natural cue would be initiated. Again, subtle fading procedures can be provided by lessening the amount of information that is provided within the verbal prompt and by providing less pronounced gestures.

In this section, antecedent change procedures—procedures that occur before the worker responds—have been discussed. Prompting procedures, including prompt sequences and pairing artificial prompts with natural cues, were also described. Consequent change procedures, including reinforcement and error correction procedures, will be covered in the next section.

CONSEQUENT CHANGES

Consequent change procedures are strategies that occur after the worker has responded or performed an action. In this section two types of consequent change procedures—positive reinforcement and error correction—will be described.

Positive Reinforcement

Positive reinforcement occurs after a response and increases the likelihood that the response will occur again. Thus, positive reinforcement is something that is provided to the worker after the response and tends to increase that response.

Positive reinforcement may occur in many forms. All of us respond to a variety of reinforcers in everyday situations. Some events are activity reinforcers such as going out to dinner after a long day at work. Other consequences are token reinforcers including money or grades in school. Food can be a reinforcer for many individuals. Social interactions are powerful reinforcers for many people. Finally, internal reinforcers such as a sense of pride or accomplishment can be powerful motivators. In order for reinforcement strategies to be effective, employment specialists should be aware that for each worker there are many levels of reinforcement. The greater an employment specialist's knowledge of what is reinforcing for a particular worker, the greater will be that instructor's ability to be successful with that worker.

How do employment specialists determine exactly what is reinforcing to the workers with whom they work? This may be a difficult task, especially with workers who have difficulty communicating preferences.

One way to discover potential reinforcers for a particular worker is to observe that person in several different situations.

Another way is to request information from people who are close to the individual, including friends, family members, and former instructors or teachers.

Finally, an employment specialist may try presenting different choices and observing any obvious preferences.

It is important for employment specialists to determine exactly what is reinforcing to the workers with whom they work so that they use these reinforcers as part of an effective training program.

Like prompts, reinforcers may be categorized as either those that occur naturally in the work environment or those that are artificial. For instance, a paycheck is a natural reinforcer in the work environment while an employment specialist's statement of "Good job" is an artificial reinforcer. As with prompting, it is important to pair artificial reinforcers (those that the instructor provides) with those that occur naturally in the work environment.

Following are important guidelines for the use of positive reinforcement:

1. In using verbal (social) reinforcers, employment specialists should use a sincere tone of voice.

2. When a worker is learning a new task, the employment specialist should provide more reinforcement (for instance, after each successful attempt).
3. Once a worker has almost learned a task, instructors should fade out their reinforcement so that the worker does not rely too much on that reinforcement (i.e., intermittent reinforcement should be provided).
4. Employment specialists need to remember that all people, including workers with disabilities, respond to a variety of types (levels) of reinforcement.
5. Employment specialists should make sure workers understand the connection between the positive actions they exhibit and the reinforcement provided. That is, reinforcement should be contingent on positive behavior.

Error Correction Procedures

The second type of consequent change strategy to be discussed is error correction. Error correction procedures are those procedures an instructor uses to respond to an incorrect demonstration of a skill by the worker. Error correction procedures are used to assist workers in identifying what they did wrong and to then respond correctly on the next attempt. Like positive reinforcement, error corrections occur after the worker has responded. Bellamy, Horner, and Inman (1979) have described three purposes for error correction procedures:

1. Error correction allows the worker to perform the step/task correctly and to be reinforced for doing so.
2. It prevents the worker from being inadvertently reinforced for completing the step incorrectly by proceeding with the activity.
3. It provides the worker with more practice on the step that she performed incorrectly.

In order to use error correction procedures effectively, Bellamy et al. (1979) suggest the following steps:

1. As soon as an error is made, stop the worker from proceeding with the activity.
2. Determine the amount of assistance (type of prompts) the worker will require to perform the step correctly.
3. Return to the task at the step just before the error was made, begin the activity at that point, and prompt the worker to complete the difficult step.

Consider our example of the operation of the commercial dishwasher. An error correction for an error made on step 5 (open door of machine) might be:

1. The instructor stops the worker as soon as he or she performs the step incorrectly.
2. The instructor determines that the worker will require a specific verbal prompt to perform the step correctly.
3. The instructor arranges the environment so that the natural cue that should set the occasion for the step to be attempted again is present. That is, the work situation is arranged to look exactly as it did before the error occurred. In this case, the natural cue that sets the occasion for step 5 is the drain lever in the shut position. The employment

specialist should then pair a prompt (artificial cue) with this natural cue so that the worker performs step 5 correctly in the presence of the natural cue (the sight of the drain lever in the shut position).

In this section, consequence change procedures, including reinforcement and error correction procedures, were described.

The final category of training strategies to be discussed in this chapter includes procedures of modification of the work task in order to facilitate learning of the task by the worker.

MODIFICATION OF THE TASK

Task modification procedures are those that involve the manner in which the various steps or components of a task are presented to the worker. This section will describe chaining procedures, shaping procedures, color coding, and modifying the environment or complexity of the task.

Chaining Procedures

Workers with severe disabilities often learn more efficiently if the tasks to be learned are presented in smaller units of behavior. With task analysis, component steps of specific tasks are delineated. One technique for conducting instruction with task analysis is to provide specific instruction on all steps of the task. In this "teach all" technique, the employment specialist instructs the worker on all steps of an activity that are not independently performed. For any individual, this technique might be effective. However, if a worker does not learn quickly with this method or becomes frustrated, techniques involving instruction on only one step at a time should be considered. In one of these methods, the employment specialist teaches the worker to initially perform the first step of the task. No other teaching would take place until the worker acquired the ability to complete this first step. Once the worker performed the first step, the employment specialist would now require the worker to complete the first step and begin work on the second step. As the worker learned how to follow each new step, the behavior chain would be lengthened until the worker performed all steps in this task analysis. An advantage of this technique is that the worker is required to learn only one step at a time. For workers who learn very slowly, this practice may be necessary to ensure acquisition.

Another type of chaining technique involves teaching the worker to complete one step at a time again proceeding from the first to the last step. However, with this technique the worker is physically assisted to complete the entire task after receiving intensive instruction on the first step. After the worker masters the first step, the employment specialist provides intensive instruction on step 2 and continues with physical assistance for the remaining steps. These procedures continue through the remaining steps.

The previously presented chaining strategies were variations of *forward chaining.* Two additional chaining techniques that may prove useful for teaching new skills are *backward chaining* methods.

In the first backward chaining method, the employment specialist assists the worker through the steps of the task analysis just prior to the last step or to where the worker can complete the rest of the task on his or her own. Intensive instruction is then provided on this one step and, if this is not the last step, the worker is allowed to complete the remaining steps by him- or herself. As that step is mastered, the step just before that step receives intensive attention/instruction. In essence, the sequence of step mastery proceeds from a "last to first step" sequence.

The second type of backward chaining is identical to the method just described with the exception that the employment specialist prepares the first part of the task on his or her own rather than physically assisting the worker. Both of these methods are similar in that they only require the worker to focus on one step at a time leading toward acquisition of the entire skill.

Shaping

Shaping involves the reinforcement of successive approximation of a step in a work task. That is, workers are reinforced each time their performance on a particular step is closer to the correct performance of the step. By reinforcing workers only when they improve in the performance of the step, the employment specialist helps them to gradually refine their skills in completing that step. For example, in using a shaping procedure to refine a worker's performance on step 13 (turn hot water faucet in counterclockwise direction), the employment specialist might first reinforce the worker for grasping the faucet handle. Subsequently, only attempts to turn the handle in the correct direction would be reinforced, and so on until the worker can turn the handle all the way without assistance. It is important that, in using shaping, the employment specialist only reinforce closer approximations of the correct performance and not ones that are more poorly performed.

Shaping is often used in conjunction with chaining; that is, the employment specialist may use a forward chaining procedure to teach the entire task, while shaping the worker's performance on steps that are being trained intensively.

Color Coding

A third way to modify the task is to provide color prompts to highlight various natural cues in the work environment. For instance, a color prompt could be added to highlight the "on" switch on the dishwashing machine to highlight that natural cue and to facilitate the worker's initiation of the task. Such a prompt could then be gradually faded so that the worker is able to respond correctly to the natural cue (the "on" switch).

In some cases, color prompts may need to be incorporated as permanent adaptations to the environment. In such cases, as with permanent picture prompts, permission should be obtained from the worksite supervisor before any permanent changes in the work environment are made.

Modifying the Environment or Complexity of the Task

In some cases, a worker may experience ongoing difficulty in learning a work task because of the way the work environment is arranged or because of the structure of the task itself. In these cases, the employment specialist may choose to modify or rearrange the work environment to facilitate skill acquisition or to modify the task by reducing its complexity as presently structured. For example, in one restaurant kitchen environment, an employment specialist reported that the removal of a section of tubular railing protruding from a counter top helped the worker with a dishwashing task because he was then better able to empty full bus-trays into the dishwashing machine. This relatively minor alteration of the work environment allowed the worker to complete a greater portion of the task unassisted. Of course, any modification of the work environment should always be approved in advance by the supervisor.

An employment specialist may also elect to modify the task itself by reducing its complexity or by adapting portions of the task to meet the unique needs of the worker. For example, if a worker was not able to complete all steps in the dishwashing task analysis as currently written, the employment specialist could rewrite the task analysis to indicate smaller steps that could be performed more easily by the worker (also referred to as *task analysis branching*). In addition, the employment specialist may elect to have the worker participate in only a portion of the task and have the rest of the task completed by a coworker or another individual in the work-site. This strategy, referred to as partial participation (Baumgart, Brown, Pumpian, Ford, Sweet, Messina, & Schroeder, 1982), allows workers to take part in work activities even though the severity of disability may prevent them from mastering the entire task and performing it independently.

SUMMARY

As workers with severe disabilities are given opportunities to perform meaningful work through supported employment, employment specialists who instruct them must acquire a number of strategies that will allow them to become effective instructors. In this chapter some of the most important instructional strategies that employment specialists need to know have been outlined. Clearly, a variety of other factors enter into an effective instructional program, including the dedication of the employment specialist to the success of the work placement as well as the values system that the employment specialist brings to the teaching effort. However, the employment specialist's skills in using systematic training strategies remain a critical component in any successful supported employment program.

Action Options

- Find out what is reinforcing to a worker with whom you work.
- Determine the best prompt sequence for one of your workers.
- Teach a complex work task using a backward or forward chaining procedure.

CHAPTER 7

Assessment Strategies in Supported Employment

A person's entry into competitive employment should not be based on traits that have limited validity for predicting progress throughout a training program. Rather than limiting work options, contemporary assessment focuses on delineating requisite behaviors that are subsequently targeted for training.

E. L. Pancsofar, "Assessing Work Behavior"

Learning Outcomes

After reading this chapter you will be able to

- Define and describe natural cues
- Define task analysis

- Complete a task analysis for an employment activity
- Define and describe a baseline procedure
- Graph a simple set of performance data

For the purposes of this chapter assessment refers to the process of obtaining information about a worker's performance in order to make a decision about what to do next. Specific to this process is the need to identify key environmental conditions within each employment setting and pair future instruction and ongoing supports with these natural cues. In addition, employment specialists use this information to complete baseline assessments for critically important activities. During instruction, assessment probes are obtained to give the instructor information to continue, modify, or stop the existing procedures. Finally, as employment specialists fade their interventions a final summary of overall effectiveness is obtained. Specific procedures for identifying natural cues, completing baseline assessments, conducting probes during instruction, and monitoring ongoing supports are the focus of this chapter.

An agency should have a catalog of assessment procedures from which to select, depending on the specific question under consideration. It is useful for evaluation specialists within each agency to conceptualize its assessment materials in terms of a funnel diagram (see Figure 7.1). A funnel contains more space at the top and narrows as it forms its spout. At the top of this funnel an agency has a multitude of assessment-gathering materials that are used to obtain *general information* about the worker. Interviews with the worker are vehicles to assess likes and dislikes, desired outcomes, and aptitudes, and to obtain general characteristics. In addition, information can be gathered from significant others that have a vested interest in the worker achieving agreed-upon outcomes. In the next level of the funnel is the agency's method of surveying the community for potential jobs with some knowledge of the general information in mind. Again, an experienced job development specialist has many tactics for obtaining this information and uses these sources to develop a job analysis survey using the factors of a compatibility analysis. In conjunction with a *survey of the community*, each

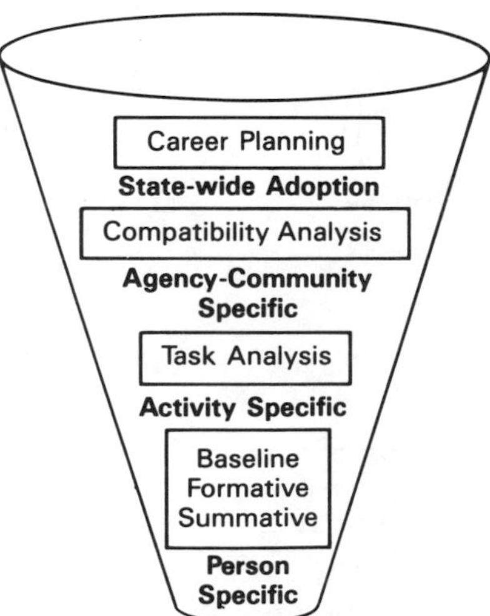

Figure 7.1 Assessment Funnel

consumer should be assessed on his or her current adherence to these *skills, attributes*, and *interests* relative to the factors that have been identified in the community job analysis. This process is best accomplished with the extensive use of situational assessments such as the format that has been described in Chapter 4. Following the accumulation of this information a *matching* process begins and a decision is made about the best jobs that could be available for each worker. Once at the employment site a *task analysis* of critical activities is conducted for additional assessment and instruction purposes. Finally, at the base of the funnel are the most specific assessments of *baseline, formative*, and *summative* processes. Baseline refers to the collection of information on the worker's reaction to the natural cues in the work setting. Formative assessment provides the employment specialist with information about whether to modify, maintain, or cease current instructional supports. Summative assessment informs the employment specialist about the relationship between supports and the changes in the worker's ability to gain more independence at the employment site. It is useful for each agency to have forms that address each of these levels of assessment. Several of these forms have been included in Appendix A.

NATURAL CUES

One of the first skills that employment specialists need to develop is the ability to identify the natural cues to which workers respond within each employment setting. Natural cues are the environmental *clues* that inform the worker about what to do next. That is, when the materials at the job site are in a certain arrangement, the worker should immediately know what to do next. Activities have natural cues that exist immediately before the activity. For example, awakening in the morning may be preceded by an alarm clock, clock radio, sound of an animal, a baby's cry, sunshine, or a knock on the door. Each of these events is a natural cue because it informs the person that it is time to get out of bed. In a similar manner, the position of the hands of a clock, a whistle, a buzzer, or coworkers leaving the room may all be natural cues for taking a break.

The process of identifying natural cues is critical for conducting a baseline assessment of a worker's current level of functioning for identified activities of importance. Prior to describing the process of baseline assessment a brief explanation of task analysis is provided.

TASK ANALYSIS

Prior to conducting a baseline assessment of a worker's current abilities on targeted activities, the employment specialist needs to develop a task analysis for each activity. A task analysis is a sequence of steps that a person completes while doing a specific work activity. Task analyses allow for

- The employment specialist to follow the expected sequence of steps as specified by a company supervisor
- Substitute employment specialists to know the proper sequence for the worker to complete
- A mechanism by which a baseline assessment can be conducted
- The identification of natural cues from which to direct instructional strategies

Guidelines for Developing a Task Analysis

Observe the Specific Activity in the Community Setting Where It Is Expected to Occur. There are several methods for completing the same activity that are unique to the location of the job. For example, the steps to operating a dishwashing machine vary depending on the style and location of each machine. Teaching someone to enter data on a computer will vary depending on the brand of computer that is available at the specific worksite. Little is accomplished by developing a sequence of steps to complete an activity from memory or for equipment with which we are familiar. Employment specialists must develop their task analyses within the exact settings where the worker is expected to complete the activity.

Contact a Supervisor at the Community Work Setting and Obtain a Previously Written Task Analysis. Some companies have already developed detailed steps to completing most jobs at the worksite under consideration. Obtain copies of all previously written task analyses and inspect them for their utility in conducting the baseline assessment that will be described later in this chapter.

List the Materials Necessary to Complete the Activity. At the top of a page, record the tools and equipment that need to be obtained prior to beginning the activity as efficiently as possible. Also, the acceptable standards of speed and accuracy can be obtained from coworkers.

Observe a Currently Employed Worker Performing the Activity. Before attempting the activity, the employment specialist observes a successfully employed worker completing the activity and asks questions about parts of the activity that need additional explanation. The worker can talk through the activity and provide hints to assist in completing it.

Complete the Activity Several Times Until You Meet the Supervisor's Satisfaction. It is important for employment specialists to be comfortable completing the activities that they will be assessing and instructing the worker with a disability to complete. Employment specialists should continue practicing the activities until the supervisor acknowledges that the quantity and quality meet company standards. For some jobs this may only require an hour or two while other, more complex activities may require one or two weeks before the employment specialist is comfortable assessing and instructing a worker to complete the activity.

List the Steps of the Activity in a Logical Sequence. Based on the observations of a currently employed worker and after completing the activity to the supervisor's specifications, the employment specialist lists the individual steps of the activity. A step refers to a specific action that is performed to complete a section of the activity. For example, turn on the machine, remove the black plate, open the container, and record the balance are all steps of different activities. It is important to write the step with words that describe an action that can be observed. A task analysis for obtaining coffee from a vending machine in a snack area could contain the following steps:

1. Choose correct amount of coins.
2. Place change in the slot marked 50¢.
3. Choose desired selection by depressing button.

4. Slide compartment door open and hold it in an open position.
5. Grasp filled cup and remove cup of coffee.
6. Release door to closed position.

Give the List of Steps for the Work Task to the Supervisor for Review. The supervisor should have the opportunity to verify that the sequence of actions that the employment specialist developed is acceptable and matches the company's guidelines for completing the activity.

Identify the Natural Cues for Each Step of the Task Analysis. Remember, natural cues are the environmental clues for what to do while completing each step of the task analysis. They set the occasion for or provide information to the worker about what to do next. A task analysis (see Table 7.1) with corresponding natural cues is provided for an activity of folding napkins according to the specifications of a local restaurant. The employment specialist followed the advice that has been presented for developing a task analysis in this chapter. Now the natural cues associated with each step of the activity are added.

Review

The steps for developing a task analysis include the following:

Observe the activity in a community work setting where the worker will actually complete the task.

Table 7.1 TASK ANALYSIS FOR FOLDING NAPKINS ACTIVITY

NATURAL CUES	RESPONSE
1. Stack of unfolded napkins is on the left side of the table.	1. Pick up one napkin from stack of napkins.
2. Napkin is in worker's hand.	2. Lay napkin in diamond shape position on the table.
3. Napkin is in diamond position.	3. Pick up top corner of napkin.
4. Top corner of napkin is in worker's hand.	4. Pull corner down to bottom corner.
5. Top corner is touching bottom corner.	5. Pick up right corner of napkin.
6. Right corner of napkin is in worker's hand.	6. Pull corner to bottom midsection of napkin.
7. Right corner is touching bottom midsection of napkin.	7. Pick up left corner of napkin.
8. Left corner of napkin is in worker's hand.	8. Pull corner to bottom midsection of napkin.
9. Left corner is touching bottom midsection of napkin.	9. Grasp lower corner of napkin.
10. Lower corner of napkin is in worker's hand.	10. Turn napkin over.
11. Napkin is on opposite side.	11. Pick up top corner of napkin.
12. Top corner of napkin is in worker's hand.	12. Pull corner down to bottom corner.
13. Top corner is touching bottom corner.	13. Grasp either left or right corner of napkin.
14. Left or right corner of napkin is in worker's hand.	14. Pull corner across to opposite corner.
15. Left or right corner is touching opposite corner.	15. Place folded napkin on stack of previously folded napkins.

Obtain a previously written task analysis from a company supervisor.
List the materials/equipment/tools for completing the activity.
Observe a currently employed worker performing the activity.
Perform the activity yourself until you meet the supervisor's requirements for quality, quantity, and speed.
List the steps of the activity in a logical sequence.
Obtain the work supervisor's validation that your steps match his or her expectations.
Identify the natural cues for each step of the task analysis.

CONDUCTING BASELINE ASSESSMENT

Baseline assessment is a process of obtaining information about a worker's current ability to complete an activity before any instruction occurs. A starting point is established from which to evaluate the worker's progress. The previous discussion on identifying natural cues is critical to conducting a baseline assessment. A record is made of the worker's performance on an activity as he or she responds to the natural cues for the steps of the identified activity. The steps for conducting a baseline assessment include

1. Tell the worker what the activity is.
2. Demonstrate the activity one time.
3. Give a nonspecific verbal prompt to begin the activity.
4. If the worker responds correctly:
   provide no direct feedback about the activity;
   record plus sign (+) on a data form.
5. If the worker responds incorrectly:
   rearrange the activity as little as possible to set up the natural cue(s) for the following step;
   record minus sign (−) on a data form;
   note if a consistent error pattern begins to develop.

Using a vending machine example, an adherence to the steps to conducting a baseline assessment follows:

1. Tell the Worker What the Activity Is

"John, this is a vending machine for coffee" or the employment specialist could make a sign for coffee while pointing to the machine.

2. Demonstrate the Activity One Time

Employment specialist performs each step as he or she talks through the activity at a level that is comprehended by the worker:
"I need 50 cents for the machine."
"I'm placing the money in the slot."
"I'll press this button for a cup of coffee."

3. Give a Nonspecific Verbal Prompt to Begin the Activity

"John, now you get a cup of coffee."

4. Situation One: Worker Responds Correctly to Each Step of the Activity

Remember, if a step is performed correctly, the environment is automatically set up with the natural cues for the next step. Also, let the coffee be the natural reinforcer for completing the activity. During a baseline assessment the employment specialist should not provide direct reinforcement for completing each step. When this occurs, the employment specialist is not obtaining an accurate picture of how well the worker responds just to the cues available within the work setting as if the employment specialist were not present. Record plus signs (+) on the data form for each step completed independently.

4. Situation Two: Worker Responds Incorrectly to Each Step of the Activity by Making No Movement to Complete Each Response

The worker may fail to initiate any movement to complete the responses of the activity. When this happens there is no opportunity for the employment specialist to observe how the worker reacts to each natural cue unless he or she intervenes. The following procedure is recommended:

Identify how much time you will allow for the worker to respond to each natural cue. A reasonable time would be three seconds. That is, for three seconds the worker makes no attempt to initiate movement toward the expected response.

The employment specialist rearranges the environment to produce the next natural cue as if the worker had correctly completed the response.

For the example of obtaining coffee from a vending machine (see pp. 61–62), the sequence of employment specialist's reaction includes the following:

Following Step:	***What the Employment Specialist Does***
1	Puts 50¢ in worker's hand
2	Takes 50¢ from worker's hand and places it in correct slot
3	Depresses button for desired selection
4	Opens compartment door and places worker's hand on door to keep it open
5	Places filled cup of coffee in worker's hand
6	If worker is still grasping compartment door, employment specialist removes his hand

The employment specialist records a minus sign (−) for each of the steps, indicating that the worker did not correctly complete the response in reaction to the natural cues.

4. Situation Three: Worker Responds Incorrectly to Each Step of the Activity by Beginning a Response That Does Not Functionally Relate to the Activity

The worker's reaction may be similar to situation two except that instead of making no movement to complete the activity the worker initiates incorrect movements to complete the response. For example, the worker could be trying to place the money in the coin return slot or could press the label above the button. To the extent possible, the employment specialist should interrupt the worker from continuing the incorrect movements and immediately arrange the environment (i.e., set up the next natural cue) for the following response. As with situation two, the employment specialist records a minus sign (−) for each step.

4. Situation Four: Worker Responds Correctly to Some Steps and Incorrectly to Others

The worker's reaction may be a combination of the previous three situations and the employment specialist should react differently to each response depending on the worker's correct/incorrect completion of each step.

It takes practice to smoothly conduct a baseline assessment. It is well worth the effort if the objective is to obtain as accurate a picture as possible of the worker's current ability to complete an activity prior to instruction.

FORMATIVE AND SUMMATIVE ASSESSMENT STRATEGIES

Introduction

The choice of data collection procedures is determined by the questions that are being asked. Are we asking the right questions? Burton Blatt, a pioneer in special education and rehabilitation, once cautioned us to stop looking for the right answers to situations but to focus instead on asking the right questions. He provided the following story to emphasize his point.

There once was a town in which property was being stolen by an unknown process. Members of the town decided to post a sentry at the only road leading from the town to check all travelers in hopes of discovering the thief. On one occasion a man arrived at the checkpoint with a wheelbarrow full of hay. The sentry searched through the hay and, finding nothing, waved the man through. This same sequence of events occurred for the following four days. At the morning briefing on the following Monday the sentry viewed the list of property that had been recently stolen from the town. Heading the list were five wheebarrows! The sentry had not asked the right question that would have resulted in confiscating the stolen property.

This concept of asking the right question is critical in a search for quality of life outcomes. This became quite clear to one of the authors at a recent presentation. He gave the following example from which to define the term *functional activity*. In this example he related that five individuals were at a table in a local sheltered workshop. The first person picked up a bolt from a box and handed it to the next person. This person picked up a nut and screwed it on the bolt and handed it to the person to his right. The third worker tightened the nut and passed it on to the next person who unscrewed the nut. The final person received the nut and bolt and placed them in separate boxes. The presenter asked the question: "Is this a functional activity?" He expected the participants to see the ridiculousness of this "make-work" as a nonfunctional activity.

One participant immediately raised his hand and said, "Yes, that's a functional activity because you have to keep them busy!" The presenter stopped for a few seconds and changed his tack. "Yes, if the question that you are asking is 'How do I keep these five workers busy?' then the activity that was described could be considered functional within that context. However, if the question is 'What work can be provided to the individuals that will assist in enhancing their quality of life?' then the 'make-work' becomes a seriously nonfunctional activity."

Marc Gold also highlighted this distinct difference in a presentation that he once delivered on a discussion of quality of life. He related that the concept of least restrictive environment becomes a useful term only if the question that is being asked is "How far has this person come? He used to live in a large institution but look at him now, he lives in a group home with eight housemates." However if the question being asked is "How far does this person have yet to go?" then the term is more aptly called *quality of life* because quality of life focuses on a vision of the future and the way things ought to be while least restrictive environment focuses on the past as we congratulate ourselves on how far the person has progressed.

Agreement on the right questions to ask takes precedence over discovering the right answers. One way to measure our own growth as professionals in supported employment is to compare the questions that we used to be asking about persons with disabilities to the questions that we are asking today. One of the authors used to ask questions like

How can I keep Beth from screaming?
How do I keep Joe busy?
What's wrong with Jill?
How much money is Bob earning?
When do I get out of here?

Now, his questions are more like

What's Beth trying to communicate to me through her screaming?
What work can Joe do that enhances attainment of his outcomes?
What's right with Jill?
What does Bob do with the money that he earns?
When is my next challenge?

In the decision-making process, the first step is agreement on the questions being addressed. If there is not a consensus on asking the right questions then the potential options and strategies are most likely to be a futile attempt at providing functional responses to unclear questions. For example, supported employment is a set of experiences that addresses a different set of questions than sheltered employment. In sheltered employment, workers have to get "ready" for the community by demonstrating competence on some predetermined exit criteria. In contrast, supported employment asks the question of what supports need to be in place for the individual to be in community-based employment right now. Unless there is a clear articulation of this new set of questions, then supported employment will run its course and be a fad whose time has gone. Only when there is a clear articulation of questions that contain a focus on enhancing an individual's quality of life will supported employment remain as the most functional and viable process of adult services for persons with severe disabilities.

In this section data collection procedures are included that help answer the following questions:

Questions	***Data Collection***
1. How many times is something occurring?	1. Frequency
2. How many times is something occurring per standard interval of time?	2. Rate

3. What part of an activity is being completed?	3. Percentage
4. How long is something happening?	4. Duration
5. How can I collect data over an extended period of time but only periodically?	5. Time sampling
6. Am I able to reduce the intensity of instruction?	6. Performance scoring

Method 1: Frequency Recording

Frequency recording is a basic procedure in which the number of specific instances of an activity is counted. Each time the behavior occurs it is recorded.

For example, Gerald's employment specialist records the number of times that Gerald leaves his worksite to go to the bathroom. The work supervisor related that Gerald was not completing all of his work assignments at the department store and that he was spending too much time away from work. The employment specialist developed a simple recording form to write the frequency of bathroom breaks during the day (see Figure 7.2).

A second example of recording frequency is when a number of completed products need to be tabulated by the worker and a golf or wrist counter can be used to tabulate the number of items that were completed for that day. In a department store, Judy needs to record the exact number of shirts that she removes from the packing box and puts on hangers for removal to the display area. Figure 7.3 illustrates how this can be recorded.

When to Use Frequency Recording. Frequency recording is a method of choice when the behavior or activity has a distinctly clear beginning and end. In addition, the observer is not concerned with the number of times that something is completed within a consistent time period.

Worker: Gerald

Activity: Number of Bathroom Breaks

Monday 4/2	Tuesday 4/3	Wednesday 4/4	Thursday 4/5	Friday 4/6
✓ ✓ ✓ ✓ ✓ ✓ ✓	✓ ✓ ✓ ✓ ✓	✓ ✓ ✓ ✓ ✓	✓ ✓ ✓ ✓ ✓ ✓	✓ ✓ ✓ ✓ ✓
7	5	5	6	5

Figure 7.2 Sample Form for Recording Frequency of Breaks

Worker: Judy
Activity: Removing and hanging shirts

Week of	Monday	Tuesday	Wednesday	Thursday	Friday
3/14	25	30	32	29	34
3/21	34	33	45	28	32
3/28	35	33	20	32	33
4/4	40	31	31	41	41

Figure 7.3 Sample Form for Recording Number of Items Completed

Method 2: Rate Recording

At times knowing the exact number of items that are completed is misleading unless all the work periods are of equal duration. For example, the shirts that were removed from the package and placed on hangers occurred during two-hour work periods. However, if this same information was collected during unequal work periods, accurate data are not being obtained.

In a situation when information is being collected over unequal work periods a rate recording system is a more accurate description of the data. *Rate* refers to the number of times an activity occurs per standard unit of time. For example, Fred works in an office where presenters deliver workshops and use overhead transparencies. When transparencies become outdated or replacements are developed for old transparencies, Fred removes the old transparency from its frame and replaces it with the newly created product. This activity does not occur during the same interval of time, nor does it occur each day. As a result, if the employment specialist wants to collect information about Fred's rate of replacing transparencies the format in Figure 7.4 would be useful.

When to Use Rate Recording. Rate recording is a method of collecting information about activities that have a clear beginning and a clear end. Additionally, the activity occurs for a short duration and is at a low enough frequency to allow the employment specialist to accurately count each occurrence. A common interval of time is used consistently across observations.

Method 3: Percentage Recording

A third method for collecting data in a more accurate format is to convert the information into a percentage presentation. This method is typically used when documenting the percentage of steps that are correctly completed from a task analysis. In an example of a task analysis for resupplying paper in a copy machine there are nine distinct steps to assess. Based on the worker's response the employment specialist can record a plus sign (+) for successful

Worker: Fred
Activity: Replacing Transparencies on Frames

Week of	Monday #	Monday Minutes	Monday rate/min.	Tuesday #	Tuesday Minutes	Tuesday rate/min.	Wednesday #	Wednesday Minutes	Wednesday rate/min.
3/14	5	3	1.67				10	8	1.25
3/21				15	15	1.0			
3/28	15	20	.75				17	20	.85
4/4				12	10	1.2			

Figure 7.4 Sample Form for Rate Recording

completion or a minus sign (−) for unsuccessful completion of the step (see Figure 7.5). A percentage score can be derived by dividing the number of plus signs by the total number of steps and multiplying by 100. For example, on April 11 there were four steps for which Beth received a plus sign and the total number of steps in this task analysis is nine.

$4 \div 9 = .44 \times 100 = 44\%$

When to Use Percentage Recording. Percentage recording is used most frequently when multiple steps of an activity are being assessed. The observer wants to compare the ratio of successfully completed steps to the total number of steps. Percentages are easy to communicate since this is the most prevalent data collection in school programs and the reader can readily note progress in the scores.

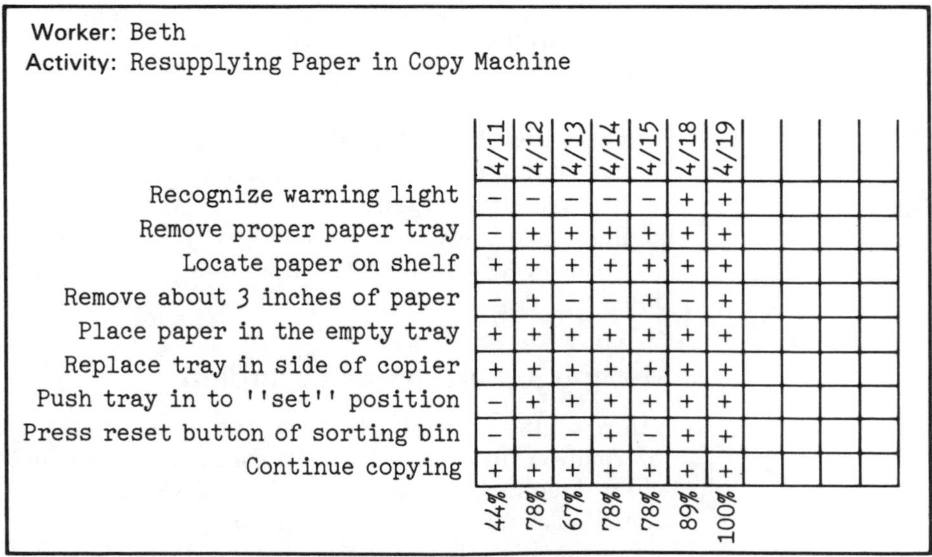

Worker: Beth
Activity: Resupplying Paper in Copy Machine

	4/11	4/12	4/13	4/14	4/15	4/18	4/19				
Recognize warning light	−	−	−	−	−	+	+				
Remove proper paper tray	−	+	+	+	+	+	+				
Locate paper on shelf	+	+	+	+	+	+	+				
Remove about 3 inches of paper	−	+	−	−	+	−	+				
Place paper in the empty tray	+	+	+	+	+	+	+				
Replace tray in side of copier	+	+	+	+	+	+	+				
Push tray in to ''set'' position	−	+	+	+	+	+	+				
Press reset button of sorting bin	−	−	−	+	−	+	+				
Continue copying	+	+	+	+	+	+	+				
	44%	78%	67%	78%	78%	89%	100%				

Figure 7.5 Sample Form for Percentage Recording

Method 4: Duration Recording

Duration recording is a procedure in which the length of the activity or behavior is documented. The amount of time of the activity and the total time in which the worker was observed are both recorded. The easiest presentation of duration data is by percent. For example, if the employment specialist needed to record the percent of time during Paul's work day that he was collating training manuals the format in Figure 7.6 could be used.

Duration information can also be recorded for the length of time between a request by a supervisor and when the activity is actually started by the worker. This information is referred to as *latency of response*. This is an important behavior on which to concentrate and a goal of the employment specialist should be to decrease this interval of time and assist the worker to respond immediately to the request to change work to meet the requirements of the immediate supervisor. Figure 7.7 illustrates one method for collecting this data for Darla.

When to Use Duration Recording. Duration recording is the method for gathering information about a worker when the important dimension is how long a behavior occurs or how long it takes for the worker to respond to a request. As with frequency recording, the activity has a clear beginning and ending.

Method 5: Interval Recording

Interval recording information involves an observation period that is divided into a number of equal time intervals. The employment specialist notes the occurrence or absence of the activity during the time interval.

Worker: Paul
Activity: Collating Training Manuals

Date	Begin	End	Total Min.	Summary	
Monday 3/11	9:30	10:15	45	Total Observation	232 min.
	11:30	12:10	40	Total Duration of Activity	92 min.
	1:15	1.22	7	Percent of occurrence	39.6%
Thursday 3/14	9:22	9:45	23	Total Observation	258 min.
	10:37	11:00	23	Total Duration of Activity	76 min.
	1:10	1:40	30	Percent of occurrence	29.4%

Figure 7.6 Sample Form for Duration Recording

Worker: Darla
Activity: Duration of time from initial request to starting the activity

Date	Time to Start Activity	Nature of the Activity
7/18	10 min.	Copy of packet of 50 pages.
	5 min.	Come into my office for a meeting.
7/19	8.5 min.	Meet me down by the car.
7/20	12 min.	Clean the conference board.
	2 min.	We have a meeting in conf. room.
7/22	20.3 min.	Put stamps on these envelopes.

Figure 7.7 Sample Form for Recording Latency of Response

Whole Interval. During whole interval recording the activity (behavior) under observation must occur during the entire interval to be scored as a plus sign (+). For example, if working steadily at the work station was targeted as an observable activity and 1-minute intervals of time were designated as the observation periods, the worker would have to be working for the entire minute for that interval to be soored with a plus sign (+). Even if the person was working for 55 seconds but stopped, a minus sign (−) would be recorded.

Partial Interval. Partial interval recording allows for a plus sign (+) if, at any time during the designated interval of time, the employment specialist observed the worker participating in the targeted activity or behavior. A targeted activity could be talking with coworkers during a break activity of 15 minutes and the individual intervals of time could be 30 seconds each. The employment specialist would record a plus sign (+) if, at any time during the 30-second interval, the worker was observed talking with a coworker. If a 30-second interval elapsed without the worker conversing with a coworker, a minus sign (−) would be scored on the data form (see Figure 7.8).

Momentary Time Sampling. When the employment specialist does not have the available time to be observing the worker during the entire interval, a momentary time sampling technique can yield useful information. In this procedure an interval of time is selected in which to observe the worker. If a 15-second interval was selected, the employment specialist would look at the worker at the 15-second mark of that interval and note the presence or absence of the targeted activity/behavior. If the behavior was occurring at that second a plus sign (+) is recorded for that interval. If the behavior was absent at that second a minus sign (−) is recorded for the interval (see Figure 7.9).

Worker: William
Activity: Conversing with coworkers during morning break

+ = conversing with a coworker
− = no conversation between William and a coworker

Date	Each interval = 30 seconds										+	%
12/12	+	−	+	+	−	+	+	+	−	−		
	+	−	−	−	+	−	−	−	+	−	12	40%
	−	+	+	+	−	−	−	−	−	−		
12/13	+	+	+	−	−	−	−	−	−	−		
	−	+	+	+	+	−	−	−	−	−	11	37%
	−	−	−	−	−	+	+	+	+	−		

Figure 7.8 Sample Form for Partial Interval Recording

When to Use Interval Recording. Interval recording is an appropriate method for obtaining information when the activities being observed are of high frequency within a short duration of time or are single events occurring over long intervals of time. In addition, these activities and behaviors may not have a clear beginning and end and would make duration or frequency recording extremely difficult.

Worker: William
Activity: Working steadily on assigned activities

+ = working steadily on assigned activity
− = wandering, staring off into space, not working

Date	Each interval = 30 seconds										+	%
8/10	+	−	+	+	−	+	+	+	−	−		
	+	−	−	−	+	−	−	−	+	−		
	−	+	+	+	+	−	−	−	−	−		
	+	+	−	+	−	+	+	+	−	+	36/70	52%
	+	+	+	+	+	+	−	−	+	−		
	−	+	+	+	+	−	−	−	−	−		
	+	−	−	−	−	+	+	+	+	−		

Figure 7.9 Sample Form for Momentary Time Sampling

Method 6: Performance Scoring

Performance scoring is a method of obtaining information about the current assistance provided to the worker by the employment specialist. By recording these data the employment specialist receives information about the effectiveness of the currently employed instructional strategies (see Figure 7.10). The individual scoring system can be uniquely adapted to meet the range of instruction that is provided to the worker. Two sample scoring formats could include scoring of:

Format 1	***Format 2***
0 = full physical assistance	0 = full physical assistance
1 = partial physical assistance	1 = gesture and diagram
2 = demonstration or model	2 = diagram only
3 = gesture	3 = nonspecific verbal instruction

When to Use Performance Scoring. Performance scoring is an appropriate method of obtaining data when the employment specialist is assessing the impact of an instructional sequence of assistance. Decisions about whether to continue, modify, or cease the current instructional procedures can best be made after viewing the performance scoring data.

Worker: Ernie
Activity: Printing from MacIntosh

0 = physical
1 = model
2 = verbal-specific
3 = verbal-nonspecific
4 = independently

	9/26	9/26	9/26	9/28	9/28	9/28
Using Mouse, move arrow to ''File''	0	0	1	2	1	3
Push down on top of Mouse	2	3	4	4	4	4
Scroll down to ''Print'' Command	0	0	2	2	3	3
Release touch from Mouse	3	3	4	4	4	4
On the Imagewriter:						
Depress ''Select'' button-light off	2	3	3	4	4	4
Place one sheet of paper in guide	3	4	4	4	4	4
Depress ''Form Feed'' button	2	3	4	4	4	4
Depress ''Select'' button-light on	3	4	4	4	4	4
On the Screen and using Mouse:						
Select ''High'' position of quality	3	3	4	4	4	4
Select ''Number of copies''	3	3	4	4	4	4
Select page range to copy	3	3	4	4	4	4
Select ''OK''	2	3	3	4	4	4
After printing, depress ''Select'' button	2	2	3	3	3	4
Remove page from top of printer	4	4	4	4	4	4
Total Score	32	38	48	51	51	54

Figure 7.10 Sample Form for Performance Scoring

GRAPHING DATA

Information that has been recorded on the worker's data collection forms, if left on the data forms, is neither easy nor quick to analyze. Displaying a picture of the data by using a graph will help with the analysis of the sequence of instruction and with future decisions to modify, stop, or continue the current strategies. The graph is the key element in the analysis of each worker's progress.

The graph will need to be arranged and marked for easy reading. Luckily there are accepted conventions for graphs so that anyone generally familiar with graphing can read other people's graphs. Graphs should be labeled so that the reader will be able to know many aspects of the data that are presented.

The nine steps that are included in this section are recommended when developing graphs.

Step 1: Obtain or prepare graphing paper of a suitable size.

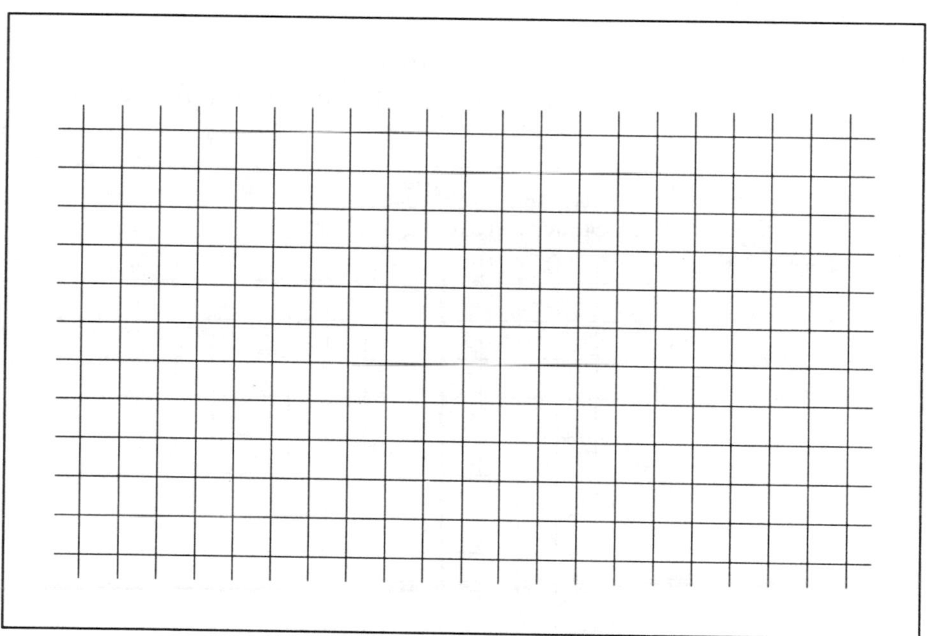

Step 2: At the top of the paper write the identifying information. This should include the worker's name and the name of the instructional activity.

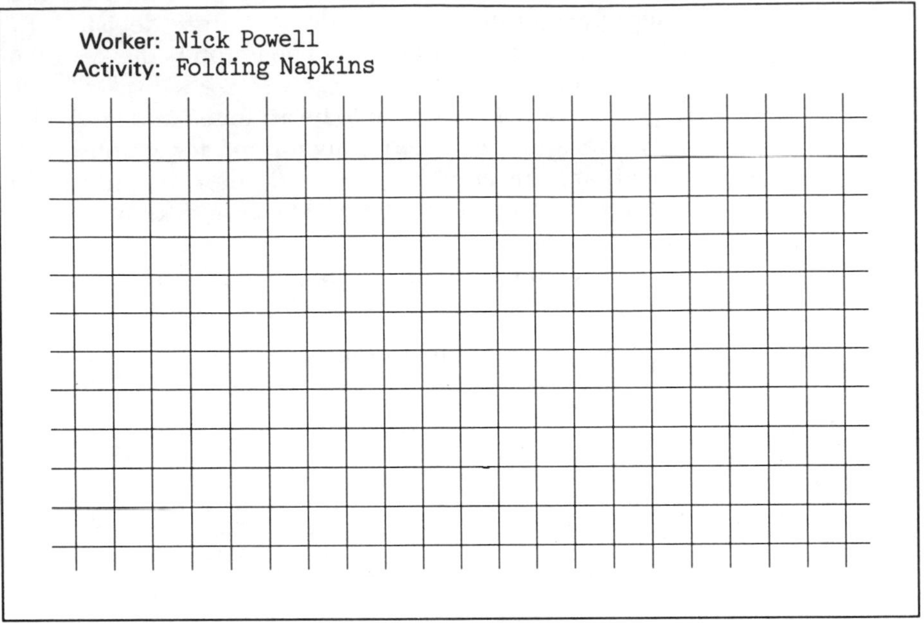

Step 3: Establish a darkened horizontal and vertical line that meet in an L arrangement. This will set the parameters of the graph.

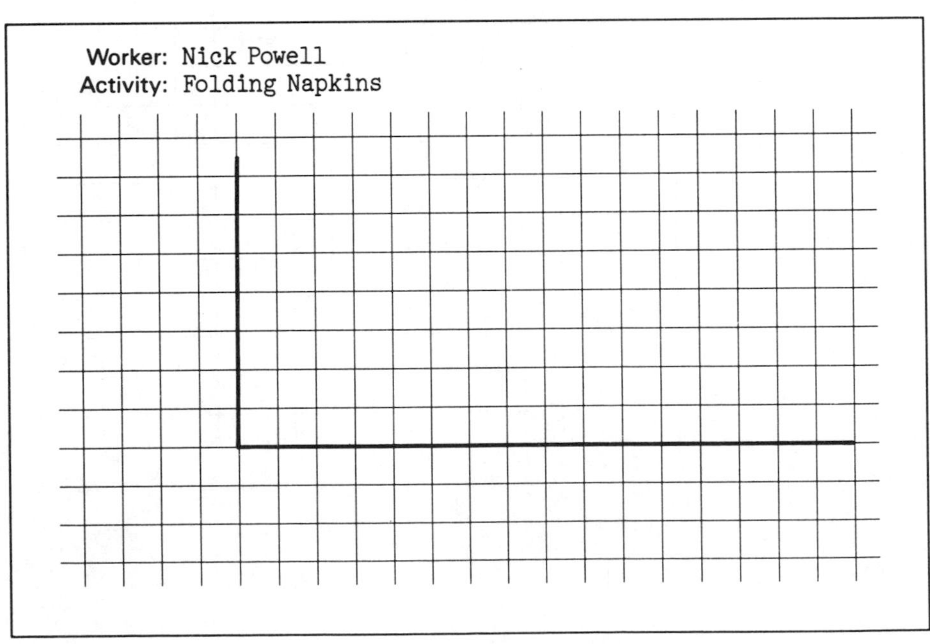

Step 4: Mark the horizontal line as a dimension of time. The horizontal line should indicate when the information is collected. Most likely it will be indicated by days or instructional sessions. The date shouid always be recorded on the graph.

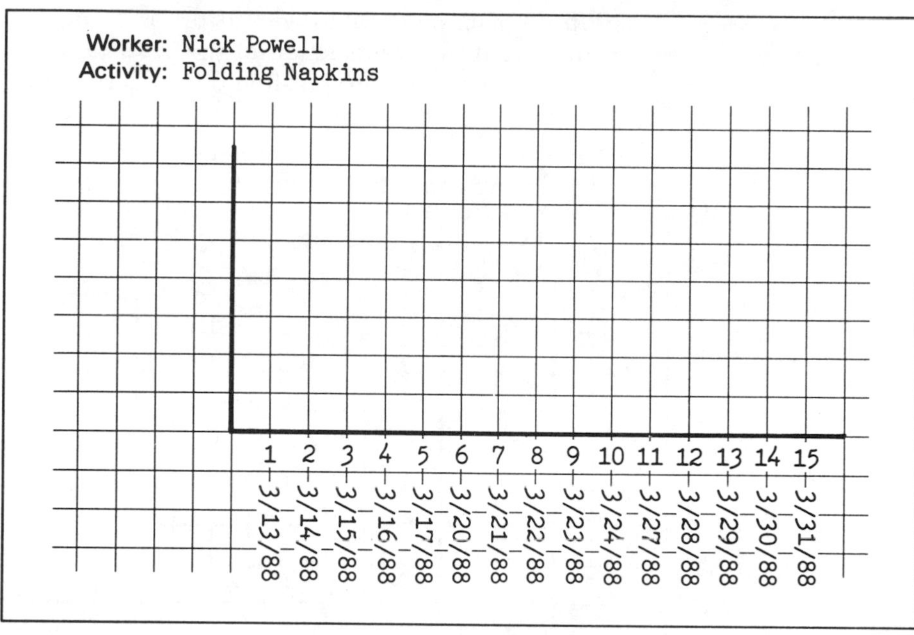

Step 5: Now mark the vertical line in a manner that represents how the behavior was measured and recorded. Most vertical lines will be marked

1. Number of __________.
2. Duration (minutes or hours) of __________.
3. Percentage of intervals in which __________.
4. Assistance score for __________.

The behavior should be stated along with the type of measurement used. Numbers are then placed along this line to represent the possible range of the behavior being measured. The zero mark is placed on the first segmented part of this line. All numbers should be readable.

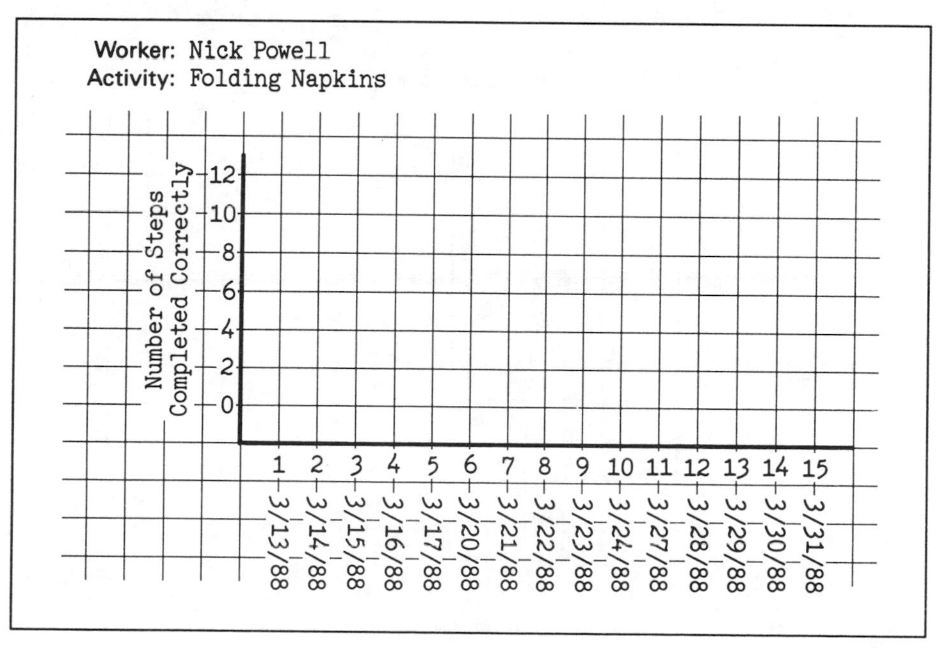

Step 6: Start plotting data from the baseline measures. All data are plotted at the intersection of the vertical and horizontal lines. The data marks on the graph should be a dark dot (●).

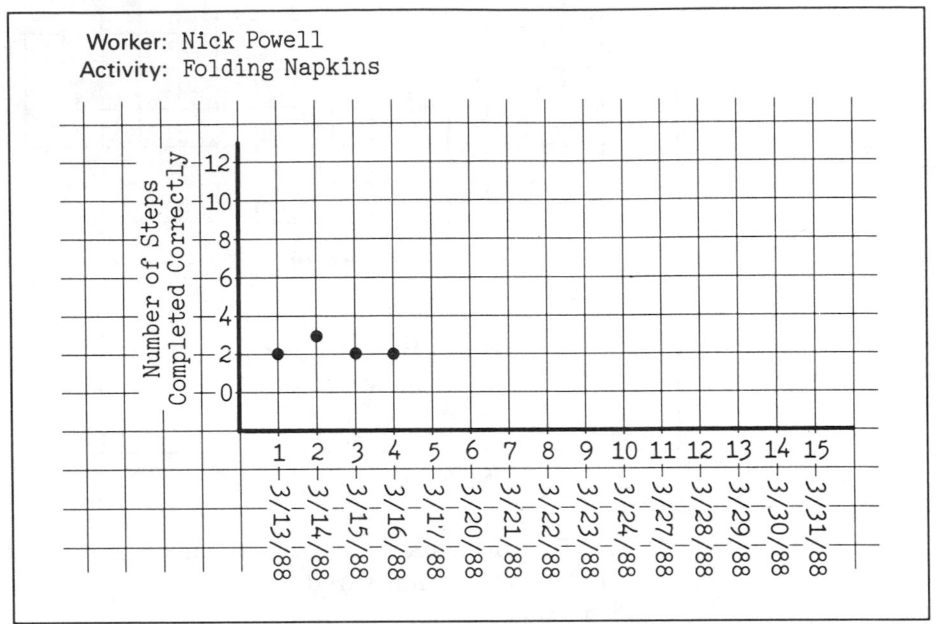

Step 7: Draw a straight line between the dots to connect them.

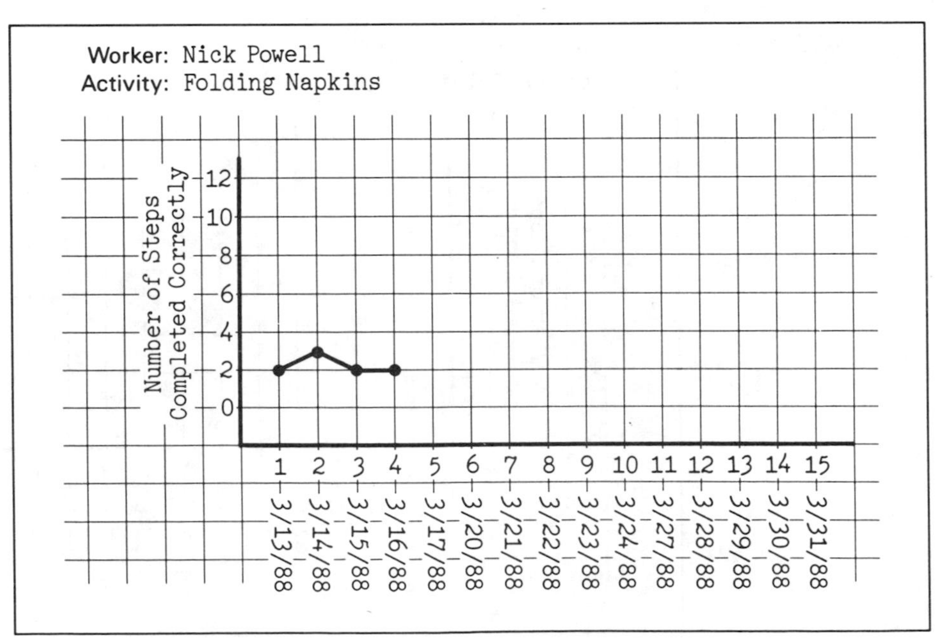

Step 8: To signify the different conditions in the instruction program, draw a vertical line on the graph. Each section of the graph should be marked at the top. These conditions can be marked Baseline or Assessment, Instruction, Revision 1, Revision 2, etc. Do not connect the line of the graph across the vertical line that separates the phases.

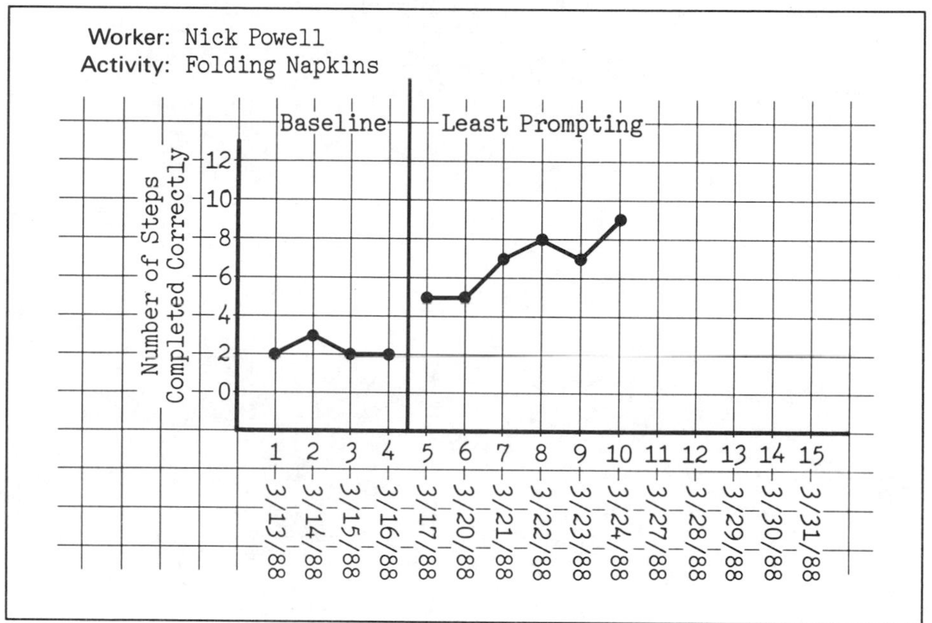

Step 9: Establish a goal line and anticipated date of completion. The goal line is the point on the vertical line that will be the measure of the behavior when the worker completes the expected activity. This line is marked with a dotted line. The anticipated date of completion is the best estimate of the date when the program will be completed. It is marked with a checkmark.

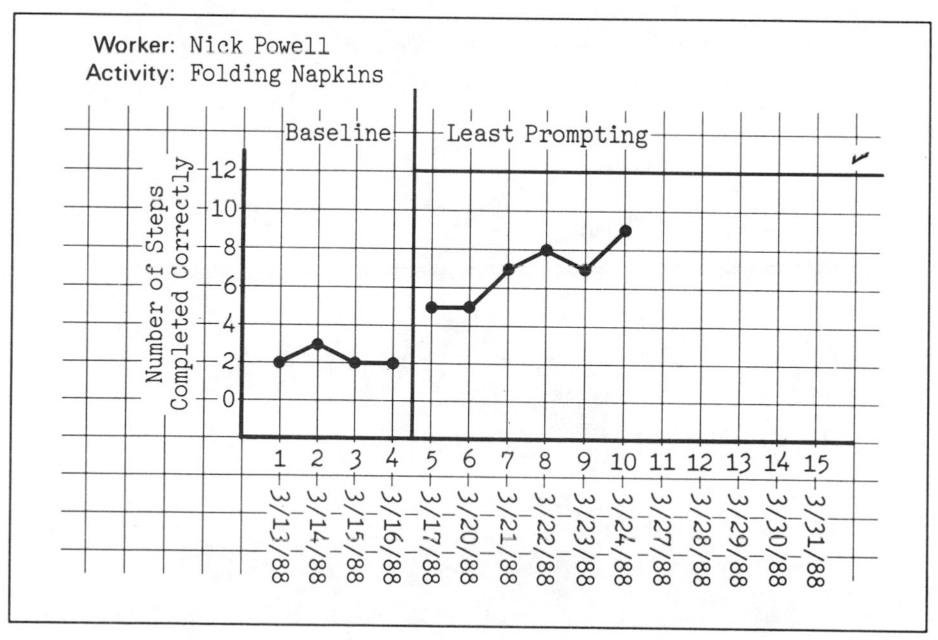

Action Options

- Describe natural cues for an activity you do regularly (make breakfast, get dressed, drive your car, etc.).
- Perform a task analysis on a novel activity.
- Record and graph your own behavior for two weeks—try measuring a behavior you want to change.

CHAPTER 8

Helping Employees with Behavioral Challenges

Every American ought to have the right to be treated as he would wish to be treated, as one would wish his children to be treated.

John F. Kennedy, television address, June 12, 1963

Randy is a 31-year-old man with mental retardation and autism. He exhibits behavior that interferes with his employment in the community; he injures himself and others, disrupts activities, and fails to remain on task for extended periods of time. Overall, Randy's behavior is problematic and poses significant challenges for professionals. Systematic behavioral interventions that had the potential to limit his participation in community-based employment have been utilized to address these behaviors. Through careful planning, data collection and analysis, and continuous evaluation, a program has evolved whereby the frequency, intensity, and duration of Randy's inappropriate behavior has decreased substantially. Randy is currently employed in an office where there are few staff, and a relatively calm and quiet ambience; here he collates, sorts, copies, and shreds documents and performs errands as needed.

Learning Outcomes

After reading this chapter you will be able to

- Identify potential behavior problems exhibited by individuals with disabilities
- Describe the behavioral intervention process in detail
- Describe the development and implementation of behavior management procedures

- Describe interventions that have been effective in dealing with problem behaviors of individuals with disabilities

INTRODUCTION

Behavioral problems exhibited by individuals with disabilities pose significant challenges for the most competent and skilled professionals. For some individuals, employment opportunities may be restricted and limited, given their problematic behavior. In some cases, individuals may even be excluded from community-based employment due to the severity of their behavior and its potential risks to themselves and to others. The terms *challenging behaviors* and *behavior problems* refer to behaviors such as aggression, self-injurious behavior, stereotypic behavior, noncompliance, pica (eating inedible objects), hyperactivity, running away, destructiveness, and disruptiveness. Within the context of work, the remediation of any of these inappropriate behaviors becomes the prime responsibility of the employment specialist and the transdisciplinary team. Unfortunately, in many circumstances, the display of inappropriate behavior becomes an excuse to prevent an individual with a disability from the opportunity to be gainfully employed in the community. Given the inherent value of work in our society, measures must be taken to assure that individuals with behavior problems have equal opportunity to be employed through supported employment.

The technology of applied behavior analysis (Sulzer-Araroff & Mayer, 1977) has been utilized to deal effectively with a wide range of problem behaviors in many situations, and with a variety of people. *Applied behavior analysis,* also referred to as behavior management and behavior modification, has developed strategies to teach people with disabilities appropriate and adaptive behavior rather than the sole elimination and suppression of undesirable or inappropriate behavior. Behavioral interventions seek to maximize skill development and assure that the rights and liberties of individuals are protected; these procedures must be implemented in accordance with the philosophy and principle of social role valorization (normalization) (Wolfensberger, 1972). The purpose of behavior modification, particularly *positive* programming (LaVigna, 1987) is to create an *instructional environment* where individuals acquire functional, age-appropriate skills across a variety of domains and develop alternative behaviors that serve the same function as the problem behaviors targeted for intervention.

This chapter serves to guide employment specialists and other professionals in the development, implementation, and refinement of behavior programs for individuals who exhibit behavior problems in work environments. There have been numerous books and articles written about the modification of behavior. Readers are encouraged to gather additional and more in-depth information from sources such as Sulzer-Azaroff and Mayer (1977), Snell (1987), and LaVigna and Donnellan (1986). All of the interventions are discussed in sufficient detail to enable individuals to use them accurately; however, caution must be exercised. Competence in the implementation of applied behavior analysis is developed through a range of modalities, including reading, observing others, using these techniques, and receiving feedback from experts.

In the development of behavioral programs for individuals like Randy, whose situation is described at the beginning of this chapter, procedures and techniques must be utilized that enhance self-esteem, develop competence, facilitate independence, promote relationships with others, and contribute to an individual's place and role within the community. To accomplish these goals, care must be taken to arrange positive events and appropriate instructional programming. Empirical research supports the notion that environmental consequences affect behavior (Sulzer-Azaroff & Mayer, 1977). Behavior followed by reinforcing consequences does increase in frequency. Employment specialists must maximize the opportunities that people have to access and receive reinforcement. It is important that people with disabilities receive positive reinforcement (feedback) for their display of appropriate behavior. Professionals' efforts must be directed toward programs that *promote success* for consumers and provide them with opportunities to access positive reinforcement.

Even with consistent and frequent positive reinforcement, some individuals may continue to display severe behavior problems that greatly interfere with the learning process and their employment opportunities. The use of other techniques, in conjunction with positive reinforcement, will also be discussed in this chapter.

In all circumstances, consideration must be given to the impact of an intervention on the dignity, respect, employment, and fundamental rights of the individual as well as his or her relationships with coworkers.

HELP IS POSSIBLE

It is possible to modify the problem behavior of persons experiencing disabilities. As professionals, we must remember the following:

The process is time consuming. The person with the disability may have engaged in the behavior for a considerable amount of time and thus the behavior will not change overnight.

Tactics must be consistently applied. All of the procedures utilized to remediate behavior must be used consistently in order to clearly communicate expectations to consumers.

An analytic approach should be taken. To determine the exact nature of problem behaviors, a careful analysis of the ecology or the environment of the person must be performed.

Cooperation and collaboration with other agencies is essential. To successfully implement any behavioral program, agency cooperation and collaboration is paramount. All aspects of the person's program demand coordination among individuals and agencies.

Patience is a virtue. As with all people, change occurs slowly. People with disabilities should not be pushed too hard at the start. A slow, steady, and consistent approach usually works best.

All programs must be success oriented. The behavior programs developed must encourage success for the person with disabilities.

Establish control for short periods and gradually extend them. It is important to establish control over behavior for short periods of time. As the individual's behavior changes, efforts to extend the behavioral control to longer periods of time, new tasks, new situations, and new people should be initiated.

GUIDING PRINCIPLES ASSOCIATED WITH BEHAVIOR CHANGE

Facilitating socially appropriate behavior is one of the most challenging tasks encountered by employment specialists and other team members. Toward the goal of community-based employment for persons experiencing disabilities, employment specialists and other professionals must be sensitive to the response by coworkers and employers to the use of certain behavioral procedures. In using behavior management strategies, the ultimate goal is to teach individual skills that are socially appropriate and functional, while simultaneously decreasing inappropriate behavior. Utilizing applied behavior analysis techniques demands competent employment specialists who have been well prepared through education, training, experience, supervision, and support. Behavior management interventions are not conducted in isolation. Rather, all efforts must be directed in a coordinated manner involving team participation, including family members.

The following principles have been adopted to assure that the rights of all individuals with disabilities are respected when behavior management interventions are developed and implemented. These tenets are necessary to protect the individual rights and liberties of all persons experiencing disabilities.

Human and legal rights are never jeopardized and are always respected when behavior management procedures are used. Since individuals with disabilities are potentially at risk for abuse and/or harm, professionals must exercise extreme caution in safeguarding their rights when behavior management procedures are utilized. To guarantee the protection, safety, and rights of all persons experiencing disabilities, the following caveats apply:

- Corporal punishment and verbal abuse (name calling, distasteful language, shouting, or any other behavior infringing on a person's rights and damaging to their self-respect) are never used as techniques to manage behavior. Instead, all procedures used are humane and communicate dignity and respect.
- Individuals experiencing disabilities should never be denied nutritionally adequate diets to manage behavior.
- Physical restraint is employed only when absolutely needed to protect the individual from harming him- or herself or others. Restraint is never used as punishment, for staff convenience, or in lieu of educational and vocational programming. If used, this procedure must be implemented in such a manner as to respect the individual's privacy and avoid discomfort on the part of coworkers. All incidents of physical restraint must be reported immediately to supervisory staff.

Interventions occur from the least to the most obtrusive. Behavior management procedures vary in the extent of their obtrusiveness or restrictiveness—that is, in how much these strategies infringe upon the rights of persons with disabilities. Procedures vary with respect to who selects the schedule and type of reinforcement, who monitors behavior and determines when the consequences are delivered, whether procedures entail any aversive components, and the situations where the procedures are implemented. All actions must be directed toward using positive approaches and eliminating aversive procedures. These efforts must occur in the least restrictive setting possible.

Specific information about the targeted behavior and the effectiveness of previous intervention strategies must be clearly documented. Prior to the implementation of any behavior management program, staff must document the existence of the interfering behavior. Evidence supporting the intense and pervasive nature of the behavior must be available. Validation of this behavior as problematic occurs through direct, daily measurements of the behavior. Frequency, percentage of time, duration, or rate are appropriate measurements to use in determining the extent of the maladaptive behavior. These data should be graphed and utilized to evaluate the outcomes of the behavior management program. All data should be reviewed by supervisory staff and the behavior management review committee.

Behavior management programs are always written prior to their implementation. Programs must make use of those practices that empirical research has demonstrated are most effective in changing behavior. Each behavior management program should consist of the following components:

- Instructional objectives
- Specific techniques to be used
- A schedule for use of the methods in the program
- The settings in which the program will be implemented
- The person(s) who will be responsible for program implementation
- The individual(s) who will supervise the program
- Data collection and graphing procedures that will be used to evaluate individual progress toward the objective
- The potential benefits and side effects of the proposed program
- Specific timelines to review the program

Behavior management programs must be reviewed systematically by competent, well-trained professionals. Prior to the implementation of any behavior management program, a review committee must evaluate the program to assure that the proposed procedures do not interfere with individual legal and ethical rights. Intervention procedures must be subject to a thorough review by the committee. This committee should consist of members who are free from any conflict of interest with the agency and/or the individual being helped. Knowledgeable professionals and advocates are likely choices. The committee, consisting of three to five members, can include

- Attorney
- Behavior management specialist
- Community member
- Community-based employer
- Direct care staff
- Family member
- Physician or nurse
- Psychologist
- Social worker
- Special educator

This committee must meet on a regular basis. A structure to ensure the expedient, yet accurate review of materials must be established. Committee members must make decisions about behavior management programs, taking into account the empirical evidence available.

All approved procedures can be implemented only by individuals who are trained and competent in the use of that particular technique. Only those individuals who are qualified in the use of a specific procedure will be allowed to implement the program. Staff must participate in training specifically designed to teach them about the proper use of the procedures. Training should include didactics (basic information), demonstration, practice, and feedback. Employment specialists should have opportunities to observe personnel utilizing these techniques correctly in real life and/or videotaped situations.

Feedback should be provided on a regular basis to assure that the accurate implementation of the program is maintained.

In the development of behavior management programs, the particular tasks, job, and work environment of an individual must be considered. Professionals should attend to the impact of proposed behavior management strategies on the individual and his or her work environment. Programs should require feedback from coworkers and employers about the appropriateness and tolerance for designated behavior management techniques within that milieu. Employment specialists must be extremely sensitive to the dynamics of the work setting and take measures to ensure the success of the program.

Consent from a parent or legal guardian must be obtained. A signed, written agreement between the agency and the individual's parent or legal guardian must be obtained. This form should detail the specifics of the program and be secured prior to the program implementation.

Documentation of program implementation and effectiveness must occur. The results of the program must be documented systematically to determine whether it is actually modifying the behavior of an individual. This documentation includes the measurement of individual behavior when the program is in effect. Usually programs should be implemented for five consecutive days prior to judgment about the overall effectiveness of the treatment. Often it is helpful to monitor several behaviors in order to determine program effectiveness.

Behavior management programs must be monitored. Since the impact of intervention techniques changes over time, it is imperative that these programs be evaluated over time. Research has revealed that the effect of certain reinforcers and mild punishment decrease over time. Subsequently, when either contingency is utilized, change in the consequences must be assessed. It may be necessary to change the event or the schedule for delivery. Therefore, continued daily monitoring of the program determines the efficacy of the program and whether changes need to be made in the program specifics. Also, monitoring provides information essential in the decision-making process concerning consequences and the introduction of less obtrusive measures.

Consultation should be requested. Suggestions and practical advice from individuals outside of an agency should be requested to assure that program implementation is smooth, effective, and producing the desired results. An educational and/or behavioral specialist can provide assistance to staff in developing, monitoring, and adapting individual behavior management programs.

THE BEHAVIORAL INTERVENTION PROCESS

The behavioral intervention process is complex; it requires extensive planning and is one of the most involved processes that employment specialists assume in their work. Preparation, planning, and careful thought are essential to the proper development of a behavioral program that will best meet the needs of an individual experiencing a disability. Since adequate preparation will assist in the acquisition of skills and amelioration of maladaptive behavior, this systematic procedure will be detailed. Figure 8.1 presents an overview of each of the necessary steps in the behavioral intervention process. Each of the steps will be discussed in detail.

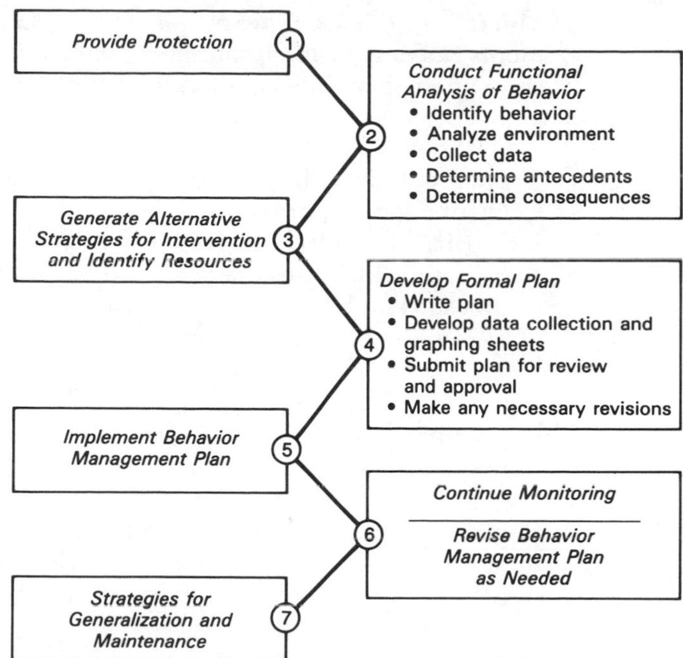

Figure 8.1 Steps to Follow in the Behavioral Intervention Process

1. Provide Protection

For some individuals with disabilities who display life-threatening behavior or behavior that is potentially damaging to themselves or others, it is imperative that action be taken to minimize if not eliminate any potential or real danger to the individual, the coworkers, and other people in the environment. Strategies include removing the individual and others from the environment; removing materials; rearranging furniture, equipment, or materials; instructing and/or interfering with the individual's movement within the environment; and under certain circumstances, physically restraining the person. If an individual requires isolation or restraint, the incident must be recorded and communicated via a written report to a supervisor.

2. Conduct Functional Analysis of Behavior

First, a behavior must be selected for change. Although several behaviors may be of concern, one behavior should be chosen that will serve as the focus of the behavior management program. This behavior should be specified in terms that are specific, observable, and measureable (Mager, 1975). Selection of the target behavior is based on the priorities for behavior change as expressed by the consumer, family members, and other team members. After the behavior is specified, an analysis of the environment or ecology can be conducted. The function of this analysis is to determine whether some isolated and/or physical events in the surrounding environment may be contributing to the maladaptive behavior. Following are environment aspects that should be considered.

Medical problems. The person with disabilities may have physical ailments causing the inappropriate behavior, including constipation, seizures, colds, dental problems, allergies, side effects of medication, or acute illnesses.

Support pattern. The individual may be reacting to the absence of support by displaying inappropriate behavior. Sometimes having too few supports for a particular individual may result in the exhibition of problem behavior. Behavioral difficulties may also be related to too much support, frequent changes in employment specialist, or differences associated with the gender of the employment specialist.

Hunger or thirst. If inappropriate behavior occurs prior to meals and/or break times on a consistent basis, the individual may be communicating hunger or thirst.

Boredom. Behavior problems may be a substitute for inactivity. Employment settings that are stimulating and rich in meaningful activity should be developed for all individuals with disabilities.

Crowding. Too many people in a small space may result in behavioral problems.

Noise. Loud and frequent noise may be responsible for some inappropriate behavior. If possible noise at the worksite should always be kept at moderate levels.

Temperature. Radical changes in temperature or extreme temperatures such as hot or cold may contribute to the display of behavior problems. It is wise to provide individuals who have disabilities with settings that have consistent, comfortable, and reasonable temperatures. Supplementing clothing in the winter may be helpful and providing sources of relief in the summer (e.g., air-conditioning, fans, cold beverages) would be advisable.

Frustration. When confronted with tasks that are too difficult or poorly presented, persons with disabilities may engage in problematic behavior. In such cases, consider extra support and teaching new work skills.

Fear. When individuals are fearful yet unable to communicate their fears, they may engage in inappropriate behavior. Analyzing the work environment with the subsequent restructuring may assist in remedying the problem behavior.

Poorly trained staff. When employment specialists attend to inappropriate behaviors, they may be teaching persons with disabilities to engage in these problematic behaviors. Employment specialists must be properly trained in systematic approaches to teach socially appropriate behavior and to extinguish inappropriate behavior. Intensive instruction is often needed to deal effectively with such problem behaviors.

Figure 8.2 highlights the factors to consider in analyzing inappropriate behaviors. The information has been adapted from Powell et al. (1985). Figure 8.3 presents key questions that can be asked to prevent the occurrence of behavior problems.

1. Individual factors such as:
   - Individual's ability to communicate
   - Person's adaptive behavior
   - Person's competence
   - Person's access to reinforcement
   - Individual's expectation of the job
2. Biological factors such as:
   - Thirst or hunger
   - Health
   - Medical problems (e.g., medications, seizures, allergies, illnesses)
   - Diet, hormones
   - Sensory disturbances (e.g., undiagnosed hearing loss, visual impairment)
3. Environmental factors such as:
   - Crowding, noise, temperature, lighting
   - Weather
   - Accommodations for handicaps
   - Changes in the environment
   - Materials and physical objects in the environment
4. Grouping and staffing factors such as:
   - Group composition (too similar, too diverse)
   - Person–staff ratio (too much/too little attention)
   - Person–employer ratios
   - Interactions between person and staff; person and coworkers; person and employer
   - Staff expertise and consistency
   - Staff/employer supervision
5. Programmatic factors such as:
   - Frustration in communication (receptive or expressive)
   - Meaningless, boring, or frustrating tasks and materials
   - Too much or too little attention
   - Too much or too little structure
   - Density of reinforcement
   - Seriousness of behavior problems
6. Family/home factors such as:
   - Changes within the home environment
   - Relationships with significant others
   - Illness or separation from significant others
   - Move from one environment to another

(Source: Information adapted from Powell et al., 1985.)

Figure 8.2 Factors That Influence Behavior

An integral component of any behavioral program is data collection. Data collection provides us with information regarding the frequency, duration, and intensity of the targeted behavior. It also enables the effects of the program to be monitored and evaluated as to its efficacy. The collection of data prior to the onset of the program or baseline and throughout the pro-

In order to prevent behavior problems, have you tried to:

- Create an atmosphere that is positive?
- Provide frequent consistent reinforcement?
- Interpret the individual's communicative intent?
- Provide appropriate opportunities for excessive energy?
- Create a more stimulating environment?
- Provide more meaningful work?
- Give assistance at critical moments?
- Increase structure and consistency?
- Decrease demands at critical moments?
- Systematically ignore attention-seeking behavior?
- Set priorities to avoid confrontations?
- Change jobs?
- Restructure the tasks?
- Restructure the work environment?
- Reduce environmental stimulation?
- Change staffing patterns?
- Increase support services?

Figure 8.3 The Prevention of Behavior Problems

gram provides for comprehensiveness in the development and implementation of a behavior management program. (See Chapter 7 on data collection.)

A functional analysis of behavior allows for the identification of the antecedents (*A*'s), and consequences (*C*'s) associated with the previously specified behaviors (*B*'s). The antecedents and consequences influence the exhibition of the behavior. *Antecedents* are those events and situations that occur directly prior to the behavior (e.g., the activity, staff demands, setting, time of day). *Consequences* are those events that immediately follow the problem behavior, such as employer attention, termination of task, or removal from the environment. An *A-B-C* analysis is useful throughout the intervention. Many programs fail due to the absence of the *A-B-C* or functional analysis of behavior (see Chapter 15).

3. Generate Alternative Strategies for Intervention and Identify Resources

A list of potential strategies to be used to deal with the problem behavior should be generated. These strategies are based on empirical evidence supporting their effectiveness. Potential strategies can be generated through a review of the literature or from input from program staff and/or consultants. (See Chapter 15 for details on determining a list of alternative strategies.)

4. Develop a Formal Plan

A comprehensive plan must be developed based on all of the information gathered. The plan should consist of the following components:

A behavior management plan is written. This plan specifies the target behavior and objectives and outlines all of the components of the behavior management program. Plans should be written so that they are easy to understand by staff and family members.

Data and graphing sheets are developed. The purpose of these data sheets is to allow staff to record the dimensions of the behavior targeted for change. The data sheets should be developed based on the specific nature of the behavior and the consumer. These forms should facilitate the collection and graphing of data with ease.

Plan is submitted for approval. The behavior management plan is submitted to the appropriate committees to assure that it does not infringe upon an individual's rights and liberties if procedures are restrictive in nature.

Make any necessary revisions. If the plan needs revisions, those are made.

5. Implement the Behavior Management Plan

Once approval of the behavior management plan has been obtained, the program can be implemented. All necessary program materials such as data sheets and procedures should be prepared prior to the onset of the program. Staff should be adequately trained in the proper use of the behavior management strategies. Additionally, consistent feedback regarding staff performance should be an integral component of any behavior management program.

6. Continue Monitoring; Revise the Behavior Management Plan as Needed

Ongoing data collection and analysis enables the employment specialist to monitor consumer performance and progress. These activities are conducted to ensure that the program is producing the desired outcomes. Upon examination of the data, revisions of the program may be apparent. Minor revisions can be made through input with other colleagues and the supervisor. Any major changes must undergo additional review and approval.

7. Strategies for Generalization and Maintenance

Procedures to facilitate generalization and maintenance must be incorporated into all behavior management programs. These systematic efforts ensure that the skills learned are maintained over time and demonstrated across materials, people, and settings. The discussion in Chapter 13 on general case programming provides a detailed discussion of tactics utilized to promote generalization and maintenance.

SELECT INTERVENTIONS

The following section provides employment specialists with descriptions regarding the implementation of select interventions. Each technique is described and then references for further information are presented.

Positive Reinforcement

Praise. Praise, also referred to as social reinforcement, is an extremely powerful technique to modify behavior. Utilizing praise involves noticing socially appropriate behavior and commenting on that behavior. The appropriate behavior is described. In essence, praise is a form of feedback or acknowledgment, informing the person about his or her behavior, its appropriateness, and its desirability. Praise is most effective when it is delivered immediately after the desired behavior, is applied consistently, and is genuine in nature. All statements are offered in a manner that is respectful to the individual and promotes self-esteem. Praise follows the desired behavior and serves to increase the frequency of that targeted behavior. If Fred has just completed an assembly task accurately, an employment specialist could say, "Way to go Fred, that's great! You finished the job."

Praise with Tangible Reinforcers. For some individuals with disabilities, praise may not be a learned or effective motivator. In these situations, rewards (primary reinforcers) such as food can be paired with social reinforcers. When tangible rewards are used, praise should always be paired with the tangibles. Efforts should be directed toward fading tangible reinforcements and utilizing only social reinforcers.

Select References

Jens, K. E., & Shores, R. J. (1969). Behavioral graphs as reinforcers for work behavior of mentally retarded adolescents. *Education and Training of the Mentally Retarded, 4,* 21–28.

Stokes, T., & Baer, D. (1977). An implicit technology of generalization. *Journal of Applied Behavior Analysis, 10,* 349–367.

Differential Reinforcement of Incompatible Behavior (DRI)

Differential reinforcement of incompatible behavior (DRI) has been referred to as the differential reinforcement of competing behavior (DRC) (Donnellan, LaVigna, Negri-Shoultz, & Fassbender, 1988) and the differential reinforcement of alternative behavior (LaVigna & Donnellan, 1986). DRI entails the reinforcement of incompatible or alternative responses that are unable to occur simultaneously with the undesirable behavior. These alternative behaviors must be incompatible with the inappropriate behavior in their intensity, duration, and topography. LaVigna and Donnellan (1986) describe their "100% rule" whereby if the alternative behavior selected for reinforcement and the undesirable behavior targeted for change add up to 100 percent of the possibilities for behavior, the behavior selected for DRI is likely to produce the desired effect. It is important to reinforce the desired behavior frequently at the outset. If the behavior selected for change is to decrease and eventually to eliminate a behavior such as a person's leaving work, the incompatible behavior to be reinforced would be all instances of remaining at or working at the work station.

Select References

Allen, K. E., Hart, B. M., Buell, J. S., Harris, F. R., & Wolf, W. M. (1964). Effects of social reinforcement on isolate behavior of a nursery school child. *Child Development, 35,* 511–518.

Datlow Smith, M., & Coleman, D. (1986). Managing the behavior of adults with autism in the job setting. *Journal of Autism and Developmental Disabilities, 16,* 145–153.

Differential Reinforcement of Other Behaviors (DRO)

Reinforcement occurs after a specified time interval of the nonoccurrence of the targeted behavior (Reynolds, 1961). According to LaVigna and Donnellan (1986), there are several variations of DRO:

1. The classic variation entails setting a timer for a designated interval. If the inappropriate behavior occurs within the specified interval, the timer is reset. However, if the individual fails to display the target behavior, reinforcement is offered.
2. The fixed interval schedule involves the earning of reinforcement if an individual does not engage in the problem behavior for a specific interval (e.g., an hour, 30 minutes).
3. The interval size is increased contingent upon the receipt of reinforcement or some reinforcement schedule. Here, the length of the interval is increased if the individual fails to demonstrate the inappropriate behavior. However, if the inappropriate behavior is observed, the interval length remains fixed.

Select References

Homor, A. L., & Peterson, L. (1980). Differential reinforcement of other behavior: A preferred response elimination procedure. *Behavior Therapy, 11*, 449–471.

LaVigna, G. W., & Donnellan, A. M. (1986). *Alternatives to punishment: Solving behavior problems with non-aversive strategies.* New York: Irvington.

Repp, A. C., & Deitz, S. M. (1974). Reducing aggressive and self-injurious behavior of institutionalized retarded children through reinforcement of other behaviors. *Journal of Applied Behavior Analysis, 7*, 313–325.

Repp, A. C., Deitz, S. M., Deitz, D. E. D. (1976). Reducing inappropriate behaviors in classrooms and in individual sessions through DRO schedules of reinforcement. *Mental Retardation, 14*(1), 11–15.

Differential Reinforcement of Low Rates of Behavior (DRL)

Reinforcement of the inappropriate behavior occurs when low rates of the behavior are emitted. Differential reinforcement of low rates of behavior (DRL) is used to reduce, not eliminate, a designated behavior. The procedure entails the delivery of reinforcement contingent upon the occurrence at or below a predetermined rate. Here the goal is to reward behavior that occurs at reasonable rates. For example, Mary constantly talks to her coworkers; this interferes with the company's productivity. In using DRL, Mary is rewarded for speaking with others at a lower rate than what she exhibited during baseline. As she decreases her talking to coworkers, expectations are shifted, and her rate of talking to others is lessened until she displays an acceptable rate of talking with others at work.

Select References

Deitz, S. M., & Repp, A. C. (1973). Decreasing classroom misbehavior through the use of DRL schedules of reinforcement. *Journal of Applied Behavior Analysis, 6*, 457–463.

Deitz, S. M., & Repp, A. C. (1974). Differentially reinforcing low rates of misbehavior with normal elementary school children. *Journal of Applied Behavior Analysis, 7*, 622.

Extinction/Ignoring (of Nonthreatening Behavior)

The purpose of extinction is to reduce a particular inappropriate behavior. In extinction, reinforcement is withheld following the specified behavior. Ignoring specifically withholds attention when an inappropriate behavior is demonstrated. This procedure gradually produces changes in the behavior and is rarely effective when used in isolation. An initial increase in the inappropriate behavior is expected when extinction is utilized. Extinction or ignoring should only be used for behaviors that are not threatening to individuals and/or coworkers. The use of ignoring of inappropriate behavior contingently with the reinforcing of appropriate behavior is an effective technique to modify behavior.

Select References

Williams, C. D. (1959). The elimination of tantrum behavior by extinction procedures. *Journal of Abnormal and Social Psychology, 59*, 269.

Gentle Teaching

Gentle teaching is a values-based approach to dealing with a range of behavior problems. The strategy precludes punishment as an option for treatment. Rather, the focus is on teaching bonding between the individual with disabilities and his or her care giver. In this case, "bonding signifies the warm and reciprocal relationship that needs to exist between care givers and persons with special needs. It is an affectional tie that one person forms with another—a tie that bonds them together and endures over time" (McGee, Menolascino, Hobbs, & Menousek, 1987, pp. 15–16). A critical component of the intervention is to create, enhance, and teach individuals to bond and relate. The assumption is that people with disabilities engage in maladaptive behavior due to the absence of bonding between themselves and their care givers. In gentle teaching, reciprocal ties of affection are developed and nurtured by teaching the values of human presence, participation, and reward. Persons with disabilities learn to associate the care givers with security and safety. Participation is reflected by human warmth and affection. The interactions between the care givers, or in this instance the employment specialist, are rewarding through their words and physical contact. Gentle teaching utilizes a range of respectful strategies that promote human contact and relationships. In dealing with severe behavior problems, professionals are encouraged to ignore the behavior, redirect the person, and provide reinforcement. In considering Randy's aggression, the following strategies could be used as indicated by gentle teaching:

Protect self as unobtrusively as possible.
Do not provide eye contact.
Ignore the hitting.
Minimize physical contact.
Make no comments about the aggression.
Redirect the person to the activity calmly.
Provide prompting to help the person resume the task.
Continue providing teaching opportunities.
Provide powerful reward.

In using all of these procedures, an integral component of gentle teaching is the relationship between individuals, a relationship consisting of mutuality, equality, human warmth, affection, and friendship.

Select References

Jordan, J., Singh, N. N., & Repp, A. C. (1989). An evaluation of gentle teaching and visual screening in the reduction of stereotype. *Journal of Applied Behavior Analysis, 22*, 9–22.

McGee, J. J. Menolascino, F. J., Hobbs, D. C., & Menousek, P. E. (1987). *Gentle*

teaching: A non-aversive approach to helping persons with mental retardation. New York: Human Sciences Press.
McGee, J. J., Menolascino, F. J., & Menousek, P. E. (in press). *Gentle teaching.* Texas: Pro-Ed.

Behavioral Contracting

A behavioral contract consists of a written agreement between two individuals, in this instance the individual and the employment specialist. An effective contracting program entails

The behavior to be increased
The behavior to be decreased
Specific consequences for each behavior
Procedures for evaluating the contract

This written agreement or commitment can be negotiated between both parties. In all cases, measures must be taken to assure that the specifications do not infringe on an individual's basic human or civil rights.

Select References

Homme, L., Csanyi, A. P., Gonzales, M. A., & Rechs, J. S. (1969). *How to use contingency contracting in the classroom.* Champaign, IL: Research Press.

Time Out (Activity)

Activity time out entails removing an individual from an activity that is reinforcing contingent on some undesirable behavior. For example, if Mark is on his coffee break and starts to talk loudly and swear, in using activity time out, a professional would remove Mark from the situation for a short period of time. This time period is one that would have been predetermined prior to the instance of inappropriate behavior.

Select References

Barton, E. S., Guess, D., Garcia, E., & Baer, D. (1970). Improvement of retardates' mealtime behaviors by time-out procedures using multiple baseline techniques. *Journal of Applied Behavior Analysis, 2,* 77.

Token Economy

A token economy is a contingency package that incorporates numerous effective behavioral procedures, primarily those utilizing reinforcement tactics (Sulzer-Azaroff & Mayer, 1977). Tokens are delivered contingent upon the desired behavior immediately after the occurrence of that behavior. Social reinforcement is offered along with the token. Later, the tokens are redeemed for a reinforcing object, event, or activity. For example, Mark sorts mail by the first number of its zip code. His productivity is measured by the number of items sorted correctly; he receives poker chips for a specified amount of items correctly sorted and then exchanges them for money at the end of the week.

Select References

Ayllon, T., & Azrin N. (1968). *The token economy: A motivational system for therapy and rehabilitation.* New York: Appleton.

Kazdin, A. E. (1977). *The token economy: A review and evaluation.* New York: Plenum.

Kazdin, A. E., & Bootzin, R. R. (1972). The token economy: An evaluative review. *Journal of Applied Behavior Analysis, 5,* 343–372.

McCuller, G. L., Salzberg, C. L., & Lignugaris/Kraft, B. (1987). Producing generalized job initiative in severely mentally retarded sheltered workers. *Journal of Applied Behavior Analysis, 20,* 413–420.

Response Cost (Mild)

Response cost is a procedure whereby reinforcers are removed based on a particular response. Mild response cost entails the withdrawal of reinforcers that are not the personal property of the individual with a disability. An example of response cost would be the removal of a token for disrupting work or loss of time from a coffee break.

Select References

Kazdin, A. E. (1972). Response cost: The removal of conditional reinforcers for therapeutic change. *Behavior Therapy, 3,* 533–546.

Verbal Reprimand

Verbal reprimand makes use of a verbal statement of disapproval for an undesirable behavior demonstrated by someone other than the person experiencing a disability. Verbal reprimands are delivered in a stern, loud manner. Staff should clearly communicate their dissatisfaction to the individual. Under no circumstances should verbal reprimands be delivered in the presence of other people.

Select References

Shultz, R., Wehman, P., Renzaglia, A., & Karan, O. (1978). Efficiency of social disapproval of inappropriate verbalizations of two severely retarded males. *Behavior Therapy, 9,* 657–662.

Time Out (Contingent Observation)

During contingent observation, an individual is removed from the opportunity to experience positive reinforcement. In some instances, individuals are removed from a reinforcing situation such as a social gathering and sit away from the group observing others. Here the person experiencing disabilities is excluded, not secluded, from the other employees. In implementing contingent observation, an employment specialist would:

State specifically what the person did to earn time out
Have the individual remain in timeout for a relatively short duration (one to five minutes)
Return the individual to the activity after one minute of appropriate behavior
Reinforce the individual's appropriate behavior immediately upon return to the situation.

Select References

Foxx, R. M., & Shapiro, S. T. (1978). The time out ribbon: A non-exclusionary time out procedure. *Journal of Applied Behavior Analysis, 11,* 125–136.

Powell, T. H., & Powell, I. Q. (1982). The use and abuse of using time out procedures for disruptive pupils. *The Pointer, 26*(2), 18–22.

Notes on the Use of Aversives and Physical Restraint

Some of the procedures discussed in this chapter, including time out, response cost, and extinction, must be used judiciously. Their use should be carefully evaluated prior to implementation by the behavior management committee. Other tactics such as punishment, negative reinforcement, overcorrection, and physical restraint are aversive and highly obtrusive in the lives of individuals with disabilities. These procedures demand extensive review and approval by the behavior management committee if they are to be utilized. In all cases, less obtrusive and dehumanizing techniques must be attempted. All of these aversive procedures should be considered only after less restrictive methods have been attempted and have failed to alter inappropriate behavior. Aversives such as electric shock, psychotropic drugs, or chemical restraint, water mist, lemon juice, ammonia, ice, mouthwash, and isolation must be avoided at all costs.

Physical restraint should only be used when the intensity and severity of behavior will cause harm to the individual or other people in the environment. These procedures must only be administered by competent professionals and must be monitored rigorously. Physical restraint is a serious procedure and should be used only in emergencies; this tactic should not be used in lieu of vocational and/or educational training or as punishment. The use of any aversive procedure must be subject to comprehensive review.

Select References

Baumeister, A. A., & Baumeister, A. A. (1978). Suppression of repetitive self-injurious behavior by contingent inhalation of aromatic ammonia. *Journal of Autism and Childhood Schizophrenia, 8,* 71–77.

Guess, D., Helmstetter, E., Turnbull, H. R., & Knowlton, S. (1987). *Use of aversive procedures with persons who are disabled: A historical review and critical analysis.* Seattle: Association for Persons with Severe Handicaps.

LaVigna, G. W., & Donnellan, A. M. (1986). *Alternatives to punishment: Solving behavior problems with non-aversive strategies.* New York: Irvington.

Lovaas, O. I., & Favell, J. E. (1987). Protection for clients undergoing aversive/restrictive intervention. *Education and Treatment of Children, 10,* 311–325.

McGee, J. J., Menolascino, F. J., Hobbs, D. C., & Menousek, P. E. (1987). *Gentle teaching: A non-aversive approach to helping persons with mental retardation.* New York: Human Sciences Press.

CLOSING REMARKS ON BEHAVIORAL INTERVENTION IN COMMUNITY-BASED EMPLOYMENT

As professionals dealing with persons who exhibit severe behavior problems, employment specialists are confronted with numerous challenges that provide lessons regarding professional values and competence. Employment specialists may utilize many of the techniques described in this chapter. The role of the employment specialist in modifying behavior is paramount. Interactions with persons with disabilities should guided by the following quotation from John F. Kennedy (1963): "Every American ought to have the right to be treated as he would wish to be treated, as one would wish his children to be treated."

Action Options

- Develop a program to modify the inappropriate behavior of an individual with a disability.
- Attend meetings of different behavior management review committees.
- Talk with employers and coworkers about appropriate behavior management procedures to use in the work environment.

CHAPTER 9

Ongoing Supports

Follow-up should not be taken lightly, nor should it center solely on problems and deficits. Follow-up services are a necessary function of a supported work program attempting to create employment opportunities for persons with handicaps.

F. Rusch, Competitive Employment Issues and Strategies

Jill has acquired the specific competencies to complete all of the required activities of being a stenographer for a local law firm. She is an individual with a chronic mental illness who obtained her current job with the collaboration of an employment specialist from a local community-based agency. This agency provided Jill with a wide array of ongoing supports that would still be available to her through individuals from the agency. These supports included the availability of a social club, financial counseling regarding the condition of her benefits and earnings, advocacy for extending clinical hours, and assistance in relocating her residence. Without these ongoing supports the probability of Jill continuing to be successfully employed diminishes. These supports are negotiated and changed as needed as part of a three-month ongoing update and a current profile is developed of current and future supports that Jill needs to maintain her employment. Jill is the recipient of the final phase of supported employment: ongoing supports.

Learning Outcomes

After reading this chapter you will be able to

- Define the term *ongoing supports* and describe its place in the supported employment process.
- List seven potential supports that could be offered by an agency that provides supported employment for consumers with disabilities.
- List five activities that could be included within the ongoing supports of financial planning, coworker involvement, and off-work-hours contact by employment specialists.

- Describe a range of options within the activity of SSI-Medicaid benefits of a financial ongoing support.
- Describe the ingredients of a monthly profile form to track the delivery of ongoing supports for a worker with a disability.

INTRODUCTION

Supported employment is perhaps best differentiated from traditional employment services by the requirement that ongoing supports be an integral part of the process. In this chapter a process for each agency to develop its own ongoing supports is presented. Several alternatives are recommended, with sample activities that are presently part of selected agencies' ongoing supports for individuals with severe disabilities. The growth of this process was pioneered by Wilcox and Bellamy (1987) in their activities catalog for family members of students with severe disabilities.

Definition

Ongoing supports are those activities that need to occur for the worker to maintain employment. These activities commence following the initial acquisition by the worker of critical work skills and begins the process of stabilization and fading of intense instructional supports. These ongoing activities can be generated by adult service agencies, family members, employers, coworkers, friends, or whoever has a vested interest in the successful employment of a person with a severe disability. There is no magical list of supports that will guarantee success. However, there is a process for developing the critical supports that will enhance the longevity of employment and open up new horizons for advancing along a career ladder to more exciting employment options.

Agency-wide Ongoing Supports

Professionals who are concerned about the long-term employment for persons with severe disabilities need to identify a range of supports that will be offered by the agency as part of their contribution to enhance each worker's continued success in community employment. Before workers receive initial services from the agency, the workers and their family members should know how that agency is going to assist them in maintaining employment once the worker acquires the essential skills to learn the critical activities of that job. All of these supports will not be necessary for each worker, but a list of potentially available supports needs to be developed by each agency.

LISTING OF SUPPORTS

It is good practice for agencies to list the supports that consumers and their families can expect to be available. In fact, it is strongly advised that these supports be included in a notebook or catalog that is presented to the consumers as they first enter the services of the agency. Form 24 in Appendix A is a useful page on which to list the agency-wide supports offered by the adult service provider.

At a recent meeting of providers of employment services the following list of supports was generated:

Advocacy	Instruction
Clinical	Materials modification
Community	Off-work hours
Coworker	Public relations
Education	Recreation
Employer	Social
Family	Transportation
Financial	Work development
Home	

The supports that are generated by agencies that provide employment services should be listed in a format that allows for the identification of activities for each of the supports that the agency is offering the consumer.

RANGE OF ACTIVITIES

For each of the supports that has been identified by the agency a range of activities needs to be developed. These activities determine the parameters of that agency's commitment toward providing a comprehensive array of services for each ongoing support. Form 25 in Appendix A can assist with this process. Three examples are provided to explore the activities that could exist within one agency that provides employment services for individuals with severe disabilities.

Financial Planning

This ongoing support is critical for family members and consumers alike and is essential to the long term success of an individual's employment. Sample activities that could be included within one agency's list of alternatives are:

Advocate for the continuation of medicaid funds and formulae for altering incentive-disincentive balance.
Attend a meeting with family members and social security representatives to establish specifics about subsidies.
Assist workers in cashing their checks.
Develop budgeting skills with each worker.
Establish a relationship between money, a job well done, and what money can buy.
Develop a financial profile for each consumer and document changes in financial status over time.

Coworker Involvement

It is becoming increasingly evident that the involvement of coworkers is essential to the maintenance of long-term employment for persons with disabilities. A potential list of activities that are included within one agency's ongoing supports includes:

Pay coworker extra salary to assume supervisory duties with the worker.
Ask coworkers for feedback about the worker.
Reinforce naturally occurring friendships.
Develop car pools with coworkers.
Encourage conversations by the worker with coworkers.
Develop specific intervention strategies that require involvement and assistance from coworkers.

Off-Work Hours Contact by Agency Representatives

Often the job coach, vocational instructor, job developer, and other personnel from the agency are involved in activities with the worker outside of the regular work hours.

Sample activities may include

Teach work related skills: transportation, banking, shopping, mobility, community outings.
Visit the workers at their home.
Participate in social clubs, job clubs, and other activities.
Invite workers to your home for dinner, parties, conversation, and develop friendships.
Call workers up by telephone to ask, "How's it going?"

ACTIVITY BY LEVEL OF INTENSITY

Some agencies may prefer to develop their range of activities in an order of presentation that reflects the level of intensity of their efforts that will be needed. For planning purposes the resources that are logistically available may be matched to the level of intensity to provide that support. Form 26 is included in Appendix A to assist with this process. One agency developed a sequence of activities that represented a degree of intensity from most to least amount of resources and time, as illustrated in Figure 9.1.

Range of Options within Selected Activities

Some of the activities within ongoing supports have a wide range of possible options that could be available to the consumer. When this is the case Form 27 in Appendix A can be useful. With this form there is room to list the designated ongoing support and an activity that is representative of this support. Beneath each activity a range of options that have been or could be available for consumers of that agency can be listed either by level of intensity or in random order. We will present two examples.

Ongoing Support: Financial
Activity: SSI-Medicaid

Range of Options
Advocate for obtaining a job that contains the necessary health insurance and benefit plans.
Meet with consumer and social security officer to investigate details of incentives-disincentives.
Develop a current/future financial profile for the individual.

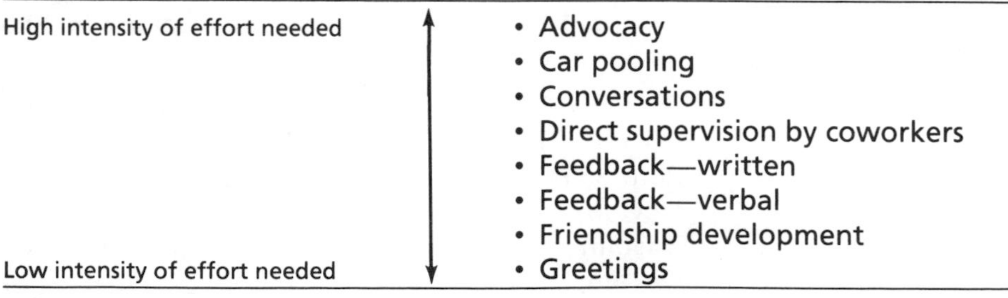

High intensity of effort needed
Low intensity of effort needed
• Advocacy
• Car pooling
• Conversations
• Direct supervision by coworkers
• Feedback—written
• Feedback—verbal
• Friendship development
• Greetings

Figure 9.1 Identified Support: Coworker Involvement

Adjust individual's work schedule to prevent jeopardizing needed subsidy support.
Communicate with representatives from neighboring agencies about how they have dealt with SSI-Medicaid situation.
Attend workshops and conferences for updates on social security policies.
Read currrent information from social security office.

Ongoing Support: Coworkers
Activity: Enhancing Friendships

Range of Options:
Provide opportunities for coworkers to participate in seminars to discuss the ways of teaching new skills to individuals with severe disabilities.
Accompany individual to company activities and assist with activities.
Answer questions from coworkers about the unique considerations of the individual.
Teach individual to initiate, sustain, and terminate social interactions.
Encourage individual to participate in off hours events and coworkers.
Arrange for car pool with a coworker.

MONTHLY PROFILE

A mechanism needs to be established to monitor the number and intensity of supports that are offered by an agency to a worker in supported employment. The activities within each support should at least be analyzed on a monthly basis for a decision about whether to cease, continue, or change the activities as they assist the worker to maintain employment.

Form 20 is included in Appendix A to assist with this process. Included in this form is the type of support, the key (contact) person, frequency of the support, and comments that are specific to that support.

WEIGHING THE BENEFITS AND CHALLENGES

Decisions about what supports need to be in place for each worker in supported employment is a question of balancing the benefits and challenges for the worker, family members, coworkers, employer, agency personnel, and society at large. There are limited resources available and negotiations will ensue between what the worker and advocates desire and what the agency can legitimately provide within its resources. However, this should not be an excuse for not pursuing the supports that are necessary for ensuring long-term employment. The agency can be a broker for additional supports or actively seek additional monies to obtain more resources than would otherwise be available. If supported employment is a commitment by the agency, then a "whatever it takes!" attitude needs to be adopted. There may not currently exist all the supports that address the needs of all workers but professionals need to advocate for the development of anticipated supports where absent.

Action Options

- Develop a financial profile for a worker and monitor changes over time.
- Develop a self-management procedure with a worker.

- Develop an ongoing feedback form to gather information from supervisors, coworkers, and family members.
- Coordinate reinforcement and instructional processes with residential staff members or family members.
- Present the ongoing supports menu of options to family members and lead a discussion of available options.
- Participate in the development and/or revision of an ongoing supports notebook.

CHAPTER 10

Goal Setting

Sometimes the new things you take on cause you anguish—but not always. At other times you experience exhilaration and excitement over the things that are coming into your life. Healthy change is always a bitter-sweet process.

R. Perske, Hope for the Families

Meredith was recently hired by a local hospital to work in the radiology department. Her job consisted of entering data from records onto the computer and filing them for later access. She acquired this task quickly but her rate was about 50 percent of that expected of a person for whom this job is intended. The employment specialist from a local mental health agency established her baseline rate and initiated a goal-setting procedure to assist her in making steady progress toward meeting the expectations of her immediate supervisor. A self-monitoring chart with goals that were realistically established by a joint conference between Meredith and the employment specialist allowed her to meet coworker rates within three months. The exact procedures that were followed by the employment specialist are outlined in this chapter on goal-setting procedures.

Learning Outcomes

After reading this chapter you will be able to

- List the critical steps to the development of a comprehensive goal-setting procedure for increasing the rate of production
- Transfer data onto a graph for decision-making purposes during a goal-setting procedure
- Describe the rationale for increasing the work requirements while maintaining the level of reinforcement for meeting the newly established goals

INTRODUCTION

A critical ongoing support that is provided by the employment specialist is to assist the worker to meet the company's productivity requirements. Efforts must be made to provide workers with the supports to complete their assignments at the rate that is expected of nondisabled coworkers. Some workers may not attain competitive standards but there should be clear documentation that the employment specialist has exhausted all avenues of support that should have been available to the worker. One such support is the development of a goal-setting program to increase a worker's rate of completing an activity up to the standards of the company. The specific steps of this procedure are presented followed by an example of a goal-setting procedure.

GOAL-SETTING STEPS

Step 1: Obtain the Competitive Standard

In a goal-setting procedure the employment specialist must establish a final goal to be obtained by the worker. This standard is obtained from the company supervisor as well as by observing currently-employed coworkers. The instructor notes any discrepancies between what the supervisor states as an expected standard and at what speed/rate currrently employed coworkers actually perform the activity.

Step 2: Establish the Baseline Rate

Once the competitive (expected) standard is derived, the employment specialist obtains the current rate of the worker within the normally occurring circumstances that exist at the worksite. These are the natural cues that would exist if the employment supervisor was absent (see the section on natural cues in Chapter 7). *Rate* is defined as how many units of the activity need to be produced within a designated time interval. Some examples of rate are 1 room to be cleaned per half-hour, 30 napkins, folded per 15 minutes, or 10 checks reviewed per minute.

Step 3: Identify a Reinforcer

A *reinforcer* is something that, once obtained, increases the likelihood that the activity that preceded the reinforcer will continue/increase in the future. Since reinforcers vary among workers, employment specialists must not assume that what is reinforcing for one worker is also reinforcing for another. This step of identifying a significant reinforcer is critical to the success of a goal-setting procedure. The employment specialist must be careful not to select something as a reinforcer that the worker has a right to obtain during the day even if there is no improvement in work performance.

Step 4: Establish an Initial Goal

An initial goal is established to be just above the average baseline rate for the worker. The employment specialist needs to make initial access to the reinforcer easy to obtain. A relationship will develop between reaching an expected rate and receiving the reinforcer.

Step 5: Determine Length of Work Time

After establishing the requirements for an initial goal, the employment specialist determines a reasonable length of time in which the goal should be reached. Some activities occur in half-hour intervals while others may be just a few minutes in duration for the completion of one full cycle of the activity.

Step 6: Establish a Policy for Change

Decision rules need to be established for determining when to increase or decrease the rate requirements for access to the reinforcer. It is extremely important to document the day-to-day progress of the worker and graphing this progress is highly recommended. Based on the data, the employment specialist will know if the current goal is within reach, if the reinforcement procedure is powerful enough, and how quickly or to what degree to make the changes in rate requirements for access to the expected reinforcer. There are no hard and fast rules for changing the rate requirements but as the worker begins adjusting his or her rate to obtain access to the reinforcement, the employment specialist should increase the requirements for reinforcement but within the continued reach of the worker.

Step 7: Provide Feedback to the Worker

After strategies have been planned during the previous steps, the program is explained to the worker in as comprehensible a way as possible. The worker's input could be extremely valuable in adapting the procedures that have been established.

Step 8: Access to the Reinforcement

If the worker's rate matches the first established goal, he or she receives access to the designated reinforcer. If the rate of work is insufficient to obtain access to the reinforcer, the employment specialist states that the person needs to work a little more quickly the next time to earn the reinforcer. No threats are made or negative statements about how slow the work has been completed. Also, the worker should not be able to access the reinforcer for other activities that are completed or it will lose its effectiveness to increase the worker's rate. For example, a selected reinforcer could be earning time to use the guitar of the employment specialist. If the worker fails to meet the established goal for work that day, access to the guitar cannot be obtained by doing any other activities.

Step 9: Monitor Progress

Progress toward attaining the competitive rate is visually represented on a graph as a decision-making aide. The goal is to slowly and successively approximate the sought for goal by reinforcing steps (goals) toward that final objective.

Step 10: Fade the Intensity of the Program

Ultimately, the reinforcement procedures should be faded and/or matched with naturally available reinforcers. Once the competitive standard is met, efforts need to occur to slowly integrate existing, more natural consequences (e.g., paycheck, words of encouragement from coworkers, self-monitoring) at the worksite.

GOAL-SETTING EXAMPLE

In this section a step-by-step example of a goal-setting program is presented to illustrate the steps that were described in the previous section (see Figure 10.1).

The work activity in Figure 10.1 is folding napkins for place settings within a restaurant. To assist in the goal-setting strategies a graph is developed to record Bill's progress in order to make appropriate instructional decisions. In this graph the bottom, horizontal line contains a sequence of consecutive work sessions of a half-hour each. The vertical line contains information about the number of napkins that will be folded within each work session.

It was determined that the acceptable, competitive standard was to fold 60 napkins within a half-hour (see Figure 10.2). The employment specialist observed currently employed workers and verified the time requirements with the restaurant's supervisor. There is room on the graph to record Bill's baseline rate before the goal-setting program (see Figure 10.3).

Sessions 1, 2, and 3

Bill folded 10 napkins for each of the three half-hour work sessions. The employment specialist put a mark above work sessions 1, 2, and 3 at the (10) designation of the vertical line. A line is drawn between each mark. Thus, the instructor has initial visual feedback to compare Bill's rate under currently existing circumstances to the competitive rate of currently employed coworkers.

Session 4

To be sure that the data recorded for sessions 1 through 3 truly reflect an accurate baseline rate, a fourth session is recorded, and since it revealed the

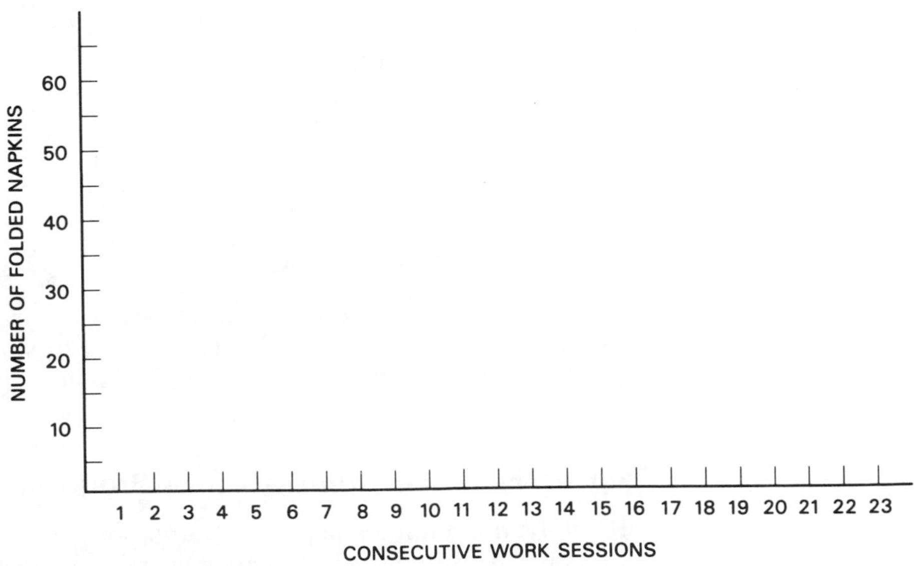

Figure 10.1 Goal-setting Form

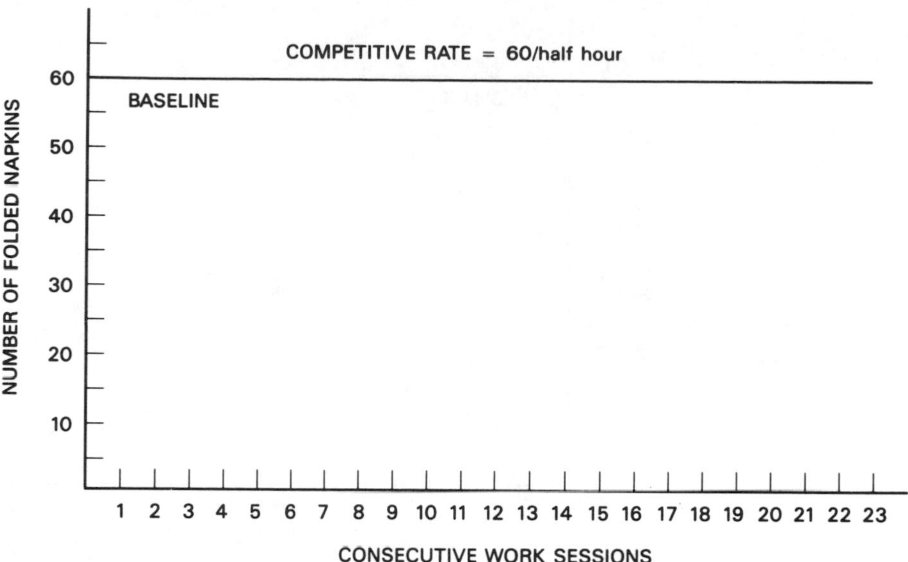

Figure 10.2 Competitive Rate

same pattern a line was drawn after session four to denote the start of a goal-setting procedure (see Figure 10.4).

Prior to explaining the goal-setting procedure to Bill, the instructor identified a reinforcer that Bill could access by attaining the established goals in the program. In this example the incentive was free tokens to use in the pinball machine in the game room during the morning break. These tokens are worth 25¢ each and Bill can participate with other coworkers and save his money for a lunch time dessert at the mobile truck. If Bill fails to meet the established goal, he can continue to use the pinball machine but he would not have the free tokens available.

An initial goal is established at 15 folded napkins per half-hour, which is slightly above the current baseline rate of 10 folded napkins per half-hour (see Figure 10.5). Access to the tokens is explained to Bill if he reaches this goal.

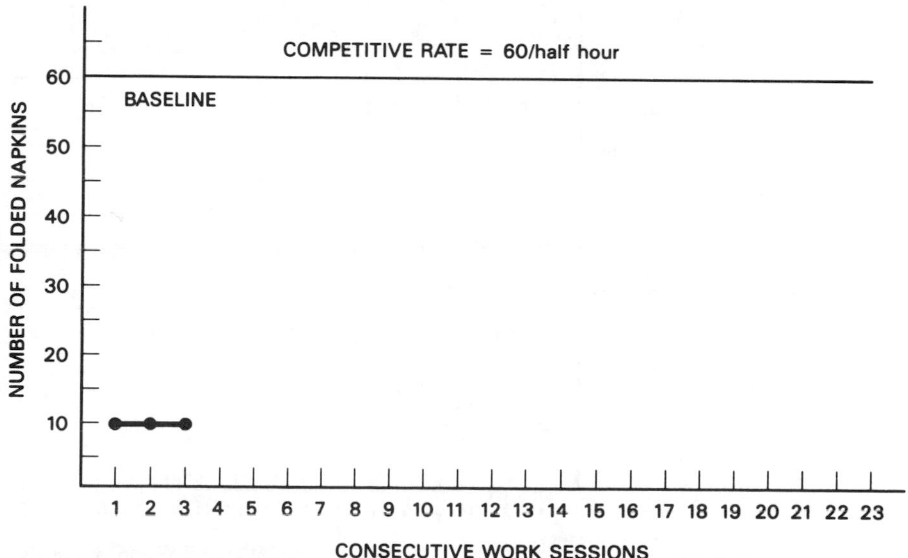

Figure 10.3 Baseline Rate

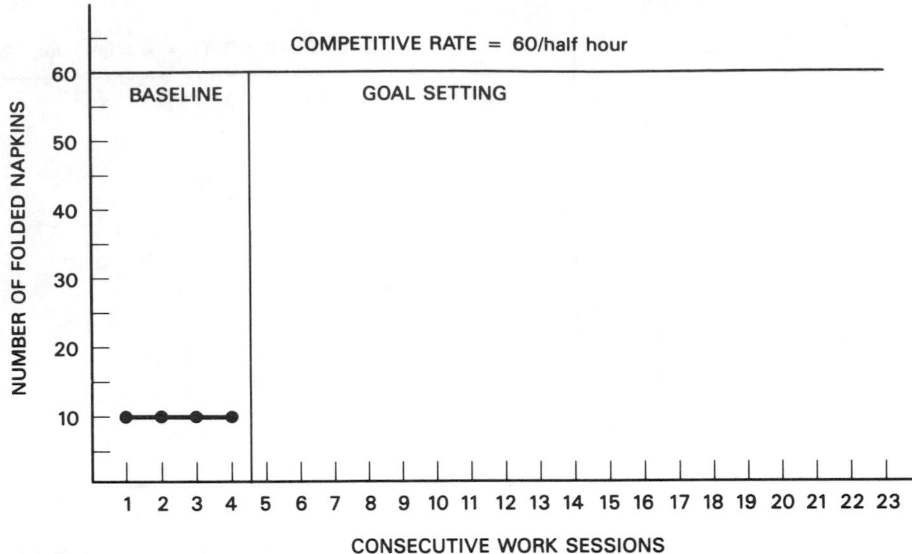

Figure 10.4 Bill's Rate

Session 5

Bill did not reach the established goal of 15 folded napkins but did improve by correctly folding 13 napkins in the allotted time period. He did not bring enough money to operate the pinball machine and the employment specialist informed him that he needed to work a little faster to earn the free tokens for the machine.

Session 6

Bill successfully folded 22 napkins and received the tokens for the pinball machine.

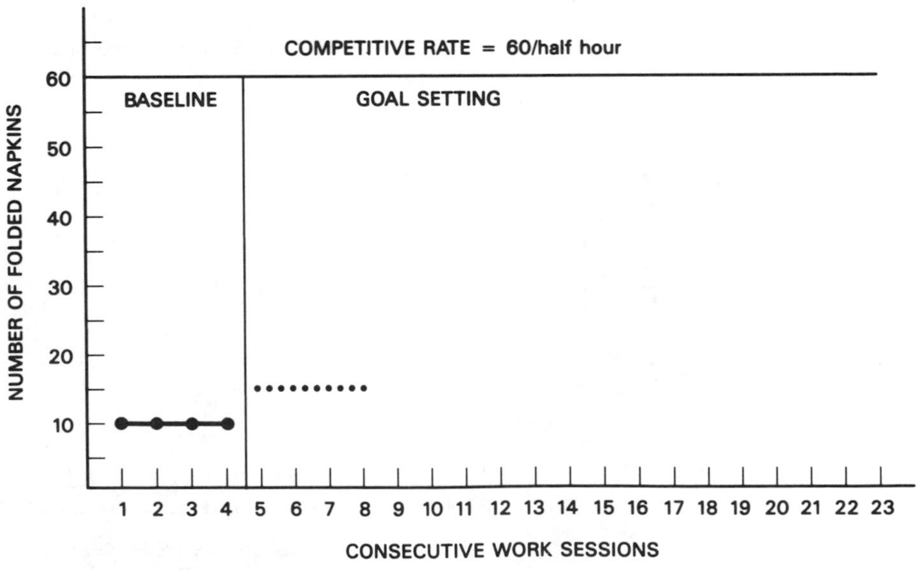

Figure 10.5 Initial Goal Setting

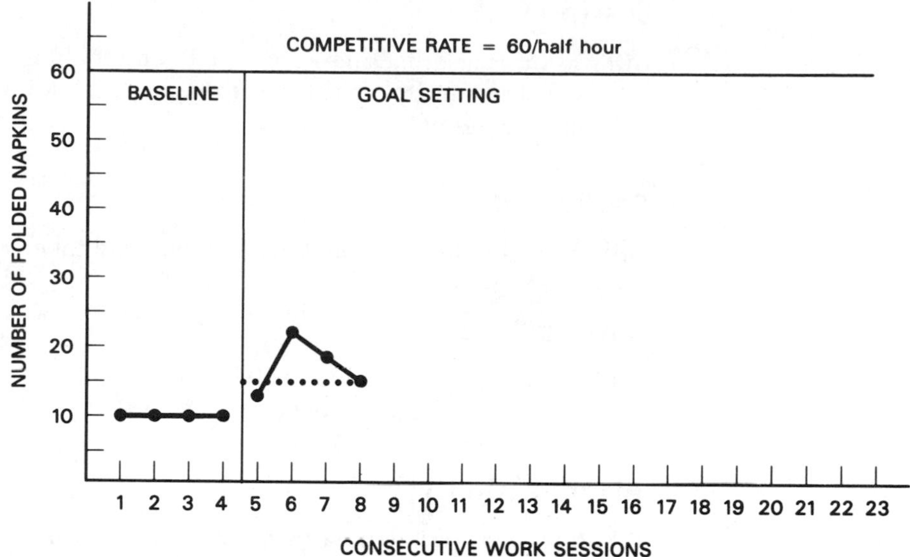

Figure 10.6 Bill's Rate after Initial Goal Setting

Sesssions 7 and 8

Bill's performance decreased although he still worked fast enough to meet the initial criterion. On day 8 his rate was exactly 15 for the half-hour work session (see Figure 10.6).

After Session 8

Since Bill demonstrated that he could work fast enough to fold 20 napkins within the allotted work session, the criterion (goal) was increased to 20 for accessing the tokens for the pinball machine beginning with session 9 (see Figure 10.7).

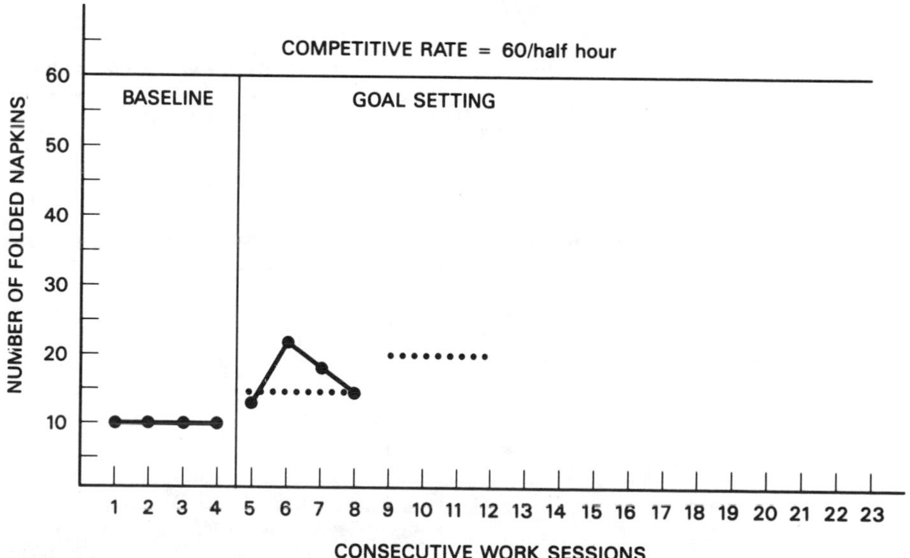

Figure 10.7 Second Goal Setting

Session 9

Bill was informed that a new goal had been set for him before he would have access to the free tokens. Even though Bill folded 17 napkins for work session 9 he did not receive the tokens.

Session 10

Bill correctly folded 27 napkins and received tokens.

Session 11

Bill's productivity dropped to 20 but he continued to receive the tokens for meeting the established goal (see Figure 10.8).

After Session 11

When we review the data that has been recorded for 11 work sessions, it appears that Bill understood the goal-setting program and that it may be time for a bigger jump in the next goal up to 30 napkins for the work session with the same access to the tokens for the pinball machine (see Figure 10.9). Bill is informed of this new goal and the need to eventually work as quickly as is expected of coworkers to complete the activity.

Session 12

Bill increased his rate to 27 folded napkins per half-hour but failed to meet the new goal of 30 established for session 12.

Sessions 13, 14, 15, and 16

Bill's data revealed that his rates of 40, 50, 44, and 36 folded napkins per half-hour exceeded the current goal and he received the tokens for the pinball machine (see Figure 10.10). Also, during these sessions the tokens were presented by a coworker who expressed his appreciation for Bill's fast

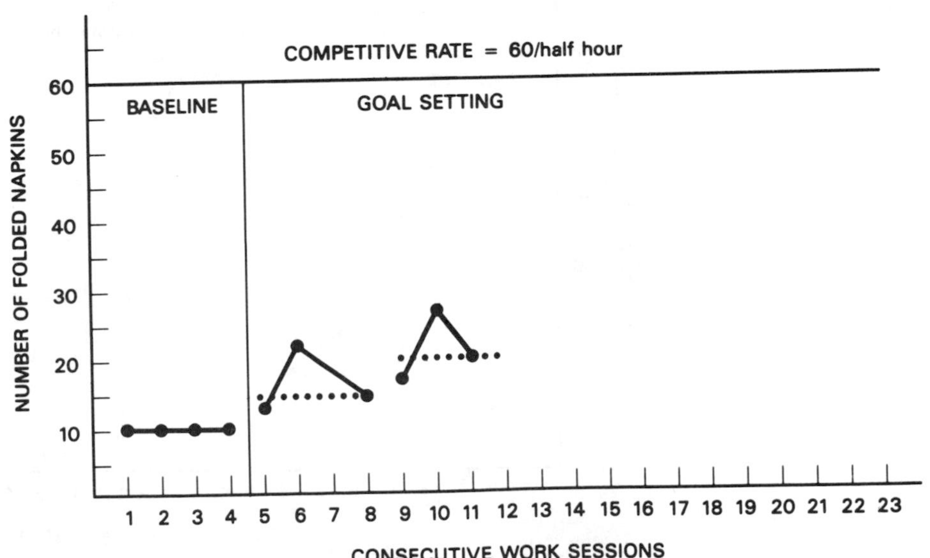

Figure 10.8 Bill's Rate after Second Goal Setting

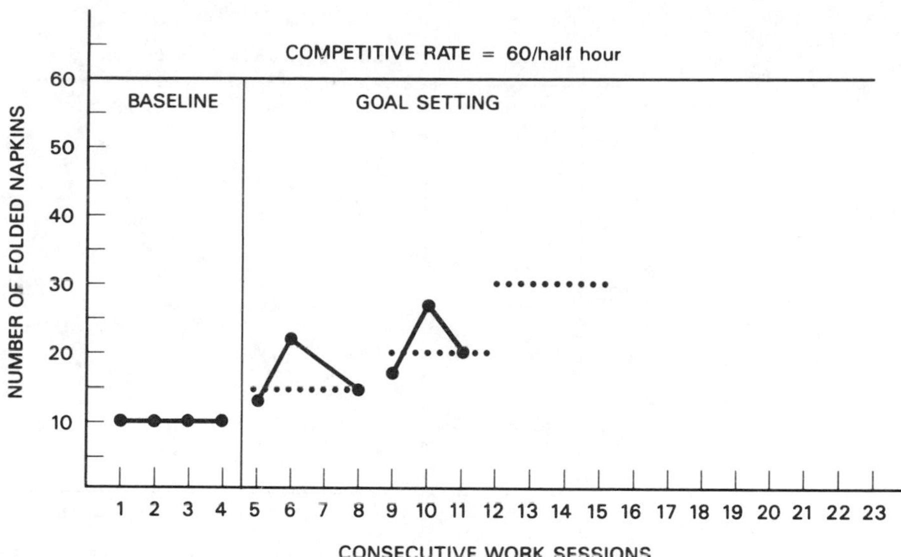

Figure 10.9 Third Goal Setting

work and he encouraged Bill to keep up the good work. As Bill continued to decrease his rate back toward the established rate of 30, the employment specialist decided to increase the goal to 50 (just 10 below the competitive rate).

Session 17

Bill met the jump to 50 by correctly folding 52 napkins in work session 17. The restaurant manager, who was a friend of Bill's, presented him with the tokens for the pinball machine. The employment specialist now must begin to plan for fading this reinforcement to more naturally occurring events. The restaurant manager was impressed with Bill's performance and decided to give him a raise. The employment specialist developed a budget plan with Bill for reserving part of his raise to play pinball and also to encourage him to participate in other break activities with coworkers.

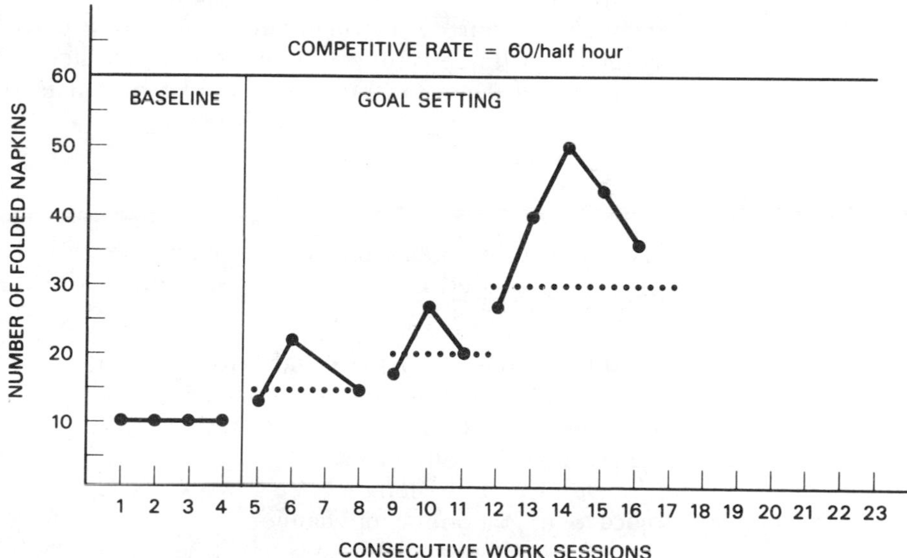

Figure 10.10 Bill's Rate after Third Goal Setting

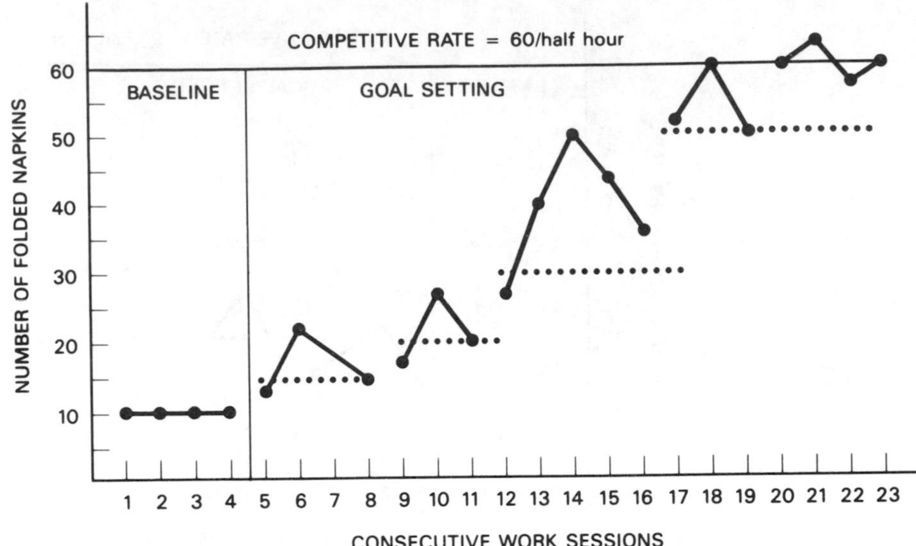

Figure 10.11 Bill's Rate after Fourth Goal Setting and at Competitive Rate

Session 18

Bill completed the activity as fast as typically performed by coworkers!

Session 19

Bill regressed to the exact rate of the currently established goal of 50 (see Figure 10.11).

Session 20

The goal is now established at the competitive rate and Bill receives an increase in his hourly wage by $1 per hour. The employment specialist, in conjunction with two coworkers, continues to interact with and provide Bill with multiple options during the break, with the pinball machine being just one of the options. The encouragement of coworkers and the permanent increase in hourly wage maintained Bill's productivity. The employment specialist still needs to record periodic data to know when to attend to any decreases that may result in disfavor or dissatisfaction by the restaurant supervisor.

SUMMARY

A brief description of a goal-setting procedure with an accompanying example was provided in this chapter. In review, the steps of this procedure include

Obtain the competitive standard.
Establish a current baseline rate.
Identify a reinforcer.
Define the initial goal.
Determine the length of each work session.
Develop a policy for change.
Provide feedback to the worker.

Provide access to the reinforcement.
Monitor the worker's progress.
Fade the intensity of the program.

Adherence to this process provides one avenue for employment specialists to allow workers to develop their rate up to the standards of the company at which they work.

Action Options

- Complete a goal-setting procedure for a worker whose production rate is below that expected of coworkers who complete the same activity.
- Develop graphs to present the data from a goal-setting procedure.
- Try the goal-setting procedure for an activity for which you are trying to increase or decrease (e.g., decreasing weight, increasing exercising, decreasing TV viewing, increasing time with family members).
- Present the steps of the goal-setting procedure at a staff meeting and have some agency-wide goals that could be achieved using this process.

CHAPTER 11

Coworkers and Supervisors

Industry participation in supported employment offers the same opportunities for community leadership, demonstration of social consciousness and commitment to affirmative action that is involved in other strategies for employing persons with disabilities."

L. Rhodes, K. D. Ramsing, and G. T. Bellamy, "Business Partnership in Supported Employment"

Shortly after Jim began work at the Silverspring Nursery, Jim's foreman requested that the employment specialist fade out so that she could provide direct training and supervision. Jim is successful at Silverspring, a nursery that specializes in growing ground covers like pachysandra, primarily because his employer and coworkers actively provide support. When Jim chooses not to work after lunch, he is taken off the clock, and coworkers have learned not to pressure him to return to work. His foreman meets regularly with the employment specialist to review progress and revise strategies for coping with Jim's unique behavioral characteristics.

Learning Outcomes

After reading this chapter you will be able to

- Discuss the role of the employment specialist in facilitating natural support and supervisory relationships in the work setting
- Define at least four roles a coworker can play in supporting a worker
- Access the social network at a worksite and prioritize employment specialist advocacy activities and instruction that will facilitate social integration and friendship formation
- Define and implement a "social validation" system for soliciting feedback on worker performance from coworkers and supervisors

- Describe three ways in which a coworker can be involved directly in the supervision or training of a worker

The ability of persons with severe handicaps to learn a wide range of sophisticated skills in community work settings has been well documented (Kierman & Schalock, 1989; Wehman & Moon, 1988). By providing the support of an employment specialist for on-the-job training and supervision, we are able to provide the assistance necessary for job acquisition to occur. Unfortunately, success in employment requires more than the acquisition of job skills. Successful job performance occurs when the employee performs the job over extended periods of time with minimal supervision (Mank and Horner, 1987). It also requires the ability to adapt to changes in job tasks, coworkers, supervisors, and operating procedures (Salzberg, Likins, McConaughy, Lignugaris/Kraft, & Stowitschek, 1986).

Success also can be measured in terms of the worker's *integration* into the social networks of the workplace. A successful employee will share the same range of relationships and social supports as his or her coworkers. In its simplest form *integration* has been defined as the presence and participation of a worker in the work culture at both the level required by the environment and desired by the worker (Shafer & Nisbet, 1989; Mank & Buckley, 1989). Knowing when true integration has occurred is more difficult. Mank and Buckley (1989) suggest we look for four levels of integration:

Physical integration. Close proximity to coworkers without disabilities.

Social integration. The presence of nonwork-related personal interactions during work and free time.

Relationships. Ongoing social interactions that are reciprocal and extend beyond work.

Social networks. Repeated contact with a number of people who identify the relationships within the group as socially important.

The statistics on job retention suggest that a substantial number of workers do not make the transition to "success" at work. Workers may lose their jobs because they don't perform work tasks satisfactorily. Ford, Dineen, and Hall (1984) report that 45 out of 53 competitive job placements made by a university-based employment training program for persons with mental retardation required on-site intervention after the first six months of employment. Further, deterioration of work skills was a factor in 47 percent of the cases when workers lost their jobs. In other cases, social or interpersonal problems appear that cause job termination (Greenspan & Schoultz, 1981). The subtlety of interacting with your boss differently than your coworkers, being on time when you would rather be fishing, or being cheerful after a rough night at home are all critical but subtle job skills.

Ensuring success in employment for persons with severe handicaps requires the active participation and support of coworkers and supervisors at the job site. For workers with and without disabilities social supports on the job clearly contribute to both quality of life and job satisfaction as well as to maintaining employment over time (House, 1981; Moseley 1988). Effective coworker and supervisor interaction with the worker *directly* address maintenance of job performance by providing a long-term source of support and supervision. More importantly, interaction provides opportunities for the relationships and social networks that define job satisfaction and ultimately affect the individual's quality of life.

THE CRITICAL ROLE OF AN EMPLOYMENT SPECIALIST

It is the emphasis of this chapter that employment specialists directly influence the development of relationships that support and maintain workers in jobs. Employment specialists often emphasize formal rules and work routines and neglect the informal social structures and relationships in the workplace (Hagner, 1987). Employment specialists need to learn and understand the informal structure of the workplace and assist the worker in entering that social network. Accomplishing this may require merely an additional emphasis for the employment specialist, or it may lead to a radically different role.

A commitment to developing supportive relationships between workers and their coworkers requires an understanding of the critical nature of the employment specialist. An employment specialist is able to provide the intensity and effectiveness of training that a worker needs in order to learn the job. At the same time, the employment specialist may unintentionally block the natural socialization process by which a new worker gets to know his or her coworkers and learn the job. Consider the following potential sources of interference (Hagner, 1987; Nisbet & Hagner, 1988):

Employees tend to pair up on job tasks. The presence of an employment specialist may prevent this natural pairing.

Employment specialist intervention may block natural mentoring and supervision.

Presence of an employment specialist creates a mystique of special expertise needed and identifies the worker as "different."

Introduction of outside expertise may create dependency on that expertise.

Employment specialist presence may cause members of the company to behave differently when the employment specialist is present.

The employment specialist needs to be conscious of assessing and controlling these influences. A second implication of a commitment to developing supportive relationships is the need to clarify the goals of supported employment. Do the worker's goals include

Increased personal competence and independence?

Significant relationships with other workers and customers who don't have disabilities?

Reduced dependence on the artifical supports we provide as a human service professional?

These goals imply that we consciously attempt to gradually eliminate the presence of employment specialists. The need to do this applies equally to all models of supported employment including mobile work crews, enclaves, and small businesses.

The successes of supported employment suggest that an employment specialist can be a facilitator of relationships that will support the worker in the specialist's absence. Employment specialists need to foster as many significant relationships as possible in the workplace. They need to support friendships over the rough spots that any new friendship passes. Employment specialists need to provide reinforcement and feedback to coworkers and to teach the coworkers to understand the person's communication.

ROLES AND FUNCTIONS OF THE COWORKER

The primary goal of any job placement is that coworkers with and without disabilities share the same support relationships. Coworkers provide us with friendship, a sounding board, and help in solving problems with the boss. More recently, researchers have also suggested concrete roles a coworker or supervisor can play in supporting a worker (Nisbet & Hagner, 1988; Shafer, 1986; Rusch & Minch, 1988). At the most basic level, a coworker is a friend or advocate, a source of informal supports and encouragement. The coworker may also be an observer, providing realistic information on a worker's progress and performance when the employment specialist isn't present. The coworker or supervisor may be an instructor, participating directly in providing reinforcement, teaching, or problem solving. Finally, the coworker could be a partner of the worker, perhaps working side by side in a job-sharing arrangement.

Each of these roles has implications for the structure and style of the supported employment service. Each of these roles must be considered in relation to the goals and strategies used by employment specialists.

COWORKERS AS FRIENDS OR ADVOCATES

Bob works at a large travelers' center, providing restaurants, stores, and services to truck drivers and travelers. His supervisor was so pleased with Bob's performance as a team member that he threatened to resign if he was not given the authority to make Bob a year-round employee. He has also purchased a piece of equipment valued at $500 specifically to make the difficult part of Bob's job easier and to allow him more time to work as part of a team with other maintenance workers.

A coworker who is a friend and advocate provides a variety of benefits, including reinforcement, feedback, instruction on new tasks, and fun.

Friendships may serve a number of specific supportive functions (Shafer, 1986):

1. Ensuring that the worker's rights are not compromised by unsupportive coworkers
2. Handling confrontation between the worker and coworkers
3. Supporting a fair distribution of job tasks
4. Assisting in communication with others in the workplace and home

The role of the employment specialist is to facilitate opportunities for supportive relationships with coworkers. While this is a delicate task that is more difficult to define than traditional systematic instruction, attention should be given to establishing a specific plan at any worksite. We will review some specific activities the employment specialist can consider.

Integration into the Work Routine

The first stage is to ensure that the new worker has every opportunity to be a full participant in the social life of the workplace. This requires a level of environmental assessment that is in more depth than traditional assessment procedures. It has been suggested that employment specialists should work in the job site for up to two weeks prior to placement (Buckley, 1986). In addition to learning the sequence of job tasks, this process is an opportunity to learn the existing network of social relationships and power structures. A role of the employment specialist should be to integrate with this social structure both at and outside of work.

Recommendations

1. Work in the job for at least one full day (up to two weeks has been recommended) before beginning the placement.
2. Assess the social network. Who has power? Who makes task decisions? Who provides reinforcement or supports?
3. Plan a work schedule that matches coworkers. If the worker needs a shorter work day, plan it to start or end with other workers or, ideally, match the schedule of other part-time workers.
4. Know when coworkers socialize, and plan for the worker to be able to participate.

Questions to Ask

1. Does the worker take breaks and lunch with coworkers?
2. Is transportation flexible enough to allow for a beer or other drink after work?
3. Does the worker participate in social gatherings?
4. Does the worker arrive and leave at the same time as coworkers?

Assistance in the Development of Relationships

Assisting in the development of relationships begins with job development and job site analysis. Workers who work cooperatively on tasks with non-disabled coworkers may develop more positive relationships than workers who work in isolation or only in physical proximity to coworkers (Johnson & Johnson, 1986; Stainback, Stainback, Courtnage, & Jaben, 1985).

During job training, the employment specialist can facilitate natural interactions and positive perceptions of the worker. Talking to coworkers and informally offering basic background information on the worker provides an opportunity to highlight strengths, as well as answer questions. Ensuring the supervisor plays a direct role in orienting and training the worker will do much to prevent problems later when the employment specialist begins to fade from the site. Considering identifying and encouraging a "mentor" who will provide ongoing informal support (Nisbet & Hagner, 1988).

Recommendations

1. Talk to coworkers, highlight the worker's strengths.
2. Be sensitive to natural friendships. Allow and encourage the supervisor to provide feedback directly to the worker. Prompt the worker to seek information or assistance from coworkers and supervisors.
3. Plan for the supervisor and coworkers to play a direct role in training. Identify the "experts" on jobs and ask for their assistance.
4. Ensure that the direct supervisor has an opportunity to interview the worker before placement and to plan the job.
5. Reinforce positive interactions with the worker. A worker may not have sufficient social skills to naturally reinforce a coworker.
6. Assist coworkers in communicating with and understanding the worker.

7. Seek out common experiences, interests, and acquaintances with coworkers. Establish a common ground.

Questions to Ask

1. Do coworkers or the supervisor always direct questions or directions through the employment specialist?
2. How often does the supervisor interact with the employee?
3. Does the employee work in isolation, or does he or she work cooperatively with a coworker?
4. Is the employee following the informal rules of the job site?

Teaching the Employee to Initiate Interactions with Coworkers

A friendship is a reciprocal relationship, involving feelings and social interaction (Stainback & Stainback, 1987). In addition to advocacy with coworkers and supervisors, an additional role for the employment specialist is to teach the worker to interact with his or her peers in a manner that leads to friendships.

Facilitating social interactions requires an understanding of what interactions typically take place. The majority of interactions in the workplace are with coworkers (Chadsey-Rusch & Gonzalez, 1988). Close to half of all of the interactions are not task related. Chadsey-Rusch and Gonzalez found that the most frequent nontask interactions were

Teasing and joking
Sharing information (e.g., about the weather, sports)
Greetings

Clearly this large percentage of nontask interactions suggests that the employment specialist should facilitate and teach a wide variety of social skills.

Two strategies may foster the development of relationships. First, the employment specialist can teach the worker to initiate specific social interactions with coworkers. Interactions can be work-specific (asking for help, asking for more work) or strictly social (saying good morning, asking about the weekend). A second strategy is to use natural events to structure interactions with coworkers. Gaylord-Ross, Haring, Breen, and Pitts-Conway (1984) taught young adults with severe handicaps to use tape players or offers of gum as tools to initiate social interaction during recess. This same principle can be applied to the work setting.

Recommendations

1. Teach the worker to approach coworkers with specific requests.
2. Teach conversational skills. Focus on asking for and responding to (reinforcing) information.
3. Provide natural tools for interaction and friendships. Teach the worker to
   Bring in cookies or doughnuts for breaks.
   Bring in a birthday card or thank-you card for a coworker.
   Offer assistance to a coworker.

Questions to Ask

1. Does the worker have a real friend? Someone to hang out with?
2. Does the worker reinforce coworkers when they initiate assistance or conversations?

3. Is there a give-and-take in the workers' relationships? Is the coworker always the initiator?
4. How frequently does the worker interact with others in the worksite? Is this more or less than coworkers? What percentage of the interactions is not task related?

Successful Fading from the Job Site

The final responsibility of the employment specialist is to make an effective transition from being a provider of training and support to not being present at all in the job site. As we have discussed, the accessibility and presence of the employment specialist at the worksite may interfere with the development of appropriate relationships with coworkers and supervisors. Frequently the worker is primarily dependent on the employment specialist for both support and reinforcement and as a cue for working effectively. The role of the employment specialist is to transfer control to supervisors and peers as soon as a worker enters a job.

Recommendations

1. Ensure supervisor and coworker participation in initial training.
2. Redirect questions and requests to the worker.
3. Fade employment specialist presence as rapidly as possible.
4. Plan periods of employment specialist absence early in the placement.

Questions to Ask

1. How much support does the worker receive from coworkers or supervisors?
2. Who provides initial orientation and training to the worker?
3. Is the employment specialist planning brief absences from the site early in the placement?

THE COWORKER AS OBSERVER: SOCIAL VALIDATION STRATEGIES

Anne worked in the dish room of a college cafeteria as part of an enclave. Her work rate was higher than any other worker, and higher than the college students who also performed the task. Despite this, the service manager complained that she was off task too much and not carrying her load. Anne worked in bursts, at high speed for several minutes, then paused to play with her hair. Her employment specialist needed to respond to the impression that Anne was not working, something she could not observe directly. Intervention addressed teaching Anne to load unobtrusively, a subtle skill.

Employment specialists often rely on coworkers and supervisors to provide an accurate picture of a coworker's performance at the job site. It has been documented anecdotally and experimentally that workers perform differently when an employment specialist is present than when they are working independently. (Rusch et al., 1984).

The standard solution to this problem is the "James Bond" approach to job training. The employment specialist sneaks in as unobtrusively as possible and tries to observe the worker without being seen. Equally important is the fact that supervisor and coworker perceptions of performance may affect job retention as much as actual performance. Research also suggests that the impressions a supervisor or coworker has of the worker's job skills are strongly related to the impressions of the worker's social relationships (White & Rusch, 1983). It is important to know how the supervisor and coworkers *think* the worker is doing.

The process of collecting information on employer and coworker impressions has been called *social validation*. Typically, collecting social validation information occurs as the employment specialist fades on-site contact. Social validation should be used throughout the supported employment process, in both group and individual employment, to ensure that employer perceptions and needs are understood.

Recommendations

1. Use a standardized format based on specific, performance-based questions.
2. Individualize administration to maximize accuracy. Administer by phone, mail, or in person.
3. Solict feedback from supervisors and coworkers often. Information may be very different.
4. Collect information formally at least monthly.

Questions to Ask Coworkers and Supervisors

1. Does the worker meet job standards?
2. Is the worker cooperative and considerate with coworkers and the supervisor?
3. Is the employment specialist present too much? Not enough?
4. Overall, how do you rate the worker as an employee?

THE COWORKER AS AN INSTRUCTOR: OVERT SUPPORT STRATEGIES

Steve worked as a janitor and utility person for a college bookstore distributor. As long as his employment specialist was with him on site, Steve worked with a high level of quality and speed. He had few problems learning the job, and could perform all of the job responsibilities by the end of his first week. As soon as the employment specialist left the job site, Steve's quality was cursory, and he rarely completed his tasks. Company staff frequently found him sleeping or loafing. Steve needed more intensive daily supervision to maintain job performance.

Frequently, informal approaches to advocacy and strengthening relationships are enough to support employment success. In certain cases, employment specialists may be unable to fade their participation in the worksite. In the case of the individual job placement, it is usually not possible to provide unlimited employment specialist intervention. For workers who are participating in a mobile crew or enclave, the continued intervention of the employment specialist may be building a long-term dependence and not fostering independent work or natural support relationships.

In these cases, a coworker may be able to replace the employment specialist as the primary source of training and support. Two levels of this participation will be discussed. The coworker may participate in this role as a natural part of his or her job responsibilities. Alternatively, the coworker can become a paid participant in the employee's service delivery.

Strategies for Coworker and Supervisor Intervention

A limited body of research has demonstrated the effectiveness of coworker- and supervisor-managed interventions (Rusch & Minch, 1988; Mank & Horner, 1987). The range of intervention strategies available is, of course, the same range used by an employment specialist tempered by the need to maintain simplicity and manageability. The role of the employment specialist is one of advisor and consultant to a coworker or supervisor.

A common problem in job sites is a low rate of feedback and reinforcement for performance. Several strategies have been used to assist supervisors or coworkers to provide more concrete or more powerful reinforcement to the worker. In one demonstration a supervisor awarded points on a daily basis for successful completion of work tasks. Points earned within a specific time period could be traded for a reinforcing event. Using this method rapid improvement in task completion and work quality was observed (Brooks, Hill, & Ponder, 1985).

Busy supervisors may not remember to provide regular feedback. A strategy for resolving this is to teach the employee to self-recruit feedback. In this approach, a coworker or supervisor is asked to participate and shown how to provide effective feedback. The employee is trained to request the feedback at specific times during the work day.

In one example, maintenance of work rate and task completion was a major problem in a busy company cafeteria. The employee received minimal feedback and reinforcement during the work day. A system was arranged where the employee gave a small index card to his supervisor at the end of the day. Printed on the card were spaces to give a plus sign (+) or minus sign (−) for completing her work and for quality. The prompt of completing the card caused the supervisor to give additional descriptive reinforcement and feedback. Mank and Horner (1987) used a similar strategy to maintain work rate. Employees maintained their own data on production during the day, and showed this to their supervisor for feedback at the end of each day.

Coworkers and supervisors may also assist by providing cues for job tasks or appropriate behavior. Employees who need assistance in maintaining the correct sequence of job tasks can receive simple "What's next?" prompts from a coworker. Rusch, Weithers, Menchetti, and Schutz (1980) used coworkers to prompt an employee to not repeat topics during breaks and lunch. Designing a strategy that is relatively painless and automatic, such as the self-recruited feedback strategies, is important.

Recommendations

1. Test for social and job skill maintenance early in a placement.
2. Identify and interact with potential instructors.
3. Design strategies that are simple and manageable:
   Self-recruited feedback

Reinforcement systems
Job task prompt

Questions to Ask

1. Are the natural supports sufficient to maintain performance?
2. Can supports be provided without interfering with the coworker's job responsibilities?

THE COWORKER AS PARTNER: DIRECT PARTICIPATION STRATEGIES

Employees may require more intensive supports than can be provided practically within the context of a coworker's normal job duties. In some cases, the supports needed may require daily responsibilities that cut into personal break times such as assistance with self-care. In these cases a more formal relationship between the coworker and worker may be necessary to ensure a successful placement and meet the needs of the employer.

Nisbet and Hagner (1988) describe two levels at which this formal relationship can be defined. In the *training-consultant model* a coworker spends a specific percentage of his or her work day providing training and supervision to the worker. While still primarily an employee of the company, a coworker who spends 10 or 15 percent of the work day in supervision and training needs specific training, support, and compensation for this responsibility. Nisbet and Hagner recommend that the human service agency pay for that portion of the work day spent in training and supervision, along with an additional stipend to compensate for the additional responsibility.

In some cases, intensive long-term support and supervision can be anticipated for a worker to succeed in a natural work setting. Nisbet and Hagner recommend a *job-sharing model* for these cases, where a worker shares a position with another employee. Typically, a human service agency could directly recruit and hire the coworker, and provide both workers to the company. Again, a portion of the coworkers' wages will be paid by the host company for work completed. The remainder of the coworker's wages would be paid by the human service agency, with an adjustment to account for the responsibilities required. In this case, the coworker is more formally assuming responsibilities as an employment specialist.

SUMMARY

Inherent in each of these approaches for supporting a worker in natural work settings is a respect for the power of human relationships. Many of the most powerful relationships are those normal friendships over which professionals have little control. Employment specialists must recognize that some of these relationships will interfere with their own relationships with workers, and thus some of the positive aspects of an employment specialist's work. Developing and supporting both friendships and business relationships may be more powerful in maintaining meaningful jobs than our training technology, and focusing our efforts on this process is critical.

Also implicit in this discussion is the recognition that we have only begun to realize and implement all of the possible strategies for supporting workers in natural work settings. All of these strategies are in their formative stages, and it is only through nuturing and extending them that we can meet the goals of full employment for people with significant handicaps.

Action Options

- Assess the social environment at work for a specific worker and identify ways in which you can enhance his or her social integration through advocacy, job design, or direct instruction with the worker. List at least three alternatives for each category before choosing an option to try.
- Design a social validation system. Establish a regular schedule for implementation.
- Recruit a coworker or supervisor to assist a worker in job skill maintenance. Work with the worker to implement a manageable procedure.

CHAPTER 12

Assisting Families

A parent is worth 10,000 school masters.

Chinese proverb

Learning Outcomes

After reading this chapter you will be able to

- List eight typical concerns parents have regarding the employment of their sons or daughters with disabilities
- Describe a system to provide regular information to family members regarding the status of a supported employment program
- List eight problems that families typically encounter with supported employment programs
- Describe three methods to facilitate family involvement in the transdisciplinary team process
- List eight steps employment specialists can take to facilitate a close working relationship with family members

Michael has spent the past 25 years living in an institution. At age 3, he was placed at this facility with the hope that the staff would be able to educate him. About 2 years ago, a group of professionals approached Michael and his family about the prospect of living and working in the community. At first, Michael and the other members of his family were apprehensive. Where would Michael live? Where would he work? What kind of work could Michael do? Could he remain at a job? Would he lose any of his benefits? Would he be accepted by his coworkers? Professionals listened to these questions and offered information, support, and encouragement. Working as a team, Michael, his family, and these professionals collaborated to create the opportunity that now enables Michael to live, work, and recreate in his local community.

Michael has a job at the local libary sorting books, shelving materials, copying materials, making sure that the library is neat and orderly, and helping with various other library jobs. He takes the bus to work each morning with some of his housemates at the home where he lives. He earns a fair wage—even enough to put some money away in a savings account.

Michael's vignette illustrates the powerful role of parents, siblings, and other family members in making community living, including employment, a reality. Given the intimate relationships between family members and their extensive knowledge of the person experiencing a disability, family members play a unique and critical role in the transdisciplinary team process and in fostering community-based employment opportunities. The relationship between the employment specialist and the family serves as the foundation for developing, implementing, and assuring that supported employment opportunities enhance the quality of life for the individual with a disability. This chapter focuses on the role of families in supported employment. First, an overview of family systems theory is presented as a foundation for understanding and better assisting families. Next, the needs of families are highlighted. A discussion of the roles of family members and what family members want from employment specialists follows. Finally, suggestions for employment specialists in their interactions with family members are discussed.

THE FAMILY SYSTEM

Family systems theory (Minuchin, 1974; Neugarten, 1976; Turnbull, & Turnbull, 1986) serves as the foundation for understanding and examining family dynamics. Families serve as a primary source of learning and social exchange for all human beings. Members learn about individual differences and similarities, relationships, values, and morals; individuals acquire skills that facilitate their competence and success in the world. One of the basic premises of family systems theory is that each family is unique; within this constellation, each member contributes to the overall composition of the family. Each member influences and is influenced by all of the other members of this system and the system as a whole.

Turnbull and Turnbull (1986) utilize family systems theory to conceptualize families with a member who has a disability. Figure 12.1 depicts this conceptual framework, which consists of four ingredients:

Family resources
Family interaction
Family functions
Family life cycle

All individual members have personal characteristics that make them distinct from the others in the family system. These descriptive characteristics, *family resources*, or *input*, are the abilities, resources, and capacity of the family to meet the needs of each individual member and the family as a whole (Turnbull & Turnbull, 1986). Characteristics pertaining to the family (e.g., size, socioeconomic status, ethnicity, geographic location), handicapping condition (e.g., type, level of ability), and personal condition (e.g., health, well-being, individual personality characteristics, coping strategies) are considered family resources, those abilities, strengths, and skills the family possesses to meet individual and family needs.

Family interaction consists of those relationships related to the daily activities of the family. Each family is a system with four major *subsystems:* marital (husband and wife interactions), parental (parent and child interactions), sibling (child and child interactions), and extrafamilial (entire family or individual member interactions with family members, friends, professionals, and persons within the community (Turnbull, Summers, & Brotherson, 1984). These subsystems reflect the interrelatedness among all members of the family.

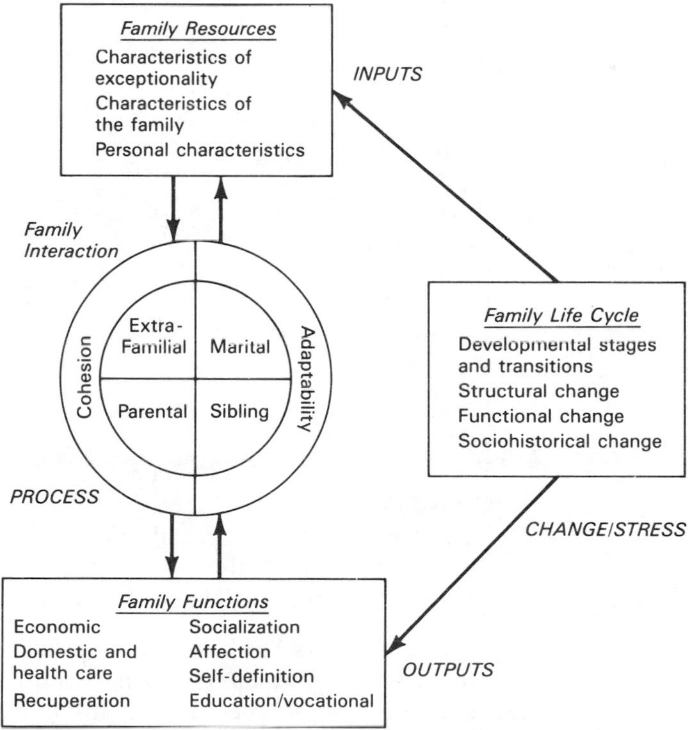

Figure 12.1 Family Systems Conceptual Framework (Source: From *Families, Professionals, and Exceptionality. A Special Partnership* by A. P. Turnbull and H. R. Turnbull, 1986, p. 20, Columbus, OH: Charles E. Merrill Publishing Co. Reprinted by permission.)

Family functions are those needs that the family possesses that must be addressed. These functions, tasks, or *output* may be economic (e.g., generating money), domestic/health care (e.g., locating health care staff), recreation (participating in community sporting events), socialization (developing friendships), self-identity (developing a thorough sense of self), affection (acknowledging others), and educational/vocational (securing a job that a person enjoys).

These needs change across the *life cycle* or developmental stages of each family. Turnbull and Turnbull (1986) suggest six stages within the family life cycle: early childhood (birth to age 5); school age (6 to 12 years); adolescence (13 to 21 years); adulthood (21 and older); empty nest; and elderly years. To meet the needs of family members with compassion and understanding, employment specialists must consider the dynamics of individual families; their needs, characteristics, strengths, values, resources; and their particular stage within the family life cycle.

NEEDS OF FAMILIES

As intricate systems consisting of individual members, families possess unique needs related to their present circumstances and their dreams for the future. These family functions vary based on the family life cycle, the individual members of the system, the family resources, and the interaction between the members of the system.

First, consider the scope of a family's present needs based on this family's hopes and aspirations for themselves and those individuals who are important in their lives. Michael's family has hopes and aspirations for him; they hope Michael will be

Happy
Healthy
Safe
Secure
Employed
Liked
Part of the community
Respected
Productive
Loved

His family also hopes he will

Have friends
Establish intimate relationships with others
Have a career
Earn a salary that allows economic self-sufficiency
Own a home
Be as independent as possible
Participate in life fully
Make a contribution

Michael's family has hopes and dreams for him; many are the same as the ones we have for ourselves and our children. Professionals have a unique opportunity to encourage family members to dream and to provide families with the support in order to reach those dreams. All members of a family have their own dreams and expectations for the future. They also have aspirations for each individual member of their family and the family as a whole. Employment specialists have numerous opportunities to assist consumers and family members to dream about the future and to assist with the realization of these dreams.

WHAT FAMILIES NEED TO KNOW ABOUT SUPPORTED EMPLOYMENT

Individual members of a family may have needs relating to information, training, and/or support to assist with their understanding of and commitment to the concept of supported employment. Since supported employment is a relatively new concept, many family members have never heard the phrase before; some have heard the phrase and find it confusing. Employment specialists often find themselves in the position of educating family members about supported employment. In providing information to families, it is important that accurate information be communicated so that each person can truly understand the concept of supported employment and its benefits.

In conversations with family members, many questions and concerns arise about community-based employment. Following are some questions posed by parents, siblings, and grandparents; proposed responses to these questions are offered.

What is supported employment?
Supported employment is a phrase used to describe the paid employment of people with developmental disabilities where competitive employment is unlikely and who, given their needs, will benefit from ongoing support to function in an employment setting.

What kind of support will individuals with disabilities receive in the community? Will it be ongoing or erratic?
The intention of supported employment is to provide individuals with a range of supports to maximize their success at work. Supports should be lifelong. However, the specific supports and the nature of the supports will change based on the unique needs of the individual and the particular job.

Is supported employment here to stay or a fad?
Supported employment is a relatively new concept. However, the commitments from the federal government and professionals in special education and vocational rehabilitation assure that supported employment is viable now and will continue.

What kinds of jobs are available?
There are many possible jobs for people with severe disabilities. Initially, many positions were in custodial, maintenance, or the food service industries. However, efforts are now being directed toward employment opportunities in offices, libraries, horticulture, and other businesses based on the preferences and strengths of each consumer.

How do people learn to do their jobs?
Individuals in supported employment acquire the skills needed to perform their jobs via on-the-job training and supervision. The employment specialist serves to train the individual in the areas that are

essential to performing the job and succeeding in the environment. Coworkers also serve as appropriate role models who assist the worker in learning the targeted skills.

How will transportation be arranged?
Will parents or other family members have to provide transportation?

The responsibility of arranging and providing transportation should not rest with the family. Typically, the responsibility rests with the provider agency. Although arrangements for transportation prove challenging, creative options can be developed; some communities have established a system whereby several businesses support a van service available to all of their employees. In other situations, the employment specialist may provide transportation.

Will the persons with disabilities make friends?
How will coworkers deal with these people?
Will they make them feel welcome?
Will they be a part of the business?

Each person has a different experience when he or she enters a new situation such as a job. The extent of feeling welcome and comfortable in a position varies based on a wide array of individual circumstances, feelings, beliefs, and interpersonal interactions. With all transitions, there is a period of adjustment and learning that occurs. Individuals' experiences vary and evolve as they become more familiar with the new situation.

What roles will family members play in the placement and follow-up process?

Family members should play an integral role in the entire supported employment process. Employment specialists should encourage active participation by family members. Family members should initiate their involvement in supported employment. It is important that all members of a family ask questions and assure that the information they receive truly addresses their questions and concerns. Accurate information for family members regarding the process, the progress, and the outcomes of supported employment is essential.

Will individuals experiencing disabilities lose SSI?
Will they lose other benefits?

It is recommended that professionals and family members secure accurate information from agencies that are well-versed in the area of benefits. In some cases, individuals may lose benefits depending on the amount of money earned. However, this information must be clarified to assure that it is appropriate to the individual situation.

What kinds of mechanisms are in place to maximize a successful transition to work?

Some states are now requiring that individualized education plans (IEPs) include vocational objectives, training, and plans for transition. Whether or not a state has such a requirement, parents and professionals can advocate for early planning and career training.

What mechanisms are in place to ensure that individuals with disabilities experience success at their jobs?

The career planning process is used to facilitate and promote success in choosing, creating, and maintaining an employment position that is in line with an individual's goals, values, strengths, and preferences. Various supports from coworkers, friends, family members, and professionals will assist in promoting an individual's success on the job. Ongoing evaluation will address whether or not a particular job is enhancing the quality of life for an individual.

What kind of training do employment specialists receive? Are these professionals truly committed to persons experiencing disabilities? Do the employment specialists have a good rapport and relationship with the workers?

Since supported employment is a relatively new concept, employment specialists in each community may have participated in various types of training. Some individuals may have degrees in special education, education, business, or vocational rehabilitation. Other individuals may have a high school education. In most cases, training is provided by the lead agency prior to and during work. As with any professional, the range of expertise and commitment varies.

Will persons experiencing disabilities be safe in the community?

Perske (1981) refers to the concept of "dignity of risk"; all individuals take risks in their lives. It is from these risks that people develop and advance in their lives. With every risk comes dignity. So, although there may be risks for people with disabilities, those risks are inherent for all of us as human beings.

This list of questions and the corresponding answers is not meant to be exhaustive. Rather, it serves to highlight some of the questions voiced by family members.

BENEFITS OF SUPPORTED EMPLOYMENT

Family members are eager to learn about the benefits of supported employment. These benefits include

- The opportunity to work and live in a "real world" environment
- Opportunities to be engaged in various meaningful work tasks on a day-to-day basis
- Opportunities to interact with and develop relationships with nondisabled adults
- A consistent amount of work to be performed
- Increased opportunities to acquire and demonstrate work-related behaviors
- Access to benefits including medical insurance, sick leave, and vacation

Additionally, supported employment provides individuals with an increased opportunity to obtain greater wages and benefits; improved perceptions by family members, friends, employers, and other individuals in the community; and increased opportunities for job enhancement. Ultimately, all of these benefits have the potential to enhance the quality of life for individuals with disabilities, the family system, and the entire community.

FAMILIES AS KEY TEAM MEMBERS

Parents, siblings, and other family members are *partners* in the process of supported employment. They make significant contributions to the overall process and offer information that is valuable and needed in order to maximize successful community-based employment. Their input must be solicited; their dreams and visions for the persons who experience disabilities must be acknowledged and considered in the overall planning and development process. Their intimate relationship with the individual experiencing disabilities is highly valued; they bring much information and insight about their family member to the team.

Family members and professionals must work together as a team. All individuals bring their specific expertise to this team. This cooperative effort reflects the potential contribution of each member and the commitment of the team to the individual experiencing disabilities. While the relationship of the professionals and the individual with disabilities may be very brief and short-lived, family members continue to be a constant force in the individual's life. Thus it is essential to welcome family members as integral team members. It is important to remember that the employment specialist must be committed to enhancing the lives of individuals experiencing disabilities. Family members and employment specialists together serve as advocates for individuals with disabilities, striving to enable these individuals to live, work, play, and be contributing members of their local community.

WHAT FAMILIES ARE LOOKING FOR

While it is difficult if not impossible to develop a list of all outcomes families desire, many family members are looking for the person with a disability to have

- Experiences that foster dignity and respect for the family as a whole
- Competent professionals
- Opportunities to perform meaningful and functional activities as independently as possible
- Security when other family members are unavailable to provide care and assistance
- Opportunities to experience one's value and to make contributions to one's community
- Meaningful relationships with other human beings and a network of community support
- A career that provides meaningful work and economic self-sufficiency
- Maximum opportunities to be integrated into all areas of local community life
- A relatively stable future that consists of participating in all aspects of community life

Employment specialists must direct their efforts to assist persons with disabilities in reaching these outcomes. Parents, siblings, and other family members play a critical role in this process.

It is important for professionals to remember that each family is unique. Some family members may convey their initial opposition to community-based employment; other family members may be excited about the opportunity. In working with families, employment specialists should recognize and respect the individuality of each family member. These individual differences must be considered when assisting families with the issues pertaining to the supported employment option.

Employment specialists are in a unique position to assist family members in discussing their concerns about supported employment and the apparent obstacles that interfere with providing quality supported employment options for persons with disabilities. As professionals, employment specialists can assist families in clarifying their dreams for the individuals experiencing disabilities. Employment specialists can encourage family members to think about future dreams for those individuals with disabilities.

Let us consider the process that professionals utilized with Michael's family. First professionals encouraged family members to participate in the career planning process described in Chapter 3. It is in this setting that family members can be encouraged to discuss their dreams for Michael's future.

What does Michael want for himself?
What are his dreams for his life?
What is the ideal scene for Michael in his life? in his career?
What vision/dream do the extended family members have for Michael's future?
What skills and strengths does Michael possess?
What are his likes and dislikes?
What type of job would he like?
What type of job would he dislike?

A first goal is to encourage family members to discuss their dreams openly and honestly within the career planning process. In developing that ideal picture, it is important to be specific. Particular attention to details such as sound, picture, feelings, and beliefs are essential.

As a part of the career planning process (see Chapter 3) and compatibility analysis (see Chapter 4), specific goals are generaged. Information pertaining to specifics about employment can be gathered, such as the following:

What kinds of jobs are available in the community?
What is the local labor market like?
What access does the individual have to transportation?
How can these potential jobs assist the person to develop greater skills and advance in his or her career?
What fringe benefits are available?
Have measures been taken to assure that the person will have opportunities for job advancement? Promotions? Salary increases?

Next, a plan of action is established to assist the individual in reaching the employment and career goals identified for him or her. Throughout these initial stages, active family involvement is essential. The employment specialist should discuss support plans that will be utilized to facilitate community employment. Family members often provide insight into the potential success of planned interventions. Family members should be consulted about any major program or strategy changes.

WHAT EMPLOYMENT SPECIALISTS CAN DO

A plan of action for employment specialists could include the following:

1. *Develop a relationship with the family.* Get to know the family. Most families welcome the opportunity to meet and visit professionals who

are helping their family member. Getting to know a family does *not* mean at a formal team meeting. Many families appreciate a home visit to limit the extra demands of time and travel. Visiting with families before team meetings may help facilitate the team process.

2. *Communicate.* Often family members want to know what is going on with the person's career and his or her job. Unfortunately, most persons who are receiving support have difficulty communicating. The employment specialist is a natural communication link. Some employment specialists call family members to let them know how the individual is performing on the job. Some find a weekly checklist of job accomplishments a helpful strategy. As time permits, a formal letter of congratulations regarding successful job performance is always welcome.

3. *Respect the confidentiality of the family.* As the employment specialist gets to know the family, he or she will be trusted with more personal information about the person and the family members. That trust is founded upon the principles that the employment specialist will keep information confidential. Confidentiality means not sharing sensitive information with coworkers, friends, spouses, or others.

4. *Respect privacy.* Sometimes the family does not want to share information with the employment specialist or other professionals. In these cases, it is best to tell the family that you are interested but allow them to make the first move to establish a relationship.

5. *Limit extra demands.* Family members have so many demands on their time and energy that additional demands by the supported employment professionals should be limited. Asking the family members to provide transportation to the worksite, conduct banking, and work with a Social Security office may be too much for a family to do. Before asking a family member to do a task it is better to ask yourself, "How else can we accomplish the task without placing a new demand on the family?"

6. *Limit "bad news" communication.* Many family members hear from professionals only when problems occur. Often the family has little control over the problem. Before sharing bad news, ask yourself, "Is this information absolutely essential to share? Can the family really help to resolve the situation? Will this information cause more hurt than serve the best interest of the individual?" Honest answers to these questions will help guide you about specific information to share with families.

7. *Minimize "surprises."* Problems *do* happen with supported employment programs. However, to really assist family members the employment specialist should minimize surprises. Problems with transportation, work schedules, and job supervision should be anticipated and, if these problems affect the family, advanced warning would always be appreciated.

8. *Provide flexible support.* The type of support provided by the employment training specialist may be varied depending on the family. For some families going out to buy special work uniforms may be problematic; for others, doing the necessary banking, or helping the individual attend a party with his or her coworkers may be too difficult to arrange. If the employment specialist considers these and other activities as part of the support needed to keep someone employed and provides this support, she or he will assist both the individual and the family.

WHAT TO DO WHEN PROBLEMS OCCUR

Sometimes an employment specialist encounters a family situation that proves to be a challenge. It is especially important to solicit feedback and information from other team members during these situations. All team members, including supervisory staff, should be recruited to assist in supporting that particular family. Special educators, psychologists, and/or social workers who have experience and expertise in working with families can also provide assistance.

Suggested Readings on Families

Featherstone, H. (1980). *A difference in the family. Living with a disabled child.* New York: Penguin Books.

Perske, R. (1981). *Hope for the families.* Nashville, TN: Abingdon.

Turnbull H. R., & Turnbull, A. P. (1985). *Parents speak out: Then and now.* Columbus, OH: Merrill.

Action Options

- Meet with family members of a person needing supported employment service. Ask them about their goals and wishes for the individual.
- Set up a supported employment communication notebook for parents or family members. In this notebook put in all of the facts about employment, special circumstances, and how family members can assist in the process.
- Attend parent meetings of advocacy groups and list 10 parental concerns about human service systems.

CHAPTER 13

Generalization of Work and Work-related Behavior

The frequent need for generalization of . . . behavior change is widely accepted, but it is not always realized that generalization does not automatically occur . . . Thus, the need actively to program generalization . . . is a point requiring both emphasis and effective techniques.

T. Stokes and D. Baer, "An Implicit Technology of Generalization"

Kathy has experienced problems recently. In her school program, she was able to wash dishes independently in the "domestic" classroom. When she graduated, she obtained employment in the kitchen of a nearby family-style restaurant. The new and different kitchen environment has produced difficulties for her, as many of her skills that were "mastered" in the school program have not generalized to the worksite. Consequently, she relies heavily on her employment specialist to assist her. She experiences even greater difficulty, however, when her regular employment specialist is absent and the substitute employment specialist attempts to work with her.

Learning Outcomes

After reading this chapter you will be able to

- Define generalization and describe its importance in working with individuals and disabilities
- Complete a generalization map for a worker for a functional work or work-related activity
- Describe the *rule of threes* and the *zero degree inference strategy*

- Conduct a general case analysis of a functional work or work-related activity

---

Up until recently, Mike had done well in his employment site. However, the vending machines in the employee's cafeteria were recently replaced with newer machines. As a result, Mike is not able to obtain his lunch because he is not able to operate the new machines.

Like many people with severe disabilities, both Kathy and Mike have experienced problems with generalization. In order to be successful in community employment, these individuals need to demonstrate certain skills within many different settings in which the conditions are different from those evident during their initial training. However, workers with severe disabilities seldom exhibit this performance without careful planning by employment specialists. Accordingly, employment specialists need effective procedures for promoting generalization.

Generalization is defined here as the demonstration of skills in situations other than those in which the original instruction occurred. There are many available strategies for employment specialists to assist workers in generalizing newly acquired skills. Two of these approaches are the use of a generalization map and general case programming. These approaches, like other procedures designed to promote generalization, are based on the recognition that community environments are complex and that workers must adapt their skills to function within these multiple, complex environments. Although generalization is not a concern for all activities (for instance, specific work tasks that are only performed one way), many work-related activities can and must be performed under different conditions if a worker is to be successful. In promoting generalization, employment specialists must use a step-by-step approach in analyzing the many factors that are present in multiple community environments to effectively promote optimum generalization.

PLANNING FOR GENERALIZATION

The first and possibly most important recommendation in promoting generalization is the following:

> Never assume that generalization will happen without planning.

Brown, Nietupski, and Hamre-Nietupski (1976) refer to this as the *zero degree inference strategy*. They state that, all too often, professionals infer or assume that workers with severe disabilities will be able to demonstrate skills in new situations when we have only seen them demonstrate these skills in an initial instructional situation. By assuming or inferring that a worker will demonstrate skills in a new situation, without actually planning for it, employment specialists often set that person up for failure in the new situation. Instead, they should practice the zero degree inference strategy and take the responsibility of planning for the successful generalization of each worker's skills.

Once employment specialists begin to plan for generalization, however, critical questions begin to surface:

How many different situations need to be planned for in considering generalization?
Should the worker be able to work with two employment specialists (or supervisors or coworkers), or with more?
How many sets of materials should the worker be able to use?
How will an employment specialist know when generalization has occurred?

There are no specific answers to these questions. However, instruction should be conducted in more than one setting, with more than one set of materials, and with more than one employment specialist or supervisor. Brown et al. (1976) state that, in order to be more confident that workers will generalize their skills, the *rule of threes* should be followed:

Conduct training in three different settings, with three different sets of materials, and with three different employment specialists/supervisors/coworkers.

In planning generalization using the rule of threes, it is important to be systematic in introducing the worker to new situations. Employment specialists should focus initially on areas of difficulty with particular workers; for instance, planning for generalization across materials for a worker who has difficulty in this area, such as Mike. In addition, the effects of generalization teaching should be carefully monitored in order to determine if the teaching has been effective. Most importantly, an employment specialist should take notice of the need for generalized skills in the worker's employment site and local community and then actively plan for generalization to occur.

THE GENERALIZATION MAP

As discussed in the previous section, employment specialists must not assume that generalization will occur unless it is specifically planned. One way to plan for generalization is to adhere to the rule of threes. An even more detailed way of planning for generalization is to complete a generalization map (Drabman, Hammer, & Rosenbaum, 1979). In using the generalization map, employment specialists can systematically plan for generalization of skills across new settings, materials, instructors, or any combination of these.

The first step to the completion of a generalization map is to record the name of the worker and the activity under consideration. Next, the original teaching setting, original instructor, and the original materials used for teaching should be recorded. Once a brief description of the original teaching situation has been recorded, the new situations to which the worker needs to generalize should be recorded. That is, the employment specialist should specify the new setting, materials, and instructor/supervisor. This information can be recorded on a form such as the one shown in Figure 13.1.

This information can be included on a generalization map (Figure 13.2). Information can be plotted by filling in each cell or box with the original or different setting, instructor, or set of materials. The sample generalization map contains boxes filled with either a numeral (I or II), a letter (A,B,C, or D), or a number (1 through 8). Each combination of numeral-letter-number represents a different way that the activity can be generalized.

WORKER'S NAME: Bob

ACTIVITY: Cleaning Restrooms

SETTINGS:

ORIGINAL: Employee's Restroom

DIFFERENT: Customer's Restroom

INSTRUCTORS:

ORIGINAL: Steve

DIFFERENT: Store Supervisor

MATERIALS:

ORIGINAL: Marshall's Materials

DIFFERENT: Sears Materials

Figure 13.1 Sample Form Leading to Generalization Map

Examples from the Generalization Map

I-A-2: Bob will work with Steve in the employees' restroom with the materials that are used at Sears.

II-C-5: Bob will now clean the customers' restroom but will continue to work with Steve and with the store's materials.

II-D-8: Bob will now clean the customer's restroom with the store supervisor instructing him and using the Sears materials. Bob has the opportunity to generalize his skills across settings, instructors, and materials.

The generalization map is a useful way of planning for the generalization of each worker's skills across two settings, instructors, or sets of materials. A generalization map can also be a handy way to keep track of the increasing abilities of workers as they generalize their skills to new situations. In the following section, an additional strategy to plan for generalization is presented.

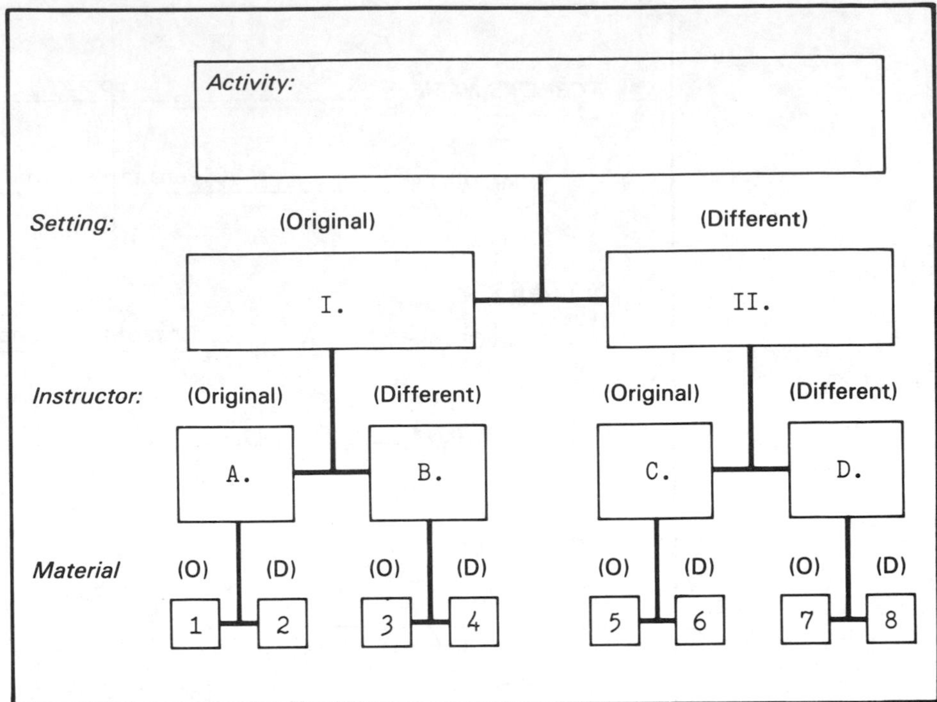

Figure 13.2 Sample Generalization Map

GENERAL CASE PROGRAMMING

Work and work-related activities are performed differently within multiple community environments. For example, there are many different kinds of coin-operated vending machines that workers are likely to encounter at or near their worksites. Employment specialists want the workers to be able to use any machine that contains a desired product. That is, they want them to generalize a skill in using vending machines to as many new vending machines as possible. A problem exists when the employment specialist has limited time to teach this skill. There may be simply too many vending machines without enough training time. However, the worker still needs to generalize this skill of operating a vending machine.

One way to address this situation is to select a few examples of vending machines for teaching that, once learned, can help the worker generalize the skill to new machines. A major question is

> Out of all the possible examples to use for teaching, which are the best examples?

Consider the following situation. An instructor needs to teach an individual to operate a coin-operated clothes washing machine. In the person's neighborhood there may be four laundromats that contain machines that are included in Figure 13.3. The employment specialist wants to limit teaching to 2 or 3 machines for actual instruction. Which of the eight examples would be the best teaching examples?

In making this decision, the employment specialist should consider a procedure known as *general case programming*. In general case programming, a few good examples of an activity are chosen for teaching because they are the most representative of all the examples in the worker's environ-

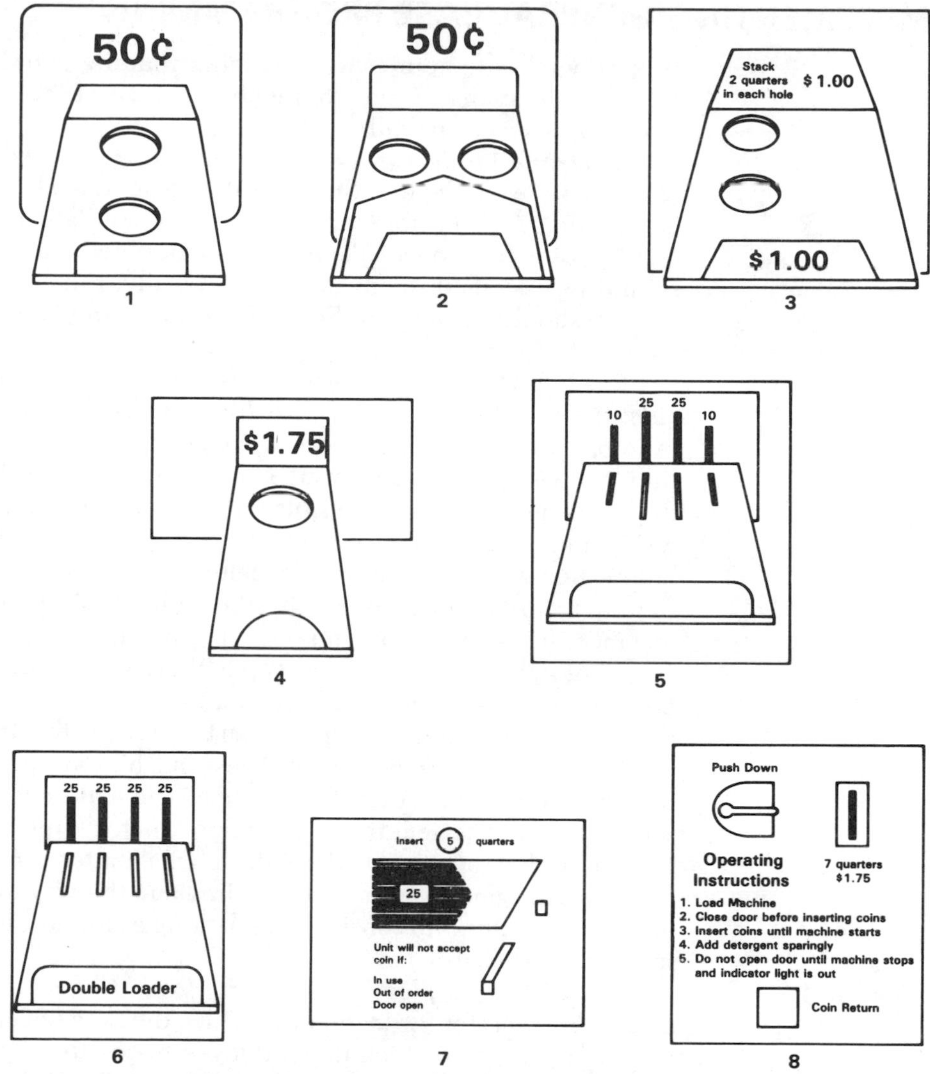

Figure 13.3 Instructions for Various Types of Coin-operated Washing Machines

ment. The number of selected examples is kept to a minimum to save valuable training time. However, employment specialists need to discover if the examples that were selected were the correct ones by presenting new examples that were not included in the instruction. By doing so, they can record whether or not the workers generalized their abilities to these new nontaught examples.

General case programming has been implemented to teach a number of diverse activities to persons with severe disabilities, including crossing streets (Horner, Jones, & Williams, 1985), obtaining soap from liquid soap dispensers (Pancsofar & Bates, 1985), operating telephones (Horner, Williams & Stevely, 1986), using screwdrivers (Colvin & Horner, 1983), bussing tables in a cafeteria (Horner, Eberhard, & Sheehan, 1986), selecting grocery items (Horner, Albin & Ralph, 1986) and opening and pouring beverages in a fast food restaurant (Steere, Strauch, Powell, & Butterworth, in press), and activating vending machines (Sprague & Horner, 1984). Activities that have many different examples within the worker's work site or community are excellent targets for general case programming.

IMPLEMENTING GENERAL CASE PROGRAMMING

In a general case approach to teaching training activities in a variety of different situations, Horner, Sprague, & Wilcox (1982) recommend that the following six steps be followed:

1. *Define the new situations to which the worker needs to generalize.* Does the employee need to be able to operate all vending machines in Connecticut? In Hartford? Or within the immediate neighborhood? There may be a big difference! Therefore, geographic boundaries for the activity should be specified in advance. Additionally, the exact parameters of the activity should be defined. For instance, does the employee need to count the exact change?

2. *Describe the range of possible features of the materials under consideration and the range of possible responses to these features.* In the example of the coin-operated clothes washer, the coins could be inserted into the machine in many ways. Some of the machines have holes in which the coins lie flat, some have slots for the coins to be inserted one at a time, while others have grooved slots for coins to be placed next to each other before being inserted into the machine. Each of these different features requires a different response by the individual using the machine. For instance, in the first type, the person must lay the coins flat in the correct spaces or must stack them two-deep in these spaces. In the second type, the person must insert the coins one at a time into the machine, while in the third type, the coins must be placed in the slots, so that they are lined up side by side on the insert mechanism. These machines require different amounts of money—another critical feature on all the materials to which the worker will be required to generalize. It is important to define the critical features of the materials as opposed to those that do not matter as much. In the previous example, the amount of money required and the way the money is inserted are critical features to consider in selecting examples, while the color of the machine is probably not.

3. *Select examples of the activity for both teaching and for assessing generalization (for use as probes).* Once the range of critical features on all of the materials to which the employee needs to generalize has been defined, the employment specialist should choose the minimum number of examples possible for use in teaching. Then a few examples that also reflect the range of critical features should be selected for use as probes, or examples that will be presented without any teaching.

These probes are extremely important and employment specialists need to present new examples of the activity to determine whether the worker can correctly complete the activity within the boundaries that were specified in the first step of this process. Horner et al. (1982) summarize these recommendations for selecting teaching and probe examples with the following six guidelines:

1. Select the minimum number of teaching examples that sample the range of features of the materials and of responses to these features.
2. Select examples that contain equal amounts of new information.
3. Select examples that do not include consistent, irrelevant features (for instance, all the same color).
4. Select examples that teach the worker what not to do as well as what to do.
5. Select examples that include important exceptions.
6. Select examples that are logistically feasible (i.e., that you can gain access to fairly easily).

4. *Sequence the teaching examples.* Now that the training examples have been selected, should the employment specialist teach the first one until it is mastered, then the next one, and so on, or should the specialist alternately present each of the examples within each teaching session (i.e., three tries on the first example, three tries on the second example, etc.)? Researchers in general case programming suggest that examples should not be taught independently until each is mastered because the worker will tend to develop error patterns that interfere with future learning. Instead, a few training examples should be presented together within each session so that the differences between the examples are clear to the learner.

5. *Teach the examples chosen for teaching.* This step relies on the effective use of prompt sequences, reinforcement strategies, and additional instructional strategies to assist the worker in acquiring the ability to use each of the teaching examples.

6. *Probe for generalization.* Once workers have learned the teaching examples, the probe examples should be presented to see if generalization to these new examples has occurred. If generalization has occurred, an employment specialist may have confidence that the worker will be able to correctly complete new examples of the activity that may be encountered in the worksite or in the community. If generalization to the new examples is absent, the selection of original teaching examples should be critically evaluated, additional examples to teach should be selected, and then probes should once again be presented.

SUMMARY

In this chapter, two methods for promoting generalization of activities to new situations were explored. Programming for generalization is extremely important to enhance the success of each worker both within the worksite and within the community. Employment specialists must never assume that generalization will happen unless its occurrence is planned for. The rule of threes was included as a guideline in promoting generalization across settings, materials, and instructors/supervisors. Also included was a discussion of the generalization map for developing detailed outcomes of generalization. Finally, general case programming procedures were described as a teaching strategy for selecting the best examples of an activity to result in optimum generalization to a variety of different situations.

Action Options

- Complete a generalization map for a worker.
- Use the steps of general case programming described in this chapter to select materials for instruction for a specific worker.

CHAPTER 14

Assisting Employees with Special Medical and Physical Needs

A person with a disability can become sick, like anyone; anyone can catch a cold or break a bone. Some disabilities may also make a person more vulnerable to illness. But the disability, itself, is not an illness to be cured. And most people who have some disability are as healthy as people who do not have disabilities.

E. Barnes, C. Berrigan, and D. Biklen, What's the Difference?

Kevin has severe spastic cerebral palsy. He requires special equipment to help him perform work tasks at a law firm in Hartford. Part of the support Kevin requires is adaptive equipment to position him in a manner that will help him complete his job task in a timely manner. Kevin's supported employment program has provided much of his special equipment. His employment specialist knows how to help Kevin utilize the special equipment to his best advantage. Because Kevin's employment specialist knows how to use adaptive equipment, Kevin is successfully employed.

Learning Outcomes

After reading this chapter you will be able to

- List five general guidelines for helping employees with physical disabilities
- List eight major safety concerns that employment specialists must consider in supported employment situations
- List five general guidelines for positioning an employee with a physical disability
- Describe grand mal and petit mal seizures and the action employment specialists should and should not take when an employee has these seizures

- Describe general first aid procedures for common injuries and illness
- List five general guidelines for lifting a person with a physical disability

Employees with disabilities may present a variety of primary or secondary medical needs, such as epileptic seizures, heart defects, and circulatory or respiratory problems. Many people with disabilities also take medications that have both desirable benefits and undesirable side effects. It is important that employment specialists anticipate and accommodate or respond to these situations, to ensure the employee's physical well-being and optimal job performance. Additionally, any employee may have an accident at the worksite that demands prompt action. For these reasons, employment specialists need to understand the various medical situations they might encounter. It is also important to distinguish between those problems that require immediate attention and those problems that require long-term treatment, monitoring, and evaluation.

The ongoing medical needs of employees with disabilities must be addressed as integral aspects of their plans for employment. The supported employment team, and the employment specialist in particular should know each employee's medical history. The team needs to determine which medical information should be shared with employers and fellow employees, whether immediately or in the future, and how information should be provided. The team also must identify and ensure the availability of medical supplies or equipment needed by individual employees (e.g., bee sting kit, special seat cushion). Finally, it is essential that the team develop procedures to respond to known and routine medical situations as well as emergencies that might occur at work.

Many large companies have employee health services available on site. In these settings, the company nurse or doctor may be an important team member who participates in planning for the employee with a disability. When an employee is known to have serious medical problems (e.g., poorly controlled seizures), the team might consider a job site close to a hospital where emergency care would be readily available. In most situations, however, specialized health services will not be available or necessary on a routine basis at the workplace. Therefore, locating community medical supports will be a critical aspect of the planning process for the majority of employees.

MEDICAL CONDITIONS

Table 14.1 describes some of the medical conditions that people with disabilities often experience. For most people, monitoring and routine treatment are sufficient to manage these medical conditions. The employment specialist should know signs that indicate the need for emergency care.

MEDICATIONS

Medications are often prescribed for people with disabilities for the management of epilepsy, emotional or behavior problems, and medical conditions such as diabetes or heart conditions. It is not unusual for some people to take several drugs in combination, to take large doses of medication,

Table 14.1 COMMON MEDICAL CONDITIONS OF PEOPLE WITH DISABILITIES

PROBLEM	SYMPTOM	TREATMENT
Seizure, grand mal	Sudden loss of motor control, involuntary movement, loss of consciousness. May fall backward or may sense seizure and lie down. Seizures are usually abrupt, beginning and ending quickly.	Clear area and help person to floor. *Do not restrain the person or put anything in the mouth.* Turn on side if possible. Provide for rest and privacy after seizure. If person loses bowel/bladder control, clean the person and provide clean clothing as soon as possible.
Seizure, status epileptious	A grand mal seizure or series of seizures that last more than 15 minutes.	Monitor duration of seizure and color. Call ambulance if seizure continues.
Seizure, petit mal	Brief loss of awareness, may be confused by lapse.	No intervention required; may resume activity, with reminder if needed. Monitor frequency; notify physician if increase or change in type.
Seizure, psychomotor	Loss of awareness, may perform movement activities with random or purposeful appearance.	Recognize movement as seizure activity (vs. behavior problem). Resume activity with reminder if needed. Monitor frequency and type of behavior. Notify physician of changes.
Heart problems	Persistent chest pain, shortness or gasping for breath, extreme pallor or bluish color to lips, skin, and fingernails. Nausea, indigestion, or vomiting may occur as well as extreme prostration or shock.	Place employee in comfortable position, usually sitting up. If not breathing, begin mouth-to-mouth resuscitation. Call for ambulance immediately.
Diabetes, insulin shock	Skin is pale, bluish, may be moist and clammy. Pulse and breathing increase. The employee may feel weak.	In the early stages, provide sugar, such as a glass of orange juice. Contact nurse/doctor.
Congestion	Employee has difficulty breathing because of phlegm in chest and throat; sounds gurgley.	Position employee to clear air passages and allow for drainage (incline 30 degrees). Reposition employee frequently. If congestion interferes with breathing or eating, it may be necessary to suction with special equipment.
Allergic reactions	May result from ingesting or coming in contact with various substances, including foods, insects, pollen, chemicals, drugs, or plants. Symptoms may include hives, itching, rash, or more severe symptoms of shock or respiratory distress.	Note any specific procedure designated by medical records. If the situation is severe as in the case of a bee sting, call for medical attention and/or administer bee sting kit immediately.

Table 14.1 continued

PROBLEM	SYMPTOM	TREATMENT
Drug toxicity	Hyperactivity, lethargy, insensitive to pain, incoordination, irritability, confusion, lack of appetite, especially when sudden or exaggerated behavior changes.	Monitor medication carefully (see section on medications). Supervise the employee and prevent injury to self and others. If behavior requires urgent intervention, seek medical assistance.
Asthma attack	Employee has extreme difficulty breathing.	Help employee assume a comfortable position, allow to rest, keep calm. If situation is acute, use asthma medication as prescribed by doctor. If employee becomes faint or loses normal color, call ambulance.
Gingivitis	Employee may have red, swollen gums that bleed while brushing teeth or eating hard foods.	Teach good dental hygiene with frequent brushing and rinsing. Dentist may suggest use of Water Pik to stimulate the gums.
Scoliosis	An abnormal sideways curve of the spine that can inhibit body movement and balance. If not recognized and treated, can be progressive, impairing heart and lungs and pinching spinal nerves.	Attend to proper handling, positioning, and use of orthopedic devices. Employment specialists should work closely with physical therapists.
Shunt infection or collapse	Blockage of the surgically implanted tube that drains fluid from the brain into the abdominal cavity. May be indicated by persistent fever, listlessness, loss of appetite, nausea, vomiting, clumsiness, headaches, or sudden, unexplained change in personality.	Physician may limit some activities. Refer illness to physician as soon as possible.
Pressure sores	Generally indicated by redness or rawness where friction, weight, or poorly fitting orthopedic equipment puts continuous pressure on skin and underlying tissues.	Prevention is the best remedy. Reposition the employee to prevent bearing weight on any part of the body for longer than 20 minutes.
Impaired sensation	Employee may fall, bump, or injure self without showing signs of discomfort.	Protect employee by making environment as safe as possible. Teach employee to take precautions.

Table 14.2 COMMON MEDICATIONS AND THEIR SIDE EFFECTS, GROUPED BY CLASS

ANTICONVULSANTS: USED IN TREATMENT AND MANAGEMENT OF SEIZURES

GENERIC NAME	TRADE NAME	SIDE EFFECTS
Mysoline	Primidone	• Drowsiness, dizziness, and clumsiness are the most common side effects. • Confusion, shortness of breath, or changes in vision may mean the dosage is too high.
Phenobarbital	Luminal	• Drowsiness, "hungover" feeling, staggering, confusion, slurred speech. • May cause behavior problems; hyperactivity.
Phenytoin	Dilantin	• Ataxia, nystagmus, slurred speech, decreased coordination and mental confusion, blurred vision. • Tiredness, drowsiness. • Tenderness, swelling, or bleeding of the gums. Coarsening of the facial features, abnormal hairiness, acne.
Depakene	Valproic acid	• Stomach upset, diarrhea, drowsiness, dizziness, unsteady walk (ataxia), blurred vision.
Carbamazepine	Tegretol	• Fatigue, nausea, headache, clumsiness, dizziness.
Ethosuximide	Zarontin	• Gastric distress, nausea, vomiting, headache, hiccups, skin rash, and itching.
Clonazepam	Klonopin	• Drowsiness, dizziness, and unsteadiness.
Acetazolamide	Diamox	• Tingling feeling in extremities, hearing dysfunction, loss of appetite, taste alteration, nausea, vomiting, diarrhea, drowsiness, and confusion.
Methsuximide	Celontin	• Nausea, vomiting, weight loss, abdominal pain, constipation, blood disorders, ataxia, blurred vision, confusion, dizziness, depression, rashes.

ANTI-ANXIETY: USED TO CALM INTRACTABILITY, MANAGE HYPERACTIVITY, CONTROL ANXIETY

Minor Tranquilizers:

GENERIC NAME	TRADE NAME	SIDE EFFECTS
Chloridiazepoxide	Librium Librax	• Drowsiness, incoordination, rash, itching, dizziness, confusion, irritability, constipation, nausea, jaundice.
Diazepam	Valium	
Clorazepate	Tranxene	• Drowsiness, dry mouth, headaches, dizziness, and confusion.

Major tranquilizers:

GENERIC NAME	TRADE NAME	SIDE EFFECTS
Chlorpromazine	Thorazine	• Tardive dyskinesia, Parkinson-like tremors, tongue-biting, sleepiness, irritability, dry mouth, nasal congestion, difficult urination, constipation, increased sensitivity to sunburn, heartbeat irregularities.
Haloperidol	Haldol	
Thioridiazine	Mellaril	

STIMULANTS: USED TO INCREASE ACTIVITY OF CENTRAL NERVOUS SYSTEM, INCREASE MOTOR ACTIVITY AND ALERTNESS, OVERCOME FATIGUE, AND ELEVATE MOOD. ALSO USED TO REDUCE HYPERACTIVITY

GENERIC NAME	TRADE NAME	SIDE EFFECTS
Methylphenidate	Ritalin	• Marked anxiety, tension, agitation, nervousness, insomnia, loss of appetite, nausea, dizziness, and weight loss.
Cylert	Pemolin	• Abdominal discomfort and insomnia.
Dextro-amphetamine	Dexedrine	• Palpitations, dizziness, insomnia, headache, dryness of mouth, gastric disturbances, impotence.

Table 14.2 continued

ANTIHISTIMINES: USED FOR RELIEF OF ALLERGIC SYMPTOMS, HAY FEVER, AND COMMON COLD. ALSO MAY BE USED AS CENTRAL NERVOUS SYSTEM DEPRESSANT		
GENERIC NAME	TRADE NAME	SIDE EFFECTS
Diphenhydramine Hydrochloride	Benadryl	• Rash, sedation, dizziness, disturbed coordination, gastric distress, nausea, thickening of bronchial secretions.
Brompheniramine Maleate	Dimetane	• Rash, sedation, sleepiness, dizziness, disturbed coordination.

ANTIDEPRESSANTS: USED TO ELEVATE MOOD		
GENERIC NAME	TRADE NAME	SIDE EFFECTS
Amitriptyline	Elavil	• Dry mouth, drowsiness, dizziness, constipation, blurred vision, difficulty urinating, shakiness, increased appetite for sweets, weakness
Imipramine (Tricyclic)	Tofranil	• Hypotension, hypertension, restlessness, nightmares, dry mouth
Phenelzine	Nardil	• Interacts adversely with some foods (bananas, wine, beer, salami, cheese, yogurt), producing high elevation in blood pressure, which could produce stroke. Toxicity includes liver damage, insomnia, tremors, and agitation.
Lithonate	Lithium	• Can be extremely toxic with above symptoms. Necessary to have frequent blood level checks.

OTHER MEDICATIONS:

Antibiotics—Used in treating bacterial infections. NOT effective for viruses (e.g., cold, flu).
Vitamins—Used as supplement to diet, especially for persons who may have dietary deficiencies due to severe feeding problems.

and/or to continue taking medication for several years. These practices have traditionally been considered necessary because of the complexity and intensity of some people's needs. Rehabilitation specialists are beginning to recognize that the benefits of such practices may be outweighed by the costs, such as adverse interactions among drugs or damage to the body's systems (Gadow, 1986). Therefore, it is essential that even "routine" use of medications is supervised by a physician, with support from the transdisciplinary team.

Team members, especially employment specialists, can assist by knowing each employee's current medications, the desired effects, and the possible side effects. When concerns about medication arise, it is appropriate to discuss them with the employee's physician and family. Providing anecdotal records and objective data on job performance can prompt a decision to modify the type or dose of an employee's medication. In the event that an employee's medication is reduced or eliminated, the employment specialist should be alert to the signs of drug withdrawal. These signs include insomnia, nervousness, numbness, faintness, poor appetite, nausea, cramps, and lack of energy. Sudden drug withdrawal can result in seizures. Because of the seriousness of these effects, drug withdrawal should only be initiated under the direction and supervision of a physician.

Table 14.2 provides basic information about medications that are frequently prescribed for people with disabilities. This information was abstracted from the *Physician's Desk Reference* (1989). Additional information can be obtained from this source, the employee's physician, or a pharmacist.

EMPLOYEE SAFETY

The safety of all employees can be enhanced by taking reasonable precautions in and around the workplace. Some employers will have established specific safety procedures, in compliance with union, state, or federal requirements. Where such standards exist, the employment specialist must be thoroughly familiar with them and incorporate them into the employee's training. At all employment settings, however, the following minimum precautions should be adopted:

Reporting emergencies. The employee will know who to report to if he or she identifies a health or safety problem when the employment specialist is not present. The employee will know the location of the fire alarm and the proper way to use it.

Emergency evacuation. The employee will know the location of emergency exits, the sound of the fire alarm, and procedures for leaving/returning to the building in the event of an emergency.

Dress. The employee will know how to dress properly for the job. Considerations should include proper weight of clothing, proper style of clothing and shoes, and protective devices. Precautions should be taken against wearing jewelry, ties, or long hair that might become tangled in equipment.

Protective devices. The employee will wear goggles, earplugs, or other gear that provides protection at the workplace.

Hazards. The employee will recognize and avoid hazards such as wet floors, sharp edges, and moving equipment.

Machinery. An employee who uses machinery will be careful of moving parts, and will know how to operate the emergency shutoff switch.

Training. The employee will only perform the jobs that he or she is competent and comfortable to perform.

First Aid Procedures

Despite the best efforts to ensure a safe workplace, emergencies will sometimes occur. The employment specialist can prepare to react promptly and effectively by becoming familiar with the following procedures:

Emergency Situation	***Response***
Asphyxia: Obstruction of air passage Drowning Electric shock Cardiac arrest Status seizures (victim not breathing)	Situation is ***life threatening.*** Administer CPR immediately. Call for emergency vehicle.
Internal bleeding Major burns Chest wounds Unconsciousness: diabetic coma Unconsciousness: head wound Severe cuts, lacerations	Situation is ***Urgent.*** Administer first aid. Call for emergency vehicle.
Cuts Bites: animal, human, insect Second-degree burns Seizures	Situation is not urgent. Notify supervisor, case manager. Administer first aid.

Fractures Eye injuries Fever Head injuries, no unconsciousness	
Diabetic insulin reaction Abdominal pain Sprains	Situation not urgent. Administer first aid until physician can be notified.
Abrasions, Splinters Insect bites (nonallergic) Common colds	Situation can be handled by employment specialists, or residential staff.

ASSISTING EMPLOYEES WITH PHYSICAL DISABILITIES

Employees with conditions such as cerebral palsy, spina bifida, traumatic brain injury, or muscular dystrophy often have physical disabilities that influence their job preparation and performance. Although the supported employment team for these employees should include occupational and/or physical therapists, the employment specialist may have the most frequent opportunity and need to position and move the employee. Occasionally an employment specialist must meet these needs without the assistance of a therapist. This section provides basic information about methods that enhance both safety and therapeutic benefit when handling employees with physical disabilities. The information must be used judiciously, however, since every person with a physical disability has different needs. The suggestions that follow are to be used as general guidelines. The employment specialist is encouraged to discuss this chapter with therapists on the employee's team, determine which methods would be most appropriate for each employee, and develop the necessary skills under the supervision of a competent team member.

Employees may present a variety of types of physical disabilities. People with progressive diseases such as muscular dystrophy have muscle weakness and eventually may become completely paralyzed. Other employees may have weakness or paralysis resulting from conditions such as spina bifida, spinal cord injury, or damage to muscles and nerves in the arms or legs. When employees have these types of physical disabilities, the employment specialist should recognize the person's limitations, but also expect the employee to work up to his or her potential. Physical activity and exercise helps the person maintain current abilities, and may increase strength enough to enable new endeavors.

Another condition associated with physical disabilities is cerebral palsy. In this condition, brain damage causes abnormal muscle tone and interferes with development of motor skills. The person with cerebral palsy is not considered weak or paralyzed, but rather has problems with muscle coordination. Cerebral palsy is categorized according to the predominant type of muscle tone and the parts of the body affected. The most common types of tone are

Spastic (high tone; stiffness and resistance to movement)
Floppy (low tone; no resistance to movement)

Athetoid (fluctuating tone; continuous writhing movement)
Mixed (this form includes a combination of spasticity and athetosis)

The most common categories of involvement are

Quadriplegia (all four limbs and the trunk)
Diplegia (all four extremities and the trunk are involved; however, the lower extremities are much more severely involved)
Hemiplegia (one side of the body)

As the person with cerebral palsy grows older, the problems of abnormal muscle tone and involvement of various body parts often are complicated by years of inactivity and poor positioning. The results may include contractures (permanent limitation in movement), deformities of the spine, and a tendency to limit activity even further. The employee with severe physical disabilities related to cerebral palsy can be a particular challenge to the employment specialist. A program of occupational or physical therapy can assist the employee to participate successfully in the employment situation.

The goals of occupational and physical therapy programs for people with physical disabilities are

To correct poor posture caused by spasticity and poor positioning
To improve coordination needed for independent mobility, functional hand use, and efficient eating
To adapt equipment and the work environment to maximize participation

Progress toward achieving these goals depends on factors such as the person's age, degree of mental impairment, degree of physical disability, and consistency of therapeutic handling. The term *therapeutic handling* refers to a specific program of therapy, but also to the way the employment specialist works with the employee, and the influence of the environment on the employee. Environmental factors such as noise, hurried activity, and temperature can affect the employee's physical abilities. For example, a person who seems to have good motor control in a quiet office with a predictable routine may exhibit severe spasticity in the staff cafeteria. Lunch with coworkers and participation in other typical work activities should not automatically be abandoned, however. The advantages and disadvantages of each situation must be weighed, and the employee's ability (and desire) to accommodate to stimulating settings must be considered.

Positioning

Occasional reminders about posture will be sufficient for some employees, but employees with severe physical disabilities will need specialized equipment and individualized programs to ensure good positioning. These efforts are supported by the increasing availability of adapted equipment designed specifically for adults with physical disabilities.

There are several factors to consider when determining how to position an employee. First and foremost are the overall safety and comfort of the employee. Positions that do not meet these criteria should be avoided. Second, preference should be given to the positions typically used by other employees who do the same job, since these are usually the most functional to perform the required tasks.

For example, collating and stapling paper are usually performed in a standing position that allows reading all materials and leaning on the stapler. An employee who does this job but needs adapted equipment in order to stand should have the equipment provided, unless the employee demonstrates that another position is more satisfactory. Unfortunately, people with physical disabilities often remain confined to static sitting positions for long periods of time, increasing the likelihood of deformity and circulation problems. Most adults do not sit throughout an entire day of work; rather, they continually shift their weight, and intermittently stretch, stand, and walk around. Employees with physical disabilities may not enjoy these normal position changes unless assisted. Therefore, it is strongly recommended that employees with physical disabilities alternate between at least two positions during the work day and that their position be changed at least once an hour.

The final consideration in determining how to position an employee is that the positions selected should be similar to those used by other people of the same age in the same environment. If health or therapeutic considerations result in positioning that does not support this criterion, the employment specialist will want to ensure that the employee's privacy is respected.

The positioning procedures outlined below are only guidelines that may be modified to meet the unique needs of the individual employee. The transdisciplinary team may identify other positioning options, particularly as new types of equipment become available and the team begins to devise its own creative solutions.

Sitting

Advantages. Sitting is a normal position offering a normal view of the world. It offers opportunities to develop control of the head, trunk, arms, and legs. It is a functional position for many vocational activities. With a variety of available chair adaptations, employees with even the most severe physical disabilities can be positioned upright.

Disadvantages. The sitting position is often overused for adults who need experience in other positions. People who spend excessive time sitting may develop hip and knee contractures. Tendencies toward scoliosis are reinforced when one sits. Properly positioning adults with severe physical disabilities is difficult without elaborate adapted chairs. The chairs are expensive, require a high level of maintenance, and may prevent independent mobility.

Procedure. The method for positioning an adult in sitting varies considerably, depending on the person's disability, the type of chair, and the adaptations available. Ideally, the hips and knees will have 90 degrees of flexion, with the hips touching the back of the seat, the full foot resting on the foot rest, and a one- to two-inch space between the front edge of the seat and the back of the knees. The head, shoulders, and hips should be aligned, which may require several straps or pads. The hips are positioned first to give a good base of support. The chair may be tipped backward so gravity assists in holding the hips until a seat belt is applied. The belt, for both safety and support, goes across the upper thigh or bend in the hip (never near the waist) and is fastened only as tightly as necessary to keep the hips back. A harness may be attached from the seat belt to the top back of the chair to keep the shoulders back. A block may be placed between the thighs to keep the legs separated. Pads may be placed on both sides of the trunk anywhere from the hip to the shoulder to support and align the trunk. A head or neck piece may be added to offer lateral support to the head. Finally, the feet are strapped to the foot rest, if necessary, for good positioning. A "lumbar roll" may be added to facilitate trunk extension, or lateral supports may be added near the shoulder to keep the arms and shoulders forward and thereby reduce excessive extension. A tray allows the person to use his or her arms to help support the trunk and often is used as a work surface. A person with very serious contractures or deformities may need a custom-made chair, molded directly to the body.

Considerations for Function. Employees with physical disabilities often use wheelchairs for transportation. Some employees will need adapted chairs during work and mealtimes (see Figure 14.1). Adapted toilet seats are available with features similar to adapted wheelchairs. Whenever possible, it is recommended that regular chairs and alternative positions be used.

Kneeling

Advantages. Kneeling offers the opportunity to improve trunk control and to develop stability in the hips for weight-bearing without also having to control the knees and ankles. People with hip or knee contractures that limit standing may be able to kneel to more normally engage in activities that are usually done standing.

Disadvantages. A person with flexor tone will have difficulty keeping the hips extended while the knees are flexed. Caution must be taken to assure that the person does not flex the hips and arch the back to maintain an upright position. Kneeling over long periods of time (months or years) may

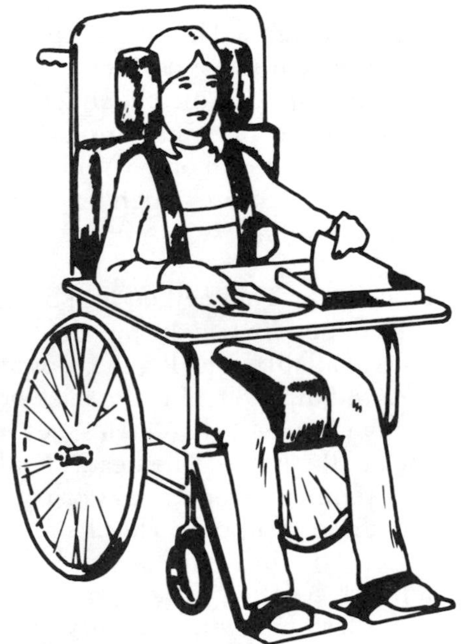

Figure 14.1 Sitting in an Adapted Wheelchair

result in bursitis of the knee. This position is not typically used by adults in work environments.

Procedure. The person is placed in a kneeling box with a base that extends out to the person's ankles and a front that extends upward to the person's chest level (see Figure 14.2). A belt is fastened across the hips or upper thighs (not across the waist) snugly enough to keep the hips extended and to prevent falling backward. A block may be placed between the knees to keep them separated for a good base of support. Pads may be placed near the hips and/or chest to align the trunk. A thick pad may be necessary under the legs to protect the knees.

Considerations for Function. By providing a variety of bases, a kneeling box can be placed at many different heights, as appropriate for working at a sink, at a table, or near the floor.

Prone-Standing

Advantages. Prone-standing offers the opportunities to improve head, arm, and trunk control while weight-bearing on the full leg. Adapted prone standers allow positioning from prone-on-elbows to almost upright while providing sufficient support to maintain alignment. It is an alternative to sitting for the person with increased flexor tone.

Disadvantages. The tonic labyrinthine prone or symmetrical tonic neck reflex may be stimulated, causing increased flexor tone. The person with extensor spasticity or poor trunk control may develop too much extension. The person with poor head and arm control will often let his or her head simply hang. Even people with good control of head, arms, and trunk have demonstrated abnormal postures when both hands are used for manipu-

Figure 14.2 Kneeling in a kneeling box

lation (i.e., when neither arm is used for support). It may be difficult to position a large adult on a prone stander.

Procedure. The person is placed on the prone stander (in a prone-lying position if possible) with feet flat of the foot rest and the shoulders, head, and arms extending off the top. A belt is placed across the hips (not the waist) and fastened tightly enough to keep the hips extended and prevent the person from falling back backward. The person who raises his or her chest off the stander may require a second strap placed loosely across the back to prevent excess or unsafe movement. A wedge or block may be placed between the legs to assure a good base of support with alignment of the trunk and legs. Pads may be placed along the hips and chest to maintain alignment of the trunk. After the person is positioned, the prone stander may be adjusted to the proper height for that person (see Figure 14.3).

Considerations for Functions. Most prone standers can be adjusted to a variety of heights for work near the floor or at a table, counter, or sink. It may be impossible for a person with severe deformities to use a prone stander, but people with dislocated hips may use them unless standing is painful. The employee should always be allowed to use one or both hands for support in prone-standing; tasks requiring two hands may be inappropriate.

Supine-Standing

Advantages. Supine-standing offers the person opportunities to improve head, arm, and trunk control while weight-bearing on the legs, without eliciting the abnormal extension patterns often seen in prone-standing. People with poor head control can also use this upright position because the head is supported. Because the arms are not needed for trunk support, they can more easily be used for vocational activities. The design of supine standers allows the person to be transferred onto a horizontal surface, and

Figure 14.3 Standing on a prone stander

positioned as two separate steps, which makes it safer and easier for large adults.

Disadvantages. Extensor tone may be elicited. The equipment is large and bulky, which interferes with storage, transportation, and positioning the employee at a variety of work surfaces.

Procedure. With the supine stander in a horizontal position, the person is placed on the back with feet flat against the foot rest and the entire body supported by the platform. Belts are placed across the person's hips and chest to ensure safety and to maintain his or her position when upright. A wedge or block may be placed between the legs for a good base of support with alignment of the trunk and legs. A belt across the knees may be necessary to keep the knees extended in the upright position. Pads may be placed next to the trunk or head to maintain alignment. After the person is positioned, the stander is slowly raised to the most upright position where the person can maintain head control (Figure 14.4).

Considerations for Function. Supine-standing is a good alternative to sitting for many employees. A tray attached to the supine stander may be the most feasible work surface. People with dislocated hips may be put in a supine-standing position unless standing causes pain.

Equipment

When a person needs a wheelchair or other piece of adapted equipment, it must be individually selected and fitted. Mobility equipment, which has not been discussed here, should also be carefully selected for and fitted to

Figure 14.4 Standing on a supine stander

individuals and used under the guidance of a physical therapist. After the employment specialist is trained to position the employee, photographs and/or written instructions can be attached to the equipment as reminders of proper positioning as well as proper adjustment of the equipment. Daily use of equipment eventually results in a loosening of pieces that must be adjusted. In addition, a regular schedule of cleaning and maintenance (e.g., oiling wheels, tightening all bolts, repairing missing, worn, or broken pieces) must be established to assure that equipment works properly and presents no danger to employees or employment specialists.

Transfers

In the course of moving people with severe physical disabilities from one position or place to another, it may be necessary to lift and carry them. In addition to the previously described principles of movement using key points of control, there are a variety of techniques of transferring that can be used. Whether lifting, carrying, or transferring an employee, it is essential that the employment specialist display confidence and maintain confidence throughout the procedure.

Two or more adults are usually needed to lift an employee. One method is for one person to reach under the employee's shoulders to grasp the wrists as the other person's arms are wrapped around the employee's bent knees (see figure 14.5a). A second method is for the lifters to position themselves on either side of the employee, supporting the employee's legs and trunk by grasping wrists under the knees and behind the back. For better balance, they can grasp the employee's legs above the knees and arms close to the shoulders (see figure 14.5b). Lifting a very large employee may require four adults. The adults can each hold one of the employee's limbs. An alternative is for the employee to sit or lie on a sheet or blanket with people lifting at each corner. When an employee must be lifted, but others are not available to assist, the employment specialist may need access to a mechanical lift designed for use by one adult. If a mechanical lift is needed at the worksite, this need should be noted in the employee's overall plan of service.

Whichever method is used for lifting, it is essential that the participants communicate their plans to the employee and to one another. It is advisable for one person to give the countdown and the order to lift. Whenever possible, employees should be taught to move themselves between the floor and a chair, between a chair and a toilet, between a chair and a car, and between a chair and a bed. When an employee transfers from a wheelchair, the first steps are always to lock the wheelchair, raise or remove the foot rests, release the seat belt, and move the hips forward to the front of the seat. The employment specialist stands in front of the employee and hold the employee's chest just under the shoulders. With the feet under the front edge of the chair, the employee leans his or her trunk forward and pushes up to stand as the employment specialist lifts and stabilizes the employee at the chest (see Figure 14.6).

Transfers from a wheelchair to another chair, a bed, a toilet or a car differ only in the setting, the height of the seats, and the amount of room available for maneuvering. While these practical differences can have a significant effect on the ease with which the transfer is made, the actual technique is the same and will be described only once. The wheelchair is positioned close to the other seat, typically arranged as depicted in Figure 14.7. The wheelchair is secured and the employee assisted to rise as de-

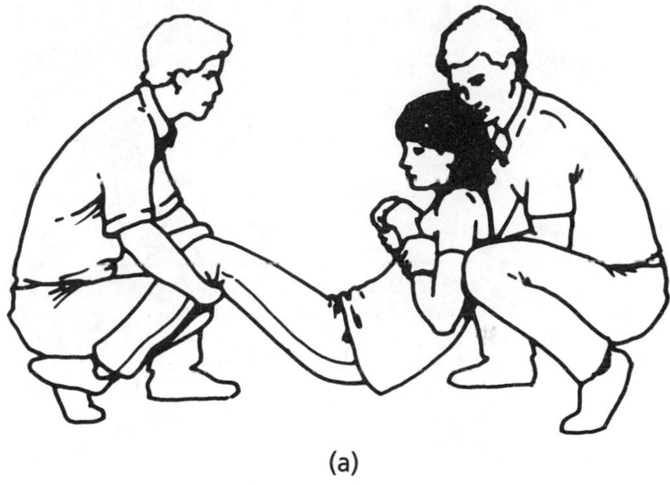

(a)

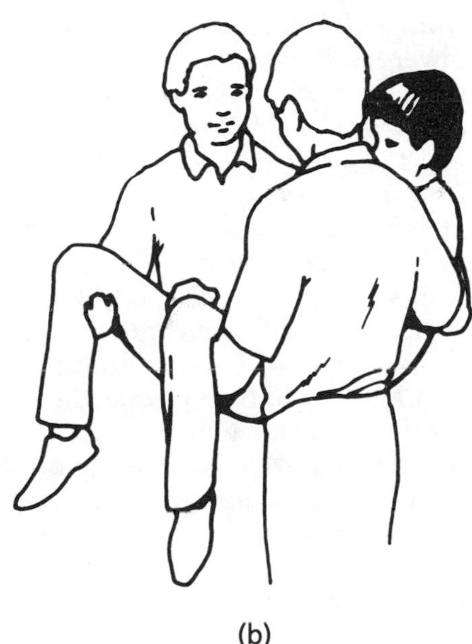

(b)

Figure 14.5 Two Methods of Lifting an Adult

scribed earlier. As the employment specialist takes a step back and toward the receiving seat, the employee pivots and then lowers into the receiving seat. It is clear that the more the employee can assist by balancing or supporting himself or herself with the hands and appropriately moving the feet, the easier the transfer is for the employment specialist. Although independence is always a goal for the employee with a physical disability, the safety of both the employee and the employment specialist is the primary concern. The methods used in these transfers can be modified so that two people work together to transfer an employee.

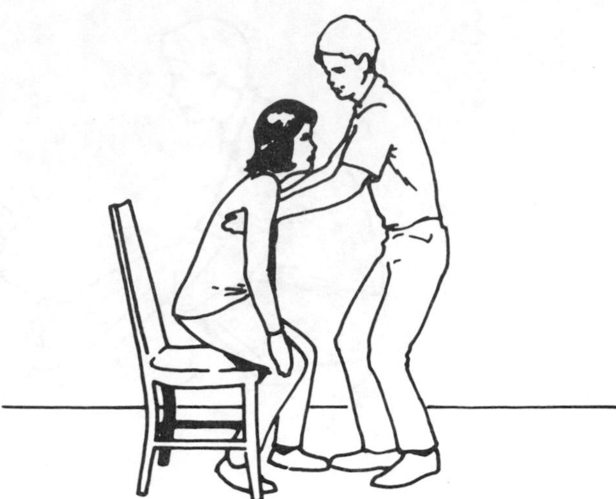

Figure 14.6 Standing Up with Assistance

Body Mechanics

Back pain is a common complaint among people whose jobs require heavy work and frequent bending and lifting. Although it commonly affects the lower back, strain on back muscles and joints may cause pain in the upper back, neck, arms, and legs. This pain can be minimized, if not prevented, by adhering to the following principles:

1. Conserve energy. Arrange the environment to minimize lifting and carrying. Push or pull wheelchairs and other positioning equipment to the employee rather than carrying the employee to them.

2. Carry weight as closely as possible to the hips to distribute the weight over the feet. The hips are usually the center of gravity. When preparing to lift someone or something, bring that person close to your center of gravity before lifting.

3. Stoop to lift by squatting with your hips and knees bent and back erect. Lift by straightening your hips and knees, keeping your back erect. Avoid sudden or jerky movement. Never rotate or bend the trunk to the side while lifting or carrying.

4. Get help when necessary. Although individuals differ, consider assistance when lifting anyone or anything more than one-fourth your weight. Carrying safely depends on skills, strength, and mobility in the trunk, arms,

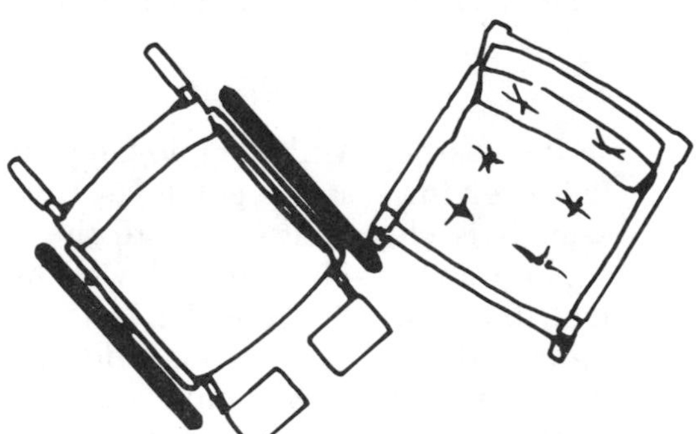

Figure 14.7 Transfer from Wheelchair to Chair

and legs. If not accustomed to lifting and carrying, build up tolerance slowly.

Guidelines for Working with Employees with Physical Disabilities

General Tips

1. Be patient.
2. Do things slowly and gently.
3. Explain to the employee what you will be doing.
4. Have the employee participate as much as possible.
5. Do not use force.

Lifting

1. If the employee is heavier than one-fourth your body weight, seek assistance.
2. Plan the lift in advance.
3. Arrange enough room for good footing.
4. Space your feet apart and get close to the employee to be lifted.
5. Lower your body to the level of the employee by bending your hips and knees.
6. Keep your trunk upright, with your shoulders over your knees.
7. Keep your back straight, with a slight arch in your lower back.
8. Grasp the employee securely before lifting.
9. Lift the employee by straightening your hips and knees in a steady upward thrust to a vertical position.
10. Hold the employee close to your body, with his or her weight over your feet.

Lowering

1. Arrange ample room for good footing.
2. Spread your feet hip width.
3. Grasp the employee securely.
4. Hold the employee close to your body.
5. Lower the employee by bending your hips and knees in a slow, gradual manner.

Wheelchairs

1. Lock both wheels of the wheelchair when conducting transfers.
2. Move the foot rests out of the way during transfers.
3. Fasten the seat belt securely across the employee's hips for travel.
4. Push the wheelchair forward unless going upstairs or over a curb.
5. Tip the wheelchair back and pull backward to go upstairs or over a curb.

Positioning

1. Position employees to minimize abnormal muscle tone, primitive reflexes, and deformities.
2. In chairs, keep the employee's hips centered and back in the chair.
3. Consider the employee's visual perspective when positioning.
4. Vary positions frequently.
5. Provide employees with opportunities for active movement.

Dressing

1. Select appropriate clothing.

2. Plan the dressing sequence.
3. Dress the employee slowly and gently.
4. Encourage the employee to participate as much as possible.

Eating

1. Position the employee properly for eating, and reposition when necessary.
2. Feed the employee slowly and calmly.
3. Give small bites of food of the consistency the employee can manage.
4. Allow time for chewing and swallowing.
5. Give the employee opportunities to indicate food preferences.

Toileting

1. Know the employee's method or symbols for communicating toileting needs.
2. Provide the employee with privacy for toileting.
3. Give only as much assistance as necessary.

Accessibility

Many community settings have architectural barriers that prevent access by people in wheelchairs and that limit access by other people with physical disabilities. Stairs, narrow halls and doorways, and bathrooms without space for maneuvering a wheelchair are examples of architectural barriers. People with disabilities may encounter architectural barriers in buildings, but also in most modes of public transportation. Public Law 93–112, the Rehabilitation Act of 1973, requires all agencies that receive federal funding to be accessible to people with disabilities. The law has several sections that pertain to architectural barriers and one that provides for adoption of national standards for accessibility. Connecticut and other states have incorporated the standards for architectural accessibility into the state building code which applies to all new commercial buildings. Many older buildings remain inaccessible, however, and the cost of some renovations is high. Developing employment opportunities for people with physical disabilities requires recognition of architectural barriers and accurate information about standards for accessibility. To assist with identification and removal barriers, an architectural assessment is contained in Appendix C.

Action Options

- Complete an accessibility assessment of two community worksites.
- Make a list of medications taken by employees you support. Next to each medication, list the dosage and times to be taken. Write down the general purpose of the medication and possible side effects.
- Spend a day in a wheelchair and list the accessibility and mobility challenges you face.

CHAPTER 15

Creative Problem Solving

Without the ability to temporarily forget what we know, our minds remain cluttered up with ready-made answers, and we never have an opportunity to ask questions that lead off the path in new directions.

R. von Oech, A Whack on the Side of the Head

Judy works in the dishroom of a large university cafeteria with two coworkers and an employment specialist as part of a small enclave. Her tendency to talk loudly, push others, and swear is an increasing problem that requires more and more staff time. The site manager has complained about her behavior and last week she hit the employment specialist and pushed a nonhandicapped coworker as she ran away. The employment specialist wants her removed from the site because she has tried "everything." The nonhandicapped coworkers at the site have been avoiding her ever since the day she hit the employment specialist.

Learning Outcomes

After reading this chapter you will be able to

- Outline a strategy for approaching problem solving as an exercise in creative thinking
- Plan a working group who will provide the best chance of finding creative solutions and implementing a decision
- Discuss the importance of beginning with a consensus on the question(s) to be answered
- Describe the importance of generating as many alternative solutions as possible and identify three strategies for facilitating this process

Effective problem solving is not really about problem solving. It is about creative thinking. Fortunately, supported employment is new and there are few established "truths" to block our thinking, but already some are sneaking in. The employment specialist model of individual placement established at Virginia Commonwealth University is an industry standard. Supported employment is typically considered to be individualized placements, enclaves, or work crews. While these models have produced outstanding results, our task is to break free of these givens and create a system of supports that leads to significant outcomes for each individual worker.

"THERE ARE NO GURUS"

The intent of this chapter is to provide a strategy for approaching problem solving. This strategy is based on the assumption that "there are no gurus" in supported employment. Existing programs and information provide important examples of effective practice, but the issues and problems encountered require unique and creative solutions. To this end, consider the following ground rules for any problem-solving effort:

Start by searching for the correct question.
Several minds are almost always better than one.
There is never one "correct" answer.
Every idea or opinion is valuable.

The emphasis on this chapter will be on the problem-solving process that applies to both individual worker issues and broader program needs. Basic to a comprehensive understanding of a worker's behavior is a thorough analysis of the relationship of the worker and the specific behaviors to the environment. This process is referred to as ecological assessment and is addressed in Chapters 6 and 8. An additional resource readers may want to review is Meyer and Evans (1989).

A SIMPLE STRATEGY

Typical questions encountered in supported employment programs span the range of possibilities. This strategy should help to address problems such as the following:

Betty does not want to be identified with other workers with disabilities and continually wanders away from her work group.
A new job site will offer year-round work but has less variety and is not preferred by the workers.
Howard does high quality work, but does not complete the job in the assigned time.

The strategy to address these problems is addressed in the section that follows.

STEPS FOR CREATIVE PROBLEM SOLVING

In this section we discuss the following steps as a guide to solving problems effectively:

1. Plan the working group.
2. Define the problem.

3. Generate alternative solutions.
4. Choose an alternative.
5. Implement.
6. Evaluate the results.

Step 1: Plan the Working Group

The first step of solving any problem is to decide who needs to be involved in the decision. It is useful to think in terms of the possible criteria for your decision.

How important is it that the decision be done in the following ways?

Made quickly. Decisions requiring a quick decision usually need to be made by one or just a few people. Groups take longer to reach a result. Recognize that you may sacrifice quality and ownership of others in the decision.

Of high quality. Clearly many of the decisions we make require the highest level of quality. Collecting the largest group of ideas and opinions possible will lead to better decisions.

Implemented thoroughly. Some decisions require commitment from a group of people for implementation to occur. Participation from the beginning fosters greater ownership in the outcome.

In supported employment most problems require both a high quality decision and commitment to implementation from a large group. In the ideal world all issues would be submitted to group problem solving. A difficult program for a worker in an individual placement may need to be implemented by a supervisor or substitute on a day the employment specialist is sick. Or it may require a longer time commitment to that job placement in the hopes of a higher likelihood of success. Decisions are made individually because we frequently are required to meet a time criterion. An employment specialist on site may not be able to rally resources for a group decision. In these circumstances, the basic rules and steps of the strategy remain the same.

Problem Definition

Who is the worker?
Judy lives in group residence with four other women; family is involved.

What is the work setting?
Dishroom of a large university cafeteria; two coworkers with disabilities supervised by employment specialist.

Who is involved?
Employment specialist, floating job trainer, residence staff (suspensions are an issue), no company staff at this time.

What is the problem?
Problem behaviors including yelling, swearing, pushing and hitting coworkers or employment specialist, and running away may jeopardize placement.

What is the question?
How can we keep Judy on task at work?

The list just given provides an example of the initial definition of a problem. Note that several people have a direct investment in the outcome. In addition to the employment specialist, Judy's residence staff are affected by the behavior if she is suspended from work. The program's floating job trainer may regularly work with Judy and should participate in the problem solving.

Rules for Step 1

Include everyone who will be directly affected by the decision.
Include anyone who needs to have ownership in implementation of the decision.

Step 2: Define the Problem

The first task of the group is to define the problem in observable and measurable terms. The purpose of this step is to clearly define the question or questions to be addressed. Each member of the group is likely to approach the problem with different questions in mind, and pursuing the correct question will focus later discussion. Consider the case of Judy.

Possible questions include

How can we stop Judy's inappropriate behaviors?
How can we keep Judy on task at work?
How can we teach Judy to tell us if she is unhappy?
Does Judy enjoy the work she is doing?

Each of these questions implies a very different approach to generating alternatives.

The working group addressed defining the problem by using an anecdotal analysis of Judy's behavior to define the antecedents and consequences that were usually present when it occurred. This process also required clearly specifying Judy's behaviors in *observable* and countable terms. A partial summary of this analysis is in Figure 15.1. Data for the analysis was collected on an Anecdotal Record Form similar to the sample found in Form 12 of Appendix A.

The result of this analysis was a consensus by team members that the primary question was "How can we keep Judy on task?"

Rules for Step 2

Define the problem in observable, measurable terms.
Make no assumption about the cause or solution of the problem.
Seek a clear consensus on the question(s) to be answered.

Step 3: Generate Alternative Solutions

The focus of step 3 is to generate as many alternative answers to the questions as possible. Basic to this step is the assumption that there is no single right answer! It should be clearly understood by the group that their measure of success is the number of solutions generated, regardless of how wild and crazy they sound. The secondary task of each member is to reinforce any new idea, and withhold judgment on every idea until the next step. The leader's role is to establish a group atmosphere that encourages dissenting opinions and guards against peer pressure. Following is a list of possible alternatives to the question "How can we keep Judy on task?"

Alternative Solutions

1. Make sure visitors distribute attention across all workers.
2. Coach Judy at the beginning of the day on appropriate behavior.

Judy: Anecdotal Analysis

Antecedents (What Happens Before)	*Behavior (Judy's)*	*Consequences (What Happens After)*
	EXCITED, Having fun: Constant	
–Any interaction with others (staff, coworkers. . . .) –Especially new or irregular people –Anywhere (van, at work, break . . .) –Praise	–Talks loudly, pushes others, spanks, swearing –Constant (daily, high frequency)	"ATTRACTS ATTENTION" –Telling her to tone down (doesn't work, leads to escalation) What stops it: –Redirect conversation –Humor her on the job –"I don't understand what to do; can you show me?" –"If you want coffee, cool down." –Ignore her (doesn't work, leads to escalation)
	ANGER: 2–3 times/week	
–Not getting attention –Negative feedback –Person giving her attention leaves –Dorothy splashed her –Receiving intensive attention, then loses it Consequence at building in the morning ⟶	–Swears at others, shakes fist –CRIES (Doesn't happen when having fun) –Blames others or authority for her problem Goes over and over the incident, escalates to anger	–Give her a con job, super sweetness, joke with her –Emphasis is on defusing the anger –GETS A LOT OF ATTENTION –Call her building and report the behavior –Be calm, give her some options ("You can work or go home.")
	AGGRESSION: 1 time/week	
–General escalates from previous stage –Same as above	–Kicks people –Raises fists toward someone –Hits out at others –Runs away May be directed at a variety of people (staff, coworkers, . . .)	–Physically block, redirect attention –Joke with her –Conversation –Talk softly –Give choices
	When doesn't she do this??	
–Attention is distributed across workers evenly –When not receiving intensive attention –Clear feedback		

Figure 15.1 Antecedent-Behavior-Consequence Analysis

3. Avoid 1 : 1 teaching or socializing.
4. Set goals for completing a specific amount of work.
5. Provide more choices at work: order of jobs.
6. Praise Judy for every pan cleaned (a low-preference job).
7. Use a timer to play "Beat the Clock."
8. Design a self-management system so Judy can check off 15-minute intervals of good behavior.

Several strategies are available to assist in this stage of problem solving. We have discussed establishing clear ground rules for a "brainstorming" session. An effective brainstorming group reinforces its own members for generating new ideas and prevents members from judging ideas. Two other approaches are presented.

Nominal Group Process. In a nominal group process each member works alone to write down solutions to a question. After answers are collected group members may be asked to vote for their top responses to narrow the list. This process helps to expand the number of alternatives considered and may be helpful at other stages such as defining the correct questions. Nominal group processes help expand the number of opinions generated and ensure equal participation by each member. The following steps outline a typical approach.

A Nominal Group Approach to Brainstorming

1. Complete the definition of the problem.
2. Give participants time to write their own solutions in private.
3. Accept one solution from each participant and record on poster paper. Continue until all solutions from the group have been recorded.
4. Reduce list by combining solutions if possible. Combining solutions requires consensus. One veto blocks combination!
5. Participants identify their top five solutions by placing a check next to them on poster paper. (Reduce list to the top 10 solutions for further discussion.)

Brainstorming Games. A common brainstorming game is to give the group a specific time limit, usually around five minutes, to list as many solutions as possible. Only new solutions are accepted during this period. All discussion is against the rules. If a group is large enough to split up, competition between teams for the most alternatives can be held.

Rules for Step 3

Maximize a range of dissenting opinions and new ideas.
Reinforce every opinion, no matter how wild and crazy.
Disallow judgment or critical comments on any idea. (An effective rule is to only allow questions requesting clarification during this step.)

Step 4: Choose an Alternative

One way to be more creative is to look for the second right answer. Often, it is the second right answer that, although offbeat or unusual, is exactly what you need to solve a problem is an innovative way (von Oech, 1983).

The first rule of decision making is that there is rarely a choice between right and wrong. The biggest mistake we can make is to look for the "right answer." If we have left the previous step with only one or two alternatives, then the group should stop, return to the previous step, or take a break. Only through the consideration of alternatives can we honestly evaluate a potential solution.

Returning to the example of Judy, review the list of the alternative solutions generated by her group. Each alternative has individual strengths and weaknesses. Through a comparison of these, a reasonable array of alternatives were chosen for implementation.

Rules for Step 4

Do not focus on the "right" decision.
Make a decision only if, on balance, the benefits clearly outweigh the costs and risks.
Consider doing nothing as a valid alternative.
Act or don't act, but don't hedge or compromise.

Step 5: Implement

Eighty percent of success is showing up.

Woody Allen

Successful problem solving or decision making does not end with the decision. Implementation is everything, the measure of the success of the project. If the problem-solving team was well selected, then most of the people involved in implementation have already been participants in the decision. It is important to step back at this point, however, to reconsider the following questions:

Who needs to know about the decision? Family? Business staff? Residence staff members?
What needs to occur?
Who does it?
Are all the skills and resources required in place?

Step 6: Evaluate the Results

One of the unfortunate rules we are conditioned to accept from early life is that to err is wrong (von Oech, 1983). No decision is foolproof, and our mistakes often teach us more than our successes. In the world of human services, reference is often made to Robert Perske's concept, the dignity of risk (1974). This idea reinforces the need to take action and learn from its consequences.

The task of job development provides a good example of the importance of accepting risk. Job developers typically canvas many businesses to find each individual job opportunity. Success is measured as much in the number of attempts as in the number of successes. A good job developer talks to many businesses, even though many of them will not produce job placements.

Rules for Step 6

Problem solving is an ongoing process. Evaluate decisions!
Recognize the value of laughing at our own mistakes.
Good decisions were made within multiple alternatives. Try again!

Decision making involves using all of the available resources to make the most creative and effective decision possible. The challenge for employment specialists is to identify and use all of the available resources to ensure not only the right decision, but implementation of the decision. Alternatives always exist. It is our job to create an opportunity to find them.

Action Options

- Convene a problem-solving work group to generate alternatives for a specific issue.
- Implement brainstorming strategies such as establishing rules for group interaction or a nominal group process in other working groups.
- Adjourn meetings if participants are not ready to make a decision with less than four viable alternatives.

CHAPTER 16

Transition from School to Supported Employment

We believe that transition programming is a concept so fundamental to the development of service delivery systems . . . that it must become a guiding force in the design and operation of programs from early intervention through adulthood. We further recognize that the combined efforts of professionals from a variety of disciplines, of family and community members, and of individuals with (disabilities) themselves are necessary if the idea of transition is to become a reality.

B. L. Ludlow, A. P. Turnbull, and R. Luckasson, Transition to Adult Life for People with Mental Retardation

---

Steve just turned 23. Since graduating from high school two years ago he has been employed in a local restaurant. Every day he rises early, dons his uniform, and takes public transportation to his job. He has received regular raises and is often asked to work overtime. Steve has Down's syndrome, severe mental retardation, and sensory disabilities. He is a productive member of his community, and his work and the $140 he earns each week contribute significantly to the quality of his life.

Learning Outcomes

After reading this chapter you will be able to

- Describe the process of transition from school to work, and identify principles and values that should guide this transition
- Identify the roles of the individual with a disability, family members, school personnel, and adult service providers in the transition from school to work

- Identify critical activities at each step of the transition process: school preparation, individualized transitional planning, and post-school opportunities

---

Richard is also 23, with Down's syndrome and severe mental retardation. After graduation from high school two years ago he was referred for adult services and financial benefits. Richard spent 18 months at home before adult services became available. His mother, who had to stay home with him, had assumed that like school services, adult services would be readily available. Richard is now enrolled in a sheltered workshop training program, and is paid approximately $30 per week.

National and regional statistics suggest that many people with disabilities have outcomes like Richard's after high school that reflect unemployment or underemployment. Hasazi, Gordon, and Roe (1985) found that only 65 percent of all students who received special education services over a four-year period were employed at the time of their survey and only 67 percent of this group were employed full time. National statistics have cited unemployment rates as high as 50 to 75 percent among people with disabilities (U.S. Commission on Civil Rights, 1983). Certainly over the last decade significant improvements have been made in the state of the art for both school and employment services. Why, then, is there such a discrepancy between Steve and Richard? And why do so many young adults sit at home or attend segregated day activity and sheltered employment programs after 18 years of special education?

Every student plans for the move from school to work. High school students choose a specialization in technical training or college preparation in their first year of school. Those who carefully organize school and work experience toward their goal move smoothly to the next stage of work or college. This process of transition begins early, includes both school and out of school experiences, and is clearly related to a specific goal (an apprenticeship, college entrance, a job).

The process of transition is even more critical for persons who need assistance and support beyond that provided by family and friends. There are significant differences between school and adult services. Following are some of them:

The legal mandate for services and support that carries a student through school ends with graduation. There is no entitlement for training, services, or supports for adults.

School-based services are organized around a curriculum, and may emphasize classroom-based skills. Adult services are organized around activites: work, recreation, etc. There may be significant discrepancies between the curriculum provided by the school and the demands of adult living and services.

Needs that were met in a coordinated way by the schools are now provided by many sources. Employment, recreation, counseling, and therapy needs may now each be provided by a separate organization.

Because resources are limited and there is no entitlement, waiting lists are common for services.

THE PROCESS OF TRANSITION

In its most specific form transition is the process of moving from school to work. Wehman, Kregel, and Barcus (1985, p. 26) provide the following definition:

> Vocational transition is a carefully planned process, which may be initiated either by school personnel or by adult service providers, to establish and implement a plan for either employment or additional vocational training . . . such a process must involve special educators, vocational educators, parents and/or the student, an adult service system representative, and possibly an employer.

Clearly, vocational transition is only one component of the transition from school to adult life. The definition has been broadened to include home and family, social, leisure, and financial domains (Halpern, 1985; Patton & Browder, 1988). This chapter will primarily address the specific goal of employment, although it is sometimes impossible to disentangle the various strands that define our lives.

Will (1984) proposed a model for the transition from school to work that includes three "bridges." The first bridge, *generic services*, includes those used by all people in the community to find employment. This bridge may include employment agencies, or family and friends. The second bridge, *time-limited services*, provides short-term assistance to persons with disabilities. Vocational rehabilitation services are a typical example. Supported employment is included in the third bridge, *ongoing services*, and represents a lifelong need for support and assistance. Will's model implies one step, from school to work. Effective transition is an ongoing process that affects an individual's opportunity to lead a high quality of life. It involves three major stages:

1. Functional preparation in school
2. Individualized transitional planning and interagency coordination
3. Appropriate post-school opportunities

TRANSITION PRINCIPLES

Most of the values that should guide the transition process have been discussed extensively in previous chapters. School and adult services should emphasize integration with persons without disabilities as well as opportunities to develop meaningful relationships. Opportunities for presence and participation in natural school and community environments is critical. Vocational training should emphasize paid employment in real jobs. It is also important to recognize several additional principles that guide transition planning.

The transition planning process must recognize and support the personal choices and preferences of the student. The transition process must be concerned with promoting participation and self-determination for the student. Independence can be defined as the ability to perform specific tasks, or to separate psychologically from parents and caregivers. It has been suggested that a more useful definition should emphasize choosing to live one's life in a way consistent with one's personal values and preferences. Such a definition emphasizes the development of both the capability and opportunity to consent directly to the events of one's own life (Knowlton, Turnbull, Backus, & Turnbull, 1988). Promoting this independence requires conscious attention to the career and life-style planning processes, teaching students to make choices, and involvement in self-advocacy.

Several additional principles must be incorporated throughout the process of transition (Schalock & Stark, 1988; Patton & Browder, 1988):

Transition planning should involve the family and be individualized to accommodate values and preferences.
Transitions are continuous events, not discrete ones. Therefore, one must think about their development, operation, and continuance.
Interagency collaboration is necessary to ensure a smooth transition of funding and no break in services.
Effective transition requires a match between school preparation and services received after graduation.

THE ROLE OF FAMILY

The transition process requires that three different levels of the service delivery network interact: the participant, service delivery providers, and the larger social system (Schalock & Stark, 1988). This simple fact creates much of the confusion and tension that is inherent in the process. Clearly the guiding principles just mentioned highlight the central role of the student and his or her family. The role of the schools and the adult service system are emphasized in the specific components of the transition process that follows.

The graduation of a child from school is a milestone in any family. Family members support the transition to independence with values, resources, and assistance in planning. The role of the family as advocate and case manager for a person with disabilities is critical during this phase. The splintering of services and resources requires a long-term vision. Only the family is in a position to demand outcomes that enhance the individual's quality of life. Anderson, Beckett, Chitwood, and Hayden (1985) have identified seven roles that the family members of a person with disabilities must play during the transition process. Family members can function as

Advocates to ensure that career education occurs in the schools
Providers of unique information on personal traits, interests, aptitudes, and behaviors
Role models for appropriate work behavior and attitudes
Case managers
Program advocates to ensure that a complete range of employment options exists, including supported employment
Risk takers
Financial planners, ensuring financial security

Most importantly, family members, especially parents, must be dreamers who help the person with a disability establish and achieve a quality adult life.

SCHOOL PREPARATION

Preparation for adult life begins with the development of a community-referenced, functional curriculum. Because adult services typically represent a relatively stable component of a person's life—work, for example—service planning revolves around goals that emphasize effective performance in a specific work setting. In the school, the assumption is that the student will move on shortly to another grade level or to adult living. The curriculum is the road map for what will be taught to facilitate that move.

Preparation for the transition from school to work should be reflected in the curriculum as early as elementary school. At this level, vocational preparation may include opportunities for social integration with nonhandicapped peers, development of simple job responsibilities such as chores, and nonclassroom and community-based instruction. It has been suggested that no more than 65 percent of instruction should be classroom-based at an elementary level, with 25 percent ocurring in other school settings (lunchroom, recess, and extracurricular activities) and 10 percent occurring in community environments (purchasing snacks, using a restaurant, etc.; Sailor et al, 1986). The distribution of time should gradually shift toward community-based instruction throughout the school career until at ages 16 through 21, immediately prior to the transition to adult services, as much as 85 percent of instruction is in community work and leisure environments.

Research has emphasized the importance of several work experiences in influencing the likelihood of employment success after school (Hasazi et al, 1985). A variety of job experiences is a critical part of the career planning process, offering the ability for the individual to make or indicate to significant others his or her preferences for specific jobs. This also establishes a résumé, characterized by a variety of job skills and demonstrated success at work. Finally, school programs typically have a higher level of staffing resources needed to provide individualized on-the-job training than adult service programs. The services provided in school represent a critical opportunity to demonstrate that a student can and should have access to community-based employment after graduation. Implementation requires a careful structuring of school resources to emphasize community-based training.

The transition process implies that school personnel are responsible for integrating plans for transition into the individual education plan process from the beginning of a student's school career. Career planning and exploration should begin early as a part of that process. Parent and family participation in creating a vision for and supporting an optimal adult life-style for the student is critical. The school must assess the opportunities available after graduation, and provide learning experiences that address these opportunities. This requires, first, an ecological approach to curriculum development and a thorough analysis of the specific job opportunities available in the community. Second, school personnel must have a complete understanding of the adult service programs and supports available after graduation. In the best of all worlds the transition to adult living is a simple handoff from one set of supports to another, with the individual already working in his or her chosen job.

Recommendations

School

Incorporate vocational education and experiences beginning in the elementary grades.

Develop curricula that are clearly preferenced to adult living.

Ensure an acceptable ratio of classroom, school, and community learning experiences throughout the school career.

Provide a variety of paid work experiences to students prior to graduation. Reorganize staffing patterns to support community-based training and work.

Develop a knowledge of local adult services, funding, and supports.

Students and Families

Advocate for an individual education plan that is clearly directed toward useful, functional skills that will enhance adult living.

Demand a variety of paid work experiences in the community.
Articulate a clear vision for the future for your family member.
Reinforce the value of paid employment and community contributions at home.

INDIVIDUALIZED TRANSITION PLANNING

As noted, planning for the transition to work and adult living should be integrated into the individual education plan process at an early age. There is still, however, a need for explicit transition planning beginning at least four or five years before graduation from school-based services. Adult services and supports are provided by an often bewildering array of organizations and sources. Financial supports are typically provided by state agencies, specific programs (personal care attendants), and the federal government (SSI/SSDI/Medicaid). Vocational training and support may be provided by an adult service agency, speech therapy by the local hospital, and counseling by a mental health center. The range of supports needed is defined individually as a part of the transition process. Accessing them in a timely manner requires long-term planning.

The first step of transition planning is identifying the range of programs and supports needed after graduation. If career planning and the individual education plan process have yielded a clear image of a positive future, this should be a straightforward task. The second step is ensuring that resources will be available. It is for this reason that the transition planning process needs to start early. Representatives of the state funding agencies need to be involved from the beginning to ensure that funding and community services are available when needed.

Recommendations

Schools

Initiate transition planning by the time a student is 15.
Work with the student and parents to develop a clear image of a preferred adult life through a career planning process.
Ensure the participation of adult service providers, funding agencies, and others.

Students and Families

Become actively involved as case manager and advocate.
Ensure that the full range of supports needed in adult life is identified and that providers participate in planning.
Ensure that funding for adult services is procured before graduation.

Adult Service Providers

Participate early to focus learning and work experiences during the last years of school.
Work to ensure a smooth transition.
Assist families and school personnel to understand the demands and structure of the adult service system.

ADULT SERVICES

Achieving a successful transition requires that an appropriate array of services exists at the end of the process. It is unacceptable for a student to receive carefully planned community-based training and employment experiences throughout school, only to graduate to a slot in a sheltered workshop. Advocacy is required to ensure that quality supported and transitional employment programs are available after graduation. Early transitional planning is part of this process.

Adult service providers also have a responsibility to ensure that school services are preparing individuals for the demands of adult life and employment. Networking with schools for curriculum development, job market analysis, and job development are strategies for expanding resources and ensuring a common focus in service delivery.

Recommendations

Student and Families

Participate in area planning boards for state agencies that fund adult services. Ensure that work opportunities like competitive and supported employment are emphasized.

Continue to provide active case management and advocacy.

Ensure an ongoing process of career planning. Demand that program decisions are made within the framework of personal quality of life outcomes.

Adult Service Providers

Advocate for improved funding for community-based employment opportunities for individuals.

Assist families in procuring an appropriate range of community living, financial, and social/recreational supports.

Advocate for individual quality of life outcomes for each consumer of services.

CONCLUSION

Clearly, the transition from school to adult living and employment is a difficult process. It requires the coordinated effort of each part of the individual's ecology over a period of five to six years. More importantly, effective transition requires a long-term attitude that recognizes that transition from one life experience to another is a continuous process that begins at birth and continues throughout our lives. Careful attention to the quality of life indicators for the individual, and consistent advocacy to ensure that these are met, provides the most useful guide through these steps.

Action Options

- Begin dreaming! Provide a vision of what each individual will be doing 10, 15, and 20 years in the future:
  - Where will he or she be working?
  - Where recreating?
  - Where living?
  - Who will be the significant others in his or her life? Friends? Family?
- Begin planning for transition today. Visit adult service providers, establish joint planning committees that cross the life span.
- Establish a curriculum that emphasizes paid employment and community experience. Structure staffing patterns and responsibilities to allow for community-based training and supervision.

CHAPTER 17

Effective Management for Supported Employment

Commitment takes form in the attitude and, more importantly, in the behavior of people in our field. The behavior is predictably energetic, productive, and unwavering in purpose. The drive is to close all the gaps that prevent consumers from being treated as full citizens.

G. Provencal, "Culturing Commitment"

Employment Services, Inc., noticed that several staff members had formed closer relationships with company staff at their worksite than with the staff of the organization. In fact, over the past month, two staff resigned to take management trainee jobs with their host company. Concerned about the isolation of their employment specialists, ESI made plans to maintain intensive face-to-face contact with each employment specialist. Supervisory ratios were reduced, and supervisors were expected to visit each site daily in addition to regular staff meetings. The psychologist, nurse, and social worker formed a resource team, and one member visited each employment specialist weekly to offer assistance and to provide an opportunity to problem solve. Finally, desk space was assigned to each employment specialist at the office. Now at the end of each day, staff gather in their office space at ESI and talk about the work day. Staff have been more involved in agency planning and functions.

Learning Outcomes

After reading this chapter you will be able to

- Define the roles and critical outcomes of an employment specialist's position

- Design an effective professional position for employment specialists, and understand the range of training needs required to support job performance and career development
- Identify and develop the critical sources of support required to maximize effectiveness, job satisfaction, and career development for employment specialists
- Identify and define critical features of organizational design that support employment specialists and foster their participation in the organization

Management of any human services program for adults with disabilities is a difficult undertaking. Both the professional literature and anecdotal reports emphasize problems in finding sufficient funding, recruitment, and retention of staff; "burnout"; and effective supervision to ensure program outcomes (Karan & Knight, 1986; Bruininks, Kudla, Wieck, and Hauber, 1980). Supported employment managers address all of these issues, as well as the unique issues created by service delivery in diverse integrated program sites.

Supported employment makes a radical departure from traditional organizational structures in vocational training. Services are primarily provided at community job sites, distant from the supervisory structure of the program. As a result, the employment specialist has almost complete control and responsibility for a worker's success, safety, and acceptance by the employer and the community at large. This independence also isolates the employment specialist from role models and support networks. Often there are no rehabilitation counselors, therapists, and production staff to provide support.

Human service agencies are faced with the challenge of providing sufficient support, training, and supervision to employment specialists. There is a direct relationship between the attainment of quality outcomes for people with disabilities and the extent to which an organization respects, communicates with, supports, and celebrates those staff members who are on the front line.

EMPLOYMENT SPECIALIST ROLES AND FUNCTIONS

What Is an Employment Specialist?

An *employment specialist* is defined as any person directly involved in training or supporting workers in integrated work settings. As introduced in Chapter 1, an employment specialist is an employee of a human service agency, but the definition leaves open the possibility of companies providing their own employment specialists. An employment specialist may work in any model of supported employment, including work crews or enclaves.

Employment specialists typically include staff identified as

Job coach
Job trainer
Crew foreman
Placement specialist
Rehabilitation counselor
Instructor

Employment specialists are the primary providers of supported employment services. The position is different from most job roles in rehabilitation because employment specialists have responsibility for the entire range of services necessary for ensuring successful entry to community-based employment. They must focus on both integration and coordination of resources and on direct instruction and support (Karan & Knight, 1986).

Employment Specialist Roles

One approach to defining an employment specialist is through a consideration of the job's primary outcomes. While these will vary somewhat from program to program, several seem critical to defining the role in supported employment. An employment specialist should be primarily responsible for ensuring that (Buckley, Albin, & Mank, 1988):

1. Paid employment is available to all workers.
2. Workers are trained in social and job skills.
3. Integration with persons who are not disabled occurs.
4. Services are coordinated across home, family, and others.
5. Work is maintained through stable ongoing support.

These job outcomes reflect the importance of a broad approach to employment. The employment specialist must interact effectively with all members of the person's ecology, including employers, family, coworkers, and professional supports.

A second approach is to consider the many roles an employment specialist plays in reaching the outcome of successful employment. As a *teacher*, the employment specialist requires skills including assessment and data collection, formulation of objectives, and systematic training. Working in a community worksite the employment specialist must also use methods that are appropriate and unobtrusive. Job analysis skills, not dissimilar to those typically used by an *industrial engineer*, are required to accurately identify the task requirements and develop job adaptations.

The employment specialist must also function as a *manager*, coordinating the efforts of home, the employer, and support services such as transportation to ensure placement success. Assistance and training of skills outside the worksite, including travel, money management, time management, or hygiene, may need to be addressed. As a *social psychologist* the employment specialist is responsible for understanding the unique culture of the job site and supporting the development of significant relationships between the worker and his or her coworkers, supervisors, and customers. The employment specialist has to be an effective *production worker*, able and willing to assist in job completion as needed. He or she must be a *trouble shooter* and public relations expert, able to handle behavioral and other crises with finesse and able to build a support system for problem solving outside of the work setting. Finally, and significantly, the employment specialist is both an *advocate* and *friend*.

Regardless of the educational and experience background of the employment specialist, the breadth of responsibilities required in the position demands that it be defined as a professional role, with responsibilities and compensation that are comparable to other rehabilitation professionals (Cohen, Patton, & Melia, 1986; Renzaglia, 1986). Professional status is reflected first in the responsibility for achieving specified outcomes, and sufficient resources of time and support to achieve the goals.

DEVELOPING THE POSITION

The Job Description: Creating Meaning

The design of a meaningful job description for high-commitment work requires attention to providing clear responsibility for achieving outcomes. Ownership for human service outcomes is increasingly given to a team. Providing clear ownership of outcomes in high-commitment work to individual staff is a critical component of providing support (Provencal, 1987).

The first implication of an outcome-focused job description is that job tasks and scheduling must be designed around the outcomes. This approach to designing a job has implications for both task responsibilities and scheduling. If an employment specialist on a mobile work crew is responsible for transporting workers to and from home, that time may interfere with the planning and coordination needed to assure real outcomes for those workers.

A second implication for job design is the placement of responsibility for case management and service coordination. In traditional vocational rehabilitation programs the case manager is a distinct professional, separate from the direct service function. Often this person is a certified rehabilitation counselor with a large caseload of "clients." Effective coordination of supports for a worker in supported employment requires that these functions be centralized with the employment specialist. Centering case management responsibility with the employment specialist is also a critical part of providing meaning to the position.

Recommendations

1. Design job descriptions and responsibilities around the critical worker outcomes an employment specialist should achieve.
2. Provide ownership through case management relationships, control, and autonomy.
3. Allocate employment specialist time for planning, service coordination and networking, and meeting participation.
4. Consciously separate support functions (transportation, equipment maintenance) from outcome-focused tasks (those directly affecting the employee).

TRAINING AND ORIENTATION

The shortage of qualified employment specialists is exacerbated by the lack of formal training programs for people entering the field. Bachelor's and graduate-level training programs have been initiated for community employment specialists at very few colleges. It is clear, however, that these programs are unlikely to meet the demand for direct service staff in supported employment services. The majority of people hired for employment specialist positions continue to be people with general college or high school backgrounds.

This manual outlines critical employment specialist functions across the four phases of supported employment. Programs need to address training in these phases either directly or through coalition arrangements. *Training* also, however, implies the socialization of a person as that person learns to adapt to the human service agency. Because of the isolation of the position, particular attention needs to be given to the entry of a person into a supported employment program to allow socialization and networking to occur. Perhaps it is most useful to consider training needs in terms of the priorities over time as a person enters a job.

First Week

Learn about the organization, its style and expectations.
Understand the organization's mission objectives, values.
Define personal job responsibilities.
Join and participate in a work group.

Most of these training needs during the first week are process and socialization focused rather than skill focused. We can learn from industrial management literature the importance of this socialization process in forging a clear and positive relationship with new staff. In supported employment, all too often new employment specialists are assigned directly to job sites. This practice requires an early emphasis on skills, and prevents socialization from occurring. In fact, it is not uncommon for a new employment specialist to become committed to the goals and personnel of the company the placement is in rather than the human service agency.

First Month

Learn basic instructional practices.
Begin data collection.
Develop relationships with host company staff.

First Quarter

Take on case management responsibilities.
Continue to develop instructional capabilities.
Develop assessment skills.
Advocate with families, supervisors, and other significant persons.

First Year

Learn job development and compatibility analysis strategies.
Learn generalization strategies.
Coordinate career planning for target workers.

CAREER DEVELOPMENT

The topic of training also includes personal career development. As professionals, employment specialists need ongoing opportunities for personal development and growth. Some of these opportunities will be internal, through task assignments and participation in agency planning and evaluation. Some will need to be external, with opportunities to learn from other sources. In the end, we have to offer clear opportunities for career advancement if we are to expect to reduce the high rate of turnover in employment specialist positions.

SOURCES OF EMPLOYMENT SPECIALIST SUPPORT

The work of an employment specialist is never dull. Supervisors change, the dishwashing machine breaks down, a worker tells his supervisor he is dissatisfied with the job, or the group home schedules a medical appointment during the work day. The way in which we support the employment specialist in his or her role will play a critical role in the success achieved.

Supervisor Supports

The human service agency supervisor is often the only source of on-site support for an employment specialist. This requires supervisors to meet several needs. They will be the primary role model that employment specialists will have an opportunity to observe with their workers. They are also the only source of direct observation and feedback as part of the employment specialist's training. Finally, on a practical note, supervisors are often a source of backup during behavioral crises or employment specialist absenteeism. Supervisors must have daily contact with each employment specialist, and visit each worksite at least two-three times per week.

Recommendations

1. Program supervisors should be working managers, providing examples for the employment specialist and direct services to workers.
2. Maintain a small ratio between supervisors and employment specialists. 1 : 3 or 1 : 4 is not too small. Even when other floating support is available, 1 : 6 or 1 : 8 is a maximum.
3. Maintain daily contact with employment specialists, and regular on-site support.

Work Team Supports

The work group or work team is the central source of socialization and peer support for an employment specialist. Without it an employment specialist frequently is forced to rely on staff at the host company for support, and they work from a different perspective and set of objectives. In the most extreme case, the internal conflicts and politics of a company can overwhelm an employment specialist. Because of problems in recruitment and retention, many new employment specialists are assigned directly to a job site. This isolation requires that specific attention be given to enhancing group membership. Ideally, contact with team members should occur daily, with ample time for both formal problem solving and planning and informal discussion. Team meetings should occur at least weekly, with an established agenda and sufficient time for both individual worker issues and group coordination and planning.

Recommendations

1. Schedule team meetings at least weekly. Two meetings with different agendas (worker issues, team issues) may be useful if possible.
2. Ensure daily opportunity for interaction with colleagues.
3. Consider 1 : 1 mentor relationship for new employees. This may also provide a growth opportunity for veterans.
4. Organize work teams around a common work schedule.

Plan for Flexibility

Can an employment specialist take a sick day? Attend a conference? Attend a quarterly case review scheduled at 11:00? In a sheltered workshop the remaining staff are able to spread out a little and cover the gap. In supported employment all of these border on crises. Programs account for these demands in several ways. Typically, effective supported employment programs have streamlined organizational structures with fewer positions in support roles, and most positions having some direct service responsibility.

This will be discussed more in the section of this chapter on administrative supports. We have discussed the need for small staffing units that allow for supervisor flexibility. Several other strategies have been used effectively to meet the need for flexibility:

Provide staff with frequent opportunities to cross between sites. Workshop staff may be support source if available.
Provide on-line experience and training to office staff.
Develop a pool of on-call substitutes.
Use "floating instructors." In some agencies, drivers serve as floating instructors during the work day.
Develop natural supports through coworkers and supervisors.

Organizational Design and Supports

It is the leader's job to lead. This requires that he or she accept the stewardship for seeing to it that a productively charged atmosphere exists in the organization. The person in charge has no more fundamental duty than to see that the agency energy level is high enough to move the organization forward to meet its objectives (Provencal, 1987).

The recurrent theme of this book is a foremost focus on values. The decision to initiate a supported employment program, whether a conversion or new program development, begins first with the agency's heart. It is certainly not a decision made on economic terms. Some funding is frequently less stable and harder to justify in bureaucratic terms. Nor is it made for ease of management. The decision to invest in supported employment is a decision to invest in people.

Developing a Mission Statement

The first and most important source of support that an organization can provide to its staff is a statement of values and objectives that provides direction and purpose. An effective mission statement or creed for a supported employment program should, according to Powell (1987),

Establish supported employment programs as different from more traditional service options
Provide an essential set of beliefs
Establish a yardstick for measuring program success
Provide direction for continued growth and development
Establish a perspective from which to solve problems

The primary work of a supported employment program is done at the individual employment specialist level. Supported employment requires an organizational design that provides strong support and resources to that position. O'Brien (1987b) describes one organization that met this need by "turning the pyramid on its side." Organizational emphasis was focused on the people being served, and the staff who had significant relationships with them. The result was a "flat" organization, with very few levels of hierarchy. Other characteristics noted by O'Brien include

Minimal distinction between administrative or professional and direct service staff
Narrowing of pay differentials between direct service workers and managers

Value for personal knowledge and contact. Managers and support staff spend significant time with the people who receive services
Strong investment in staff development for all positions

Communication and Participation

The isolation of employment specialists affects not only the functioning of small work teams, but the administration of the organization. It is the responsibility of the leader of the organization to ensure that employment specialists remain valued participants in the organization.

Recommendations

1. Ensure that organizational decisions are not made without the participation of each person.
2. Design committee structures that give each person a role in the larger organization, outside of his or her work team.
3. Take meetings into the field. Hold individual and small group meetings at job sites whenever possible.
4. Collect every staff person in one place often. Consider luncheons, in-services, retreats.
5. Celebrate successes! Send up balloons, hold parties, give out prizes.
6. MBWA: Practice "management by walking around." Communicate your commitment to employment specialists by visiting sites, listening to employment specialists, and observing the results.

Administrators and Managers

Finally, managers and administrators need to attend to maintaining for themselves the "productively charged" energy level that is their primary responsibility. Provencal (1987) offers four proverbs to program managers and administrators that help him maintain an appropriate perspective on his work:

1. Be careful not to isolate yourself. Reach out to friends and supporters who you know will give you hope when hope is needed.
2. Reacquaint yourself with the heroes and reading that led you to this field. The lives of men and women who had the conviction to revolt against, to reform some part of their society, can serve to ignite the spirit again and again.
3. Stand for something. Be sure that people come to recognize what your commitment is, what your obsession is.
4. Take care of yourself, but avoid self pity. If any group of professionals should know about the debilitating effects of labeling, we should. There is no burn-out.

Living these proverbs will go a long way toward meeting the support needs of the organization.

Action Options

- Initiate a review of the employment specialist job description and responsibilities. Make sure that the critical outcomes of the position match the task responsibilities and time allocation in the employment specialist's work day.

- Review the training and orientation package for new employment specialists. Ensure that integration with the organization is as much of a priority as skill acquisition.
- Review the support structures and needs of employment specialists with particular attention to the role of the direct supervisor, participation in a work team, and program flexibility.
- Review the design and structure of the organization to ensure it efficiently addresses the needs and goals of supported employment services. Begin by ensuring a common understanding of the mission of the organization.

CHAPTER 18

Governmental and Regulatory Issues

Thou shalt know the law with all thine heart.

M. Mooslin, Presentation at Connecticut Developmental Disabilities Council Conference 1985

Gary, who has a severe disability, does not have a job. Although he would certainly be successful at a number of different jobs if provided with the necessary supports, he and his family are both afraid of losing government benefits that pay for Gary's ongoing medical needs. Gary's family has not investigated his situation in detail, but they feel that if he works, his increased income will jeopardize these benefits and will therefore have a negative impact on his financial resources and those of his family. As a result, Gary continues to be unemployed.

Learning Outcomes

After reading this chapter you will be able to

- Assist workers and their families in predicting the impact of supported employment on subsidies
- Describe the Targeted Jobs Tax Credit and its use as an incentive for employers
- Describe the Supplemental Security Income (SSI) and Social Security Disability Insurance (SSDI) programs

Marge and her family faced apprehensions similar to Gary's about her benefits but found that she could work and retain specific insurance benefits that were critical for her to be successfully employed. In her case, the ability to work while maintaining certain benefits has had a positive impact on her life and has allowed her to increase her independence. Marge and her family recognize that, as her abilities at work increase, she may reach a point where she will be able to earn benefits through her job and will no longer require governmental subsidies.

As persons with severe disabilities enter integrated employment settings, a number of related issues that may affect the success of employment need to be considered. Among the most frequently mentioned issues are the relationship between increased earnings and the loss of federal subsidies (SSI/SSDI), the payment of subminimum wages, and the use of tax credits as incentives for employers. It is not the intent of this brief chapter to discuss all facets related to these issues. Instead, we would like to alert the employment specialist to the need to investigate these issues and suggest critical steps that need to be completed.

In general, specific situations will probably require individualized solutions. For instance, the outcome of time studies to determine the rate of pay below minimum wage that a worker should earn will depend on the nature of work activity, the prevailing wage for nondisabled workers performing the activity, and the method used to determine the rate. Similarly, the question of benefits determination for a worker entering supported employment depends on unique circumstances of the worker, possible work-related expenses that may be deducted, the wages paid and benefits offered by the job, and so forth. In general, then, the best advice is to investigate each case on an individual basis with representatives of the appropriate agency (such as the local Social Security office for subsidies issues and the Department of Labor for wage determination issues). This is particularly true in light of the changes that often occur in regulations and of which agency representatives may be unaware.

Always check cases on an individual basis before job placement.

This chapter will provide an overview of the following governmental/regulatory issues:

Supplemental Security Income (SSI)
Social Security Disability Insurance (SSDI)
PASS (Plan for Achieving Self-Support)
Volunteering
Subminimum wage payments/certificates
Employer incentives

Each of the following issues will be addressed using the following format:

Specific issues.
Description of the issues to be discussed.
Why is this an issue?
Who might be affected most by this issue?
What steps should be taken?

ISSUE: SSI

Many individuals with severe disabilities are recipients of Supplemental Security Income cash benefits as well as Medicaid benefits. For some individuals, the Medicaid insurance coverage is as important if not more so than the cash benefit.

Why Is This an Issue?

As individuals earn more money through supported employment, cash subsidies are reduced. Before July 1987, loss of cash benefits may have also resulted in loss of Medicaid benefits, thus providing a strong disincentive to earning too much. However, with the signing into law of Sections 1619 a and b of the Social Security Act, recipients can earn up to $793.00 per month before losing cash benefits altogether and can retain Medicaid benefits if certain criteria are met. (It should be noted that in several states, eligibility for Medicaid differs from SSI eligibility criteria. Therefore, eligibility for Medicaid benefits not under the SSI program is possible for some individuals. Social Security representatives should be consulted on this issue.)

Who Might Be Affected?

The worker with a disability
The worker's family
The agency trying to develop a job for the worker

What Steps to Take

The worker and an agency representative should meet with a representative from the local Social Security office prior to committing to a particular job. At that time, the impact of the potential job on that particular worker's benefits should be determined.

ISSUE: SSDI

Individuals may receive benefit checks and/or receive Medicare coverage through the Social Security Disability Insurance (SSDI) program. Because an individual may receive benefits under either SSDI, SSI, or both, the issues in terms of impact on workers in supported employment are closely related.

Why Is This an Issue?

The SSDI program entitles an individual to a trial work period during which the person's ability to work can be assessed. If the individual works at or above a level of "substantial gainful activity" (currently $300 a month) following the trial work period, then benefits will be terminated. There is a provision for the continuation of Medicare coverage for 24 months beyond the end of the eligibility period under certain conditions.

Who Might Be Affected?

In SSDI, the same individuals as might be affected under SSI issues.

What Steps to Take

Again, the worker (or family member or advocate) and the agency representative should research the specific impact of a job on the worker's benefits prior to accepting the job. This should be accomplished by meeting with a Social Security representative.

ISSUE: PASS

PASS (Plan for Achieving Self-Support) is an employment incentive available through the Social Security Administration that allows a portion of income targeted for services necessary to attain greater independence to be excluded from consideration of earned income. This allows workers with disabilities to set aside a portion of their income for needed services, like continued education or even hiring an employment specialist, and at the same time reducing the amount of earned income that is used in calculating federal benefits.

Why Is This an Issue?

As workers with disabilities earn more through supported employment, benefits are reduced in accordance with preestablished formulas. This can provide a disincentive for many workers or their families. The PASS system provides one option for minimizing such a disincentive while providing an incentive for pursuing greater self-sufficiency.

Who Might Be Affected?

Individuals receiving federal benefits through the Social Security Administration might be affected under PASS.

What Steps to Take?

All cases must be discussed on an individual basis with local SSD representatives, as the PASS system is not beneficial to all workers.

ISSUE: VOLUNTEERING

Some individuals have such severe disabilities that finding paid employment to enhance community integration is problematic. Because of this, some agencies believe that these workers should be allowed to volunteer their services without compensation. However, the Fair Labor Standards Act, the law that governs many of the issues of employment for individuals with disabilities, prohibits volunteering except under very specific conditions.

Why Is This an Issue?

If an agency allows workers to volunteer illegally, then the employers of the individuals will be liable for retroactive unpaid wages as well as a penalty. Clearly, this would have a disastrous impact on a human service agency's relationship with area employers and on the lives of the workers. Volunteering is permissible in certain situations, such as in churches and libraries, in which any individual, regardless of disability, might choose to donate services. In addition, the Department of Labor lists six criteria to be met for individuals to be able to volunteer in community placements as a training option:

1. The training, even though it includes actual operation of the facilities of the employer, is similar to that which would be given in a vocational school.
2. The training is for the benefit of the trainees.

3. The trainees do not displace regular employees, but work under their close supervision.
4. The employer who provides the training derives no immediate advantage from the activities of the trainees, and on occasion the employer's operations may actually be impeded.
5. The trainees are not necessarily entitled to a job at the conclusion of the training period.
6. The employer and the trainees understand that the trainees are not entitled to wages for the time spent in training.

All six criteria need to be met before individuals with disabilities can work in community businesses without pay. Again, specific situations should be investigated in advance with the Department of Labor prior to placement.

Who Might Be Affected?

Workers with disabilities
Area employers
Human service agencies

What Steps to Take

Always check with state and federal representatives of the Department of Labor if you are unsure as to when a worker may legally volunteer.

ISSUE: SUBMINIMUM WAGE

Many individuals with severe disabilities are unable, either initially or long-term, to work at a rate necessary to earn minimum wage. Some individuals with more severe disabilities may never work at such a rate. In order for their workers to have the opportunity to work for pay but at a rate below minimum wage, an agency or the employer (depending on who actually pays the worker) must obtain a certificate from the Department of Labor (DOL) that allows them to pay below the minimum wage. In addition, specific wages that are equitable for identified individuals in particular jobs need to be verified through time studies. The major issue in the completion of time studies is one of comparability. That is, the prevailing wage (the wage paid to experienced persons completing the same job in the same geographic area) is the basis for the time study. For example, an individual may be performing at 75 percent of the prevailing wage; if this amount is less than minimum wage, then a certificate from the DOL would be necessary. If 75 percent of the prevailing wage was more than minimum wage, then no certificate would be necessary.

It should be mentioned that, whenever possible, workers with severe disabilities should be paid minimum wage or above. While this is not always possible, every effort should be made to secure minimum wage prior to investigating the use of certificates.

Why Is This an Issue?

Failure to obtain a certificate from the DOL or to pay equitable wages can result in severe penalties from the DOL. These penalties may affect both employers and the human service agency.

What Steps to Take

Clearly, an agency needs to make sure that all certificates, whether held by the agency or by an employer, are up to date. In addition, for any job in which an individual is paid less than minimum wage, time studies need to be completed to verify wage levels in compliance with DOL mandates. Again, whenever in doubt, contact state and/or federal DOL representatives (state and federal laws may differ on certain points, so both need to be taken into consideration) to verify or clarify procedures for the payment of sub-minimum wages.

ISSUE: INCENTIVES FOR EMPLOYERS

1. Targeted Jobs Tax Credits

The Targeted Jobs Tax Credit (TJTC) program provides incentives for employers to hire workers from targeted groups of individuals, including persons with severe disabilities, who have had difficulty obtaining and retaining employment. The tax credits under TJTC play a part in the development of some supported employment programs in that they provide a possible incentive for employers to hire workers with severe disabilities. Specifically, the TJTC provides employers with a tax credit of 40 percent of first-year wages (up to $6,000 per employee) to a maximum credit of $2,400 per employer (if the employee works a minimum of 120 hours).

Why Is This an Issue? The use of TJTC as an employer incentive may play a part in job development efforts for persons with severe disabilities. If TJTC is to be used, it must be applied for by the employer for an eligible worker prior to the first day of employment; hence, the use of this program involves advanced planning with the employer.

Steps to Be Taken. If an employer expresses interest in TJTC as a stipulation for hiring a particular worker, then the agency representative should contact a representative of the Department of Labor *before* the worker begins employment. The eligibility of the worker will need to be determined by Job Service in advance, and the employer will need to apply for the tax credit in advance, as mentioned earlier.

2. On-the-Job Training

On-the-job Training (OJT) is a wage subsidy program available through state vocational rehabilitation agencies that allows employers to be reimbursed for additional costs related to the training of employees with disabilities. Although there is variation from state to state regarding the way specific OJT agreements are written, typically the amount of reimbursement to employers reduces over a period of time as workers gain proficiency. An underlying expectation is that the employer will hire the individual with a disability following the termination of the OJT.

Why Is This an Issue? The use of OJT as an employer incentive can be an effective tool for entry into the labor market for individuals with disabilities. This paid employment opportunity allows workers with disabilities the opportunity to receive training in specific areas of employment.

Steps to Be Taken. When using an OJT as an employer incentive, the agency representative should contact a representative of the state vocational rehabilitation agency to determine in advance the eligibility of the worker. Cooperative negotiations and proper forms will be completed by an agency representative, a state vocational rehabilitation counselor, and the employer.

SUMMARY

This chapter has provided a brief overview of some of the major governmental and regulatory issues that may affect supported employment programs. Clearly, we have only scratched the surface in terms of clarifying specific issues. Because of the individual nature of many of these issues, and the rapid changes in regulations, it is difficult to make meaningful generalizations about these topics. Indeed, the only general statement that can be made with confidence is that individual cases should always be investigated on an individual basis. This approach is the best way to avoid unnecessary problems that result from incomplete planning or incorrect assumptions regarding the application of general issues to specific cases.

Action Options

- Accompany a worker and his or her family in meeting with representatives at the local Social Security office in order to determine impact of income from a job on that person's subsidies (SSI/SSDI).
- Develop contacts within the state and federal offices of the Department of Labor who will be able to address specific questions that you may have.
- Identify an agency staff member who will become the "expert" in each of the areas discussed in this chapter.

BIBLIOGRAPHY

Albano, M. L. (1983). *Transdisciplinary teaming in special education: A case study.* Unpublished doctoral dissertation, University of Illinois, Urbana-Champaign.

Allan, K. E., Hart, B. M., Buell, J. S., Harris, F. R., & Wolf, W. M. (1964). Effects of social reinforcement on isolate behavior of a nursery school child. *Child Development, 35,* 511–518.

Anderson, W., Beckett, C., Chitwood, S., & Hayden, S. (1985, summer). Next steps: planning for employment: A workshop for parents. *Coalition Quarterly, 4*(4), 1–7.

Ayllon, T., & Azrin, N. (1968). *The token economy: A motivational system for therapy and rehabilitation.* New York: Appleton.

Barcus, M. (1985). Personal communication. Glastonbury, Connecticut.

Barnes, E., Berrigan, C., & Biklen, D. (1978). *What's the difference?* Syracuse, NY: Human Policy Press.

Barton, E. S., Guess, D., Garcia, E., & Baer, D. (1970). Improvement of retardates' mealtime behaviors by time-out procedures using multiple baseline techniques. *Journal of Applied Behavior Analysis, 2,* 77.

Baumeister, A. A., & Baumeister, A. A. (1978). Suppression of repetitive self-injurious behavior by contingent inhalation of aromatic ammonia. *Journal of Autism and childhood Schizophrenia, 8,* 71–77.

Baumgart, D., Brown, L., Pumpian, I., Ford, A., Sweet, M., Messina, R., & Schroeder, J. (1982). Principle of partial participation and individualized adaptation in educational programs for severely handicapped students. *Journal of the Association for the Severely Handicapped, 7,* 17–27.

Bellamy, G. T., Horner, R. H., & Inman, D. P. (1979). *Vocational habilitation of severely retarded adults: A direct service technology.* Baltimore: University Park Press.

Bobath, K., & Bobath, B. (1972). Cerebral palsy. In P. H. Pearson & C. E. Williams (Eds.), *Physical therapy services in the developmental disabilities.* Springfield, IL: Charles C. Thomas.

Brickey, M., Browning, L., & Campbell, K. (1982). Vocational histories of sheltered workshop employees placed in Projects With Industry and competitive jobs. *Mental Retardation, 19,* 113–116.

Brooks, V., Hill, J., & Ponder, C. (1985). A demonstration of the acceptibility of applied behavior analysis in a natural job environment. In P. Wehman & J. Hill (Eds.), *Competitive Employment for Persons with Mental Retardation: From Research to Practice.* Richmond, VA: Rehabilitation Research and Training Center.

Brown, L., Neitupski, J., & Hamre-Nietupski, S. (1976). Criterion of ultimate functioning. In M. A. Thomas, (Ed.), *Hey! don't forget about me! Education's investment in the severely and profoundly handicapped.* Reston, VA: Council for Exceptional Children.

Bruininks, R., Kudla, M., Wieck, C., & Hauber, F. (1980). Management problems in community residential facilities. *Mental Retardation, 18,* 125–130.

Buckley, J. (1988). Personal communication.

Buckley, J., Albin, J., & Mank, D. (1988). Competency-based staff training for supported employment. In G. T. Bellamy, L. Rhodes, D. Mank, & J. Albin, *Supported employment: A community implementation guide.* Baltimore, MD: Paul H. Brookes.

Campbell, P. (1983). Individualized team programming with infants and young handicapped children. In D. P. McClowry, A. M. Guildford, & S. Richardson (Eds.), *Infant communication: Development, assessment, and intervention.* New York: Grune and Stratton.

Chadsey-Rusch, J., & Gonzalez, P. (1988). Social ecology of the workplace: Employer's perceptions versus direct observation. *Research in Developmental Disabilities, 9,* 229–245.

Cohen, D., Patton, S., & Melia, R. (1986). Staffing supported and transitional employment programs: Issues and recommendations. *American Rehabilitation, 12*(2), 20–24.

Colvin, G. T., & Horner, R. H. (1983). Experimental analysis of generalization: An evaluation of a general case program for teaching motor skills to severely handicapped learners. In J. Hogg & P. J. Miller (Eds.), *Advances in Mental Handicap Research. Vol. 2.* London: Wiley.

Connor, F. P., Williamson, G. G., & Siepp, J. M. (Eds.), *Program guide for infants and toddlers with neuromotor and other developmental disabilities.* New York: Teachers College Press.

Datlow Smith, M., & Coleman, D. (1986). Managing the behavior of adults with autism in the job setting. *Journal of Autism and Developmental Disabilities, 16,* 145–153.

Deitz, S. M., & Repp, A. C. (1973). Decreasing classroom misbehavior through the use of DRL schedules of reinforcement. *Journal of Applied Behavior Analysis, 6,* 457–463.

Deitz, S. M., & Repp, A. C. (1974). Differentially reinforcing low rates of misbehavior with normal elementary school children. *Journal of Applied Behavior Analysis, 7,* 622.

Donnellan, A. M., La Vigna, G. W., Negri-Shoultz, N., & Fassbender, L. L. (1988). *Progress without punishment. Effective approaches for learners with behavior problems.* New York: Teachers College, Columbia University.

Drabman, R. S., Hammer, D., & Rosenbaum, M. S. (1979). Assessing generalization in behavior modification with children: The generalization map. *Behavioral Assessment, 1,* 203–219.

Evans, I. M., & Meyer, L. H. (1985). *An educative approach to behavior problems: A practical decision model for interventions with severely handicapped learners.* Baltimore: Paul H. Brookes.

Federal Register (1984, September 25) Developmental Disabilities Act of 1984. Report 98–1074, Section 102 (11) (F).

Federal Register (1987, August 14) The state supported employment services program: Final Regulations. Vol. 52. No. 157. 34 CRF Part 363.

Finnie, N. R. (1974). *Handling the young cerebral palsied child at home.* New York: Dutton.

Ford, L., Dineen, J., & Hall, J. (1984). Is there life after placement? *Education and Training of the Mentally Retarded, 19,* 291–296.

Foxx, R. M., & Shapiro, S. T. (1978). The time out ribbon: a non-exclusionary time out procedure. *Journal of Applied Behavior Analysis, 11,* 125–136.

Gadow, K. D. (1986). *Children on medication.* San Diego: College Hill Press.

Gaylord-Ross, R., Haring, T., Breen, C., & Pitts-Conway, V. (1984). The training and generalization of social interaction skills with autistic youth. *Journal of Applied Behavior Analysis, 17,* 229–247.

Gold, M. (1981). *"Did I say that?"* Champaign, IL: Research Press.

Greenspan, S., & Shoultz, B. (1981). Why mentally retarded adults lose their jobs: Social competence as a factor in work adjustment. *Applied Research in Mental Retardation, 2,* 23–38.

Guess, D., & Helmstetter, E. (1986). Skill cluster instruction and the individualized curriculum sequencing model. In R. H. Horner, L. H. Meyer, & H. D.

Fredericks (Eds.), *Education of learners with severe handicaps: Exemplary service strategies* (pp. 221–228). Baltimore, MD: Paul H. Brookes.

Guess, D., Helmstetter, E., Turnbul, H. R., & Knowlton, S. (1987). *Use of aversive procedures with persons who are disabled: An historical review and critical analysis.* Seattle: Association for Persons with Severe Handicaps.

Hagner, D. (1987, October). *The meaning of social integration for adults labelled mentally retarded: Relationships at work and home.* Paper presented at the meeting of the Association for Persons with Severe Handicaps, Chicago, IL.

Halpern, A. (1985). Transition: A look at the foundations. *Exceptional Children, 51,* 479–486.

Haring, N., & Billingsley, F. F. (1984). Systems-change strategies to ensure the future of integration. In Certo, N. Haring, N., & York, R. (Eds.), *Public school integration of severely handicapped students.* Baltimore, MD: Paul H. Brookes.

Hart, V. (1977). The use of many disciplines with the severely and profoundly handicapped. In E. Sontag, J. Smith, & Certo (Eds.), *Educational programming for the severely/profoundly handicapped.* Reston, VA: Council for Exceptional Children.

Hasazi, S., Gordon, L., & Roe, C. (1985). Factors associated with the employment status of handicapped youth exiting high school from 1979–1983. *Exceptional Children, 51,* 455–469.

Homer, A. L., & Peterson, L. (1980). Differential reinforcement of other behavior: A preferred response elimination procedure. *Behavior Therapy, 11,* 449–471.

Homme, L., Csanyi, A. P., Gonzaes, M. A., & Rechs, J. S. (1969). *How to use contingency contracting in the classroom.* Champaign, IL: Research Press.

Horner, R. L., Albin, R., & Ralph, G. (1986). Generalization with precision: The role of negative teaching examples in the instruction of generalized grocery item selection. *Journal of the Association for Persons with Severe Handicaps, 11,* 300–308.

Horner, R. L., Eberhard, J., & Sheehan, M. (1986). Teaching generalized table bussing; The importance of negative teaching examples. *Behavior Modification, 10,* 457–471.

Horner, R. H., Jones, D. N., & Williams, J. A. (1985). A functional approach to teaching generalized street crossing. *Journal of the Association for Persons with Severe Handicaps, 10,* 71–78.

Horner, R. H., Sprague, J., & Wilcox, B. (1982). General case programming for community activities. In B. Wilcox & G. T. Bellamy (Eds.), *Design of high school programs for severely handicapped students.* Baltimore: Paul H. Brookes.

Horner, R. H., Williams, J. A., & Stevely, J. D. (1986). Acquisition and maintenance of generalized telephone use by students with moderate and severe mental retardation. *Research in Developmental Disabilities, 8,* 229–247.

House, J. S. (1981). *Work stress and social support.* Reading, MA: Addison-Wesley.

Hutchinson, D. (1978). The transdisciplinary approach. In J. B. Curry & K. K. Peppe (Eds.), *Mental retardation: Nursing approaches to care.* St. Louis: Mosby.

Jens, K. E., & Shores, R. J. (1969). Behavioral graphs as reinforcers for work behavior of mentally retarded adolescents. *Education and Training of the Mentally Retarded, 4,* 21–28.

Johnson, D. W., & Johnson, R. T. (1986). Mainstreaming and cooperative learning strategies. *Exceptional Children, 52,* 553–561.

Jordan, J., Singh, N. N., & Repp, A. C. (1989). An evaluation of gentle teaching and visual screening in the reduction of stereotype. *Journal of Applied Behavior Analysis, 22,* 9–22.

Karan, O., & Knight, C. (1986). Training demands of the future. In W. Kiernan & J. Stark (Eds.), *Pathways to employment for adults with developmental disabilities* (pp. 253–269). Baltimore, MD: Paul H. Brookes.

Kazdin, A. E. (1972). Response cost: The removal of conditional reinforcers for therapeutic change. *Behavior Therapy, 3,* 533–546.

Kazdin, A. E. (1977). *The token economy: A review and evaluation.* New York: Plenum.

Kazdin, A. E., & Bootzin, R. R. (1972). The token economy: An evaluative review. *Journal of Applied Behavior Analysis, 5,* 343–372.

Kennedy, J. F. (1963). Address, June 12, 1963 (on civil rights after the registration of two black students at the University of Alabama—cited in *Bartlett's Familiar Quotations*).

Kiernan, W. E., & Bruininks, R. H. (1986). Demographic characteristics. In W. E. Kiernan & J. A. Stark (Eds.), *Pathways to employment for adults with developmental disabilities.* Baltimore: Paul H. Brookes.

Kiernan, W. E., & Schalock, R. L. (1989). *Economics, industry & disability: A look ahead.* Baltimore: Paul H. Brookes.

Kiernan, W. E., & Stark, J. (1986). *Pathways to employment for adults with developmental disabilities.* Baltimore: Paul H. Brookes.

Knowlton, Ed., Turnbull, A., Backus, L., & Turnbull, R. (1988). Letting go: Consent and the "yes, but . . ." problem in transition. In B. Ludlow, A. Turnbull, & R. Luckasson (Eds.) *Transitions to adult life for people with mental retardation: Principles and practices.* Baltimore: Paul H. Brookes.

LaVigna, G. W. (1987). Non-aversive strategies for managing behavior problems. In D. J. Cohen & A. M. Donnellan (Eds.), *Handbook of autism and disorders of atypical development* (pp. 418–429). New York: Wiley.

LaVigna, G. W., & Donnellan, A. M. (1986). *Alternatives to punishment: solving behavior problems with non-aversive strategies.* New York: Irvington.

Lovaas, O. I., & Favell, J. E. (1987). Protection for clients undergoing aversive/restrictive intervention. *Education and Treatment of Children, 10,* 311–325.

Ludlow, B. L., Turnbull, A. P., & Luckasson, R. (1988). *Transition to adult life for people with mental retardation: Principles and practices.* Baltimore: Paul H. Brookes.

Lyon, S., & Lyon G. (1980). Team functioning and staff development: A role release approach to providing integrated educational services for severely handicapped students. *Journal of the Association for the Severely Handicapped, 5,* 250–263.

Mager, R. (1975). *Preparing instructional objectives.* Palo Alto, CA: Fearon.

Mank, D. M., & Buckley, J. (1989). Strategies for integrated employment. In W. E. Kiernan & R. L. Schalock (Eds.), *Economics, industry & disability: A look ahead.* Baltimore: Paul H. Brookes.

Mank, D., & Horner, R. (1987). Self-recruited feedback: A cost-effective procedure for maintaining behavior.*Research in Developmental Disabilities, 8,* 91–112.

McCuller, G. L., Salzberg, C. L., & Lignugaris/Kraft, B. (1987). Producing generalized job initiative in severely mentally retarded sheltered workers. *Journal of Applied Behavior Analysis, 20,* 413–420.

McGee, J. J., Menolascino, F. J., Hobbs, D. C., & Menousek, P. E. (1987). *Gentle teaching: A non-aversive approach to helping persons with mental retardation.* New York: Human Sciences Press.

McGee, J. J., Menolascino, F. J., & Menousek, P. E. (in press). *Gentle teaching.* Texas: Pro-Ed.

Meyer, L. H., & Evans, I. M. (1989). *Non-aversive intervention for behavior problems: A manual for home and community.* Baltimore: Paul H. Brookes.

Minuchin, S. (1974). *Families and family therapy.* Cambridge, MA: Harvard University Press.

Moon, S., Goodall, P., Barcus, M., & Brooks, V. (Eds.) (1986). *The supported work model of community employment for citizens with severe handicaps: A guide for job trainers.* Richmond, VA: Virginia Commonwealth University.

Mooslin, M. (1985, May). Transcript of presentation at Connecticut's Developmental Disabilities Council Conference, Danbury, CT.

Moseley, C. R. (1988). Job satisfaction research: Implications for supported employment. *Journal of the Association for Persons with Severe Handicaps, 13,* 211–219.

National Information Center for Children and Youth with Handicaps (1987). Transition—the role of parents, students, and professionals. *Transition Summary, 4,* 1–7.

Neugarten, B. (1976). Adaptations and the life cycle. *The Counseling Psychologist, 6*(1), 16–20.

Nisbet, J., & Hagner, D. (1988). Natural supports in the workplace. A reexamination of supported employment. *Journal of the Association for Persons with Severe Handicaps, 13,* 260–267.

O'Brien, J. (1987a). A guide to life-style planning: Using the activities catalog to integrate services and natural support systems. In B. Wilcox, and G. T. Bellamy (Eds.), *The activities catalog: An alternative curriculum for youth and adults with severe disabilities.* Baltimore: Paul H. Brookes.

O'Brien, J. (1987b). Embracing ignorance, error, and fallibility: Competencies for leadership of effective services. In S. Taylor, D. Biklen, & J. Knoll (Eds.), *Community integration for people with severe disabilities* (pp. 85–108). New York: Teacher's College Press.

O'Connor, G. (1983). Social support of mentally retarded persons. *Mental Retardation, 21,* 187–196.

Pancsofar, E. L. (1986). Assessing work behavior. In F. Rusch (Ed.), *Competitive employment issues and strategies* (pp. 93–102). Baltimore: Paul H. Brookes.

Pancsofar, E., & Bates, P. (1985). The impact of acquisition of successive training exemplars on generalization. *Journal of the Association for Persons with Severe Handicaps, 10,* 95–104.

Pancsofar, E., & Blackwell, R. (1986). *A user's guide to community entry of the severely handicapped.* Albany, NY: SUNY Press.

Patton, J., & Browder, P. (1988). Transitions into the future. In B. Ludlow, A. Turnbull, & R. Luckasson (Eds.), *Transitions to adult life for people with mental retardation—principles and practices* (pp. 293–312). Baltimore: Paul H. Brookes.

Perske, R. (1974). *The dignity of risk and the mentally retarded.* Arlington, TX: National Association for Retarded Citizens.

Perske, R. (1981). *Hope for the families.* Nashville, TN: Abington.

Peters, T., & Austin, N. (1985). *A passion for excellence.* New York: Knopf.

Peterson, C. (1980). Support services. In B. Wilcox & R. York (Eds.), *Quality educational programs for the severely handicapped: The federal investment.* Washington, DC: U.S. Department of Education, Office of Special Education.

Physician's Desk Reference. (1989). Oradell, NJ: Medical Economics.

Powell, T. (1987). Do you have a supported employment creed? *Interact, 1*(2), 1.

Powell, T. H., & Powell, I. Q. (1982). The use and abuse of using time out procedures for disruptive pupils. *The Pointer, 26*(2), 18–22.

Powell, T. H., Rainforth, B., Hecimovic, A., Steere, D. E., Mayes, M. G., Zoback, M. S., & Singer, A. L. T. (1985). *Connecticut's data-based model. Developing integrated public school programs for students with severe handicaps.* Storrs, CT: Connecticut's University Affiliated Program, University of Connecticut.

Provencal, G. (1987) Culturing commitment. In S. Taylor, D. Bilken, & J. Knoll (Eds.), *Community integration for people with severe disabilities* (pp. 67–84). New York: Teacher's College Press.

Renzaglia, A. (1986). Preparing personnel to support and guide emerging contemporary service alternatives. In F. Rusch (Ed.), *Competitive employment: Issues and strategies.* Baltimore, MD: Paul H. Brookes.

Repp, A. C., & Deitz, S. M. (1974). Reducing aggressive and self-injurious behavior of institutionalized retarded children through reinforcement of other behaviors. *Journal of Applied Behavior Analysis, 7,* 313–325.

Repp, A. C., Deitz, S. M., & Deitz, D. E. D. (1976). Reducing inappropriate behaviors in classrooms and in individual sessions through DRO schedules of reinforcement. *Mental Retardation, 14*(1), 11–15.

Reynolds, G. S. (1961). Behavioral contrast. *Journal of the Experimental Analysis of Behavior, 4,* 57–71.

Rhodes, L., Ramsing, K. D., & Bellamy, G. T. (1988) Business partnership in supported employment. In G. T. Bellamy, L. Rhodes, D. Mank, & J. Albin (Eds.), *Supported employment: A community implementation guide* (pp. 247–261). Baltimore: Paul H. Brookes.

Rusch, F. (1986). *Competitive employment issues and strategies*. Baltimore: Paul H. Brookes.

Rusch, F., Menchetti, B., Crouch, K., Riva, M., Morgan, T., & Agran, M. (1984). Competitive employment: Assessing employee reactivity to naturalistic observation. *Applied Research in Mental Retardation, 5*, 339–351.

Rusch, F. R., & Minch, K. E. (1988). Identification of co-worker's involvement in supported employment: A review and analysis. *Research in Developmental Disabilites, 9*, 247–254.

Rusch, F., Weithers, J., Menchetti, B., & Schutz, R. (1980). Social validation of a program to reduce topic repetition in a non-sheltered setting. *Education and Training of the Mentally Retarded, 15*, 208–215.

Sailor, W., Halvorsen, A., Anderson, J., Goetz, L., Gee, K., Doering, K., & Hunt, P. (1986). Community intensive instruction. In R. H. Horner, L. H. Meyer, & H. D. Fredericks (Eds.), *Education of learners with severe handicaps: Exemplary service strategies* (pp. 251–288). Baltimore: Paul H. Brookes.

Salzberg, C., Likins, M., McConaughy, K., Lignugaris/Kraft, B., & Stowitschek, J. (1986). In N. Ellis, *International Review of Research in Mental Retardation, Volume 14*. New York: Academic Press.

Schalock, R., & Stark, J. (1988). Identifying programming goals for independent living. In B. Ludlow, A. Turnbull, & R. Luckasson (Eds.), *Transitions to adult life for people with mental retardation—principles and practices* (pp. 85–100). Baltimore: Paul H. Brookes.

Schalock, R. L., & Hill, M. L. (1986). Evaluating employment services. In W. E. Kiernan & J. A. Stark (Eds.), *Pathways to employment for adults with developmental disabilities*. Baltimore: Paul H. Brookes.

Shafer, M. (1986). Utilizing co-workers as change agents. In F. Rusch (Ed.), *Competitive Employment Issues and Strategies*. Baltimore: Paul H. Brookes.

Shafer, M., & Nisbet, J. (1989). Integration and empowerment in the workplace. In M. Barcus, S. Griffin, D. Mank, L. Rhodes, & S. Moon (Eds.), *Supported employment implementation issues*. Richmond: Rehabilitation Research & Training Center, Virginia Commonwealth University.

Shultz, R., Wehman, P., Renzaglia, A., Karan, O. (1978). Efficiency of social disapproval of inappropriate verbalizations of two severely retarded males. *Behavior Therapy, 9*, 657–662.

Snell, M. E. (1987). *Systematic instruction of persons with severe handicaps*. Columbus, OH: Merrill.

Sprague, J. & Horner, R. H. (1984). The effects of single instance, multiple instance, and general case training on generalized vending machine use by moderately and severely handicapped students. *Journal of Applied Behavior Analysis, 17*, 273–278.

Stainback, W., & Stainback, S. (1987). Facilitating friendships. *Education and training in mental retardation, 22*, 18–25.

Stainback, W., Stainback, S., Courtnage, L., & Jaben, T. (1985). Facilitating the mainstream by modifying the mainstream. *Exceptional Children, 52*, 144–152.

Steere, D. E., Strauch, J. D., Powell, T. H., & Butterworth, J. (in press). Promoting generalization from a teaching setting to a community based setting among persons with severe disabilities: A general case programming approach. *Education and Treatment of Children*. Pittsburgh: Pressley Ridge Schools.

Sternat, J., Messina, R., Nietupski, J., Lyon, S., & Brown, L. (1977). Occupational and physical therapy services for severely handicapped students: Toward a naturalized public school service delivery model. In E. Sontag, J. Smith, & N. Certo (Eds.), *Educational programming for the severely and profoundly handicapped*. Reston, VA: Council for Exceptional Children.

Stokes, T., & Baer, D. (1977). An implicit technology of generalization. *Journal of Applied Behavior Analysis, 10*, 349–367.

Sulzer-Azaroff, B., & Mayer, G. R. (1977). *Applied behavior-analysis procedures with children and youth*. New York: Holt, Rinehart and Winston.

Turnbull, A. P., Summers, J. A., & Brotherson, M. J. (1984). *Working with families with disabled members: A family systems approach.* Lawrence, KS: Kansas University Affiliated Facility, University of Kansas.

Turnbull, A. P., & Turnbull, H. R. (1986). *Families, professionals, and exceptionality. A special partnership.* Columbus, OH: Merrill.

Turnbull, F. P., & Turnbull, H. R. (1988). Toward great expectations for vocational opportunities: Family-professional partnerships. *Mental Retardation, 26,* 337–342.

United States Commission on Civil Rights (1983). *Accommodating the spectrum of individual abilities.* Clearing House Publishing (list 81.)

von Oech, R. (1983). *A whack on the side of the head: How to unlock your mind for innovation.* New York: Warner.

Wehman, P. (1981). *Competitive employment: New horizons for severely disabled individuals.* Baltimore: Paul H. Brookes.

Wehman, P., Kregel, J., & Barcus, M. (1985). From school to work: A vocational transition model for handicapped students. *Exceptional Children,* 52, 237.

Wehman, P., & Moon, M. S. (1988). *Vocational rehabilitation and supported employment.* Baltimore: Paul H. Brookes.

Wehman, P., Renzaglia, A., & Bates, P. (1985). *Functional living skills for moderately and severely handicapped individuals.* Austin, TX: Pro-Ed.

White, D., & Rusch, F. (1983). Social validation in competitive employment: Evaluating work performance. *Applied Research in Mental Retardation, 4,* 343–354.

Wilcox, B. & Bellamy, G. T. (1987). *The activities catalog: An alternative curriculum.* Baltimore: Paul H. Brookes.

Will, M. (1984). Let us pause and reflect—but not too long. *Exceptional Children, 51,* 11–16.

Williams, C. D. (1959). The elimination of tantrum behavior by extinction procedures. *Journal of Abnormal and Social Psychology, 59,* 269.

Wolfensberger, W. (1972). *The principle of normalization in the human services.* Toronto, Canada: National Institute on Mental Retardation.

SSA (1987). *A summary guide to social security and supplemental security income work incentives for the disabled and blind.* Washington: Social Security Administration, Office of Disability.

NARF (1987). *Federal wage and hour law: A guide for vocational rehabilitation facilities.* Washington: National Association of Rehabilitation Facilities.

APPENDIX A

Forms for Program Implementation

FORMS AND WORKER DOCUMENTATION

Comprehensive implementation of supported employment requires a flexible and interactive system for maintaining individual worker information. This appendix will outline a structure for individual worker records and provide samples of forms.

A blank copy of each form is included. The supported employment agency is encouraged to use and adapt these forms.

INDIVIDUAL WORKER RECORDS

A comprehensive worker record system includes 3 major parts:

Permanent file
Worker notebook
On-site data and information

Permanent Files

The permanent file is the formal file, usually located in a locked file cabinet in the program offices. This file usually must meet specific contractual requirements and program needs.

Worker Notebook

The Worker Notebook is the critical resource for the employment specialist. It should contain any information pertaining to instructional strategies, worker goals and objectives, progress monitoring, and job placement decisions. It is important to emphasize that this notebook is intended to be used on a daily and weekly basis to make employment decisions. It is maintained in the employment specialist's office, and at times (if a secure and private cabinet is available) may be kept at the job site. A 1-inch loose-leaf notebook should be organized with dividers into 5 sections. The following outline provides guidelines for organizing information within each section.

A. Worker Information. This section includes general information about a worker's learning style, preferences, and career plans. It is intended as a reference point for instructional and employment decision making.

1. Worker information (Form 01)
2. Career planning information (Meeting notes and form 02)
3. Worker Resume (Form 03)

B. Job Development. Information and narratives specific to job development for the worker.

1. Participant Screening Form (Form 04)
2. Single Factor Analysis Form (Form 05)
3. Compatibility Analysis Summary (one for each job considered) (Form 06)

C. Instruction. This section will typically be the most active section on a daily and weekly basis. It is organized according to the specific instructional objectives being addressed. It is recommended that the Weekly Schedule of Job Responsibilities and the Objectives Summary (Forms 07 and 08) be used in each notebook as an outline of the instructional focus for that worker. The rest of the forms provide alternative methods of planning, collecting data, and summarizing progress on specific objectives.

1. Weekly Schedule (Form 07)
2. Objective Summary (Form 08)
3. Individual Objectives
   Instructional Plan (Forms 09, 10, and/or 11)
   Task Analysis of generalization plan if appropriate (Forms 13 and 19)
   Data (Forms 13 and 19)
   Data (Forms 12 and 14 to 18)

D. Ongoing Supports. This section details the range of supports identified to support the worker on the job. The Ongoing Supports Summary (Form 20) summarizes each support, when it is provided, and who is responsible. Additional information or narrative records of the supports may also be appropriate. In most cases a record of follow-up contacts will also be maintained using the Worker Performance Record (Form 21).

1. Ongoing Supports Summary (Form 20)
2. Worker Performance Records (Form 21)

E. Narratives and Correspondence. Miscellaneous narrative, meeting minutes, and correspondence are maintained in this section. Information that is not needed by the job coach should be filed in the permanent file.

1. On-Site Data and Information. Systems for maintaining raw data on site need to be highly individualized in supported employment. Typically, worker information and raw data sheets can be maintained on site. The employment specialist needs to be sensitive to the appropriateness and intrusiveness of data forms in each work place.

2. General Administrative Forms. Additional forms (Forms 22 and 23) for use in job development have been included. The creation of an employer file, with contact and job analysis information for each employer and/or job opportunity will prove helpful.

In addition, forms to be used to list and clarify the ongoing supports offered by an agency are included. These forms (Forms 24 through 27) are to be used to develop a notebook that can be used to acquaint parents, guardians and consumers with those supports that are typically offered by the agency.

WORKER INFORMATION

Name: ______________________ **Program:** ___________________________

Social Security No: __________________________

Medical Alerts:

____

____

____

____

Reinforcement Information:

Activities: ____

____

Social: ____

____

Objects: ____

____

Food/Beverages: ____

____

Token/Money: ____

____

5/88

Language Information:

Receptive: ______________________________

____

____

Expressive: ______________________________

____

____

____

Interfering Behaviors:

Behaviors: ______________________________

____

____

Typical Correction: ______________________________

____

____

Prompt Sequence:

____

____

____

General Comments:

____

____

____

____

____

5/88

WORKER INFORMATION

Name: Nick Powell **Program:** EHR, Inc.

Social Security No: 075-49-6234

Medical Alerts:

Seizure disorder - Takes Dilantin 200 mg twice a day

Reinforcement Information:

Activities: Listening to music - Reading T.V. Guide - Walking with family; Art

Social: Praise statements - "How proud are we?"

Objects: Tapes; colored pencils; Art supplies

Food/Beverages: Diet sodas Hot dogs Ice Cream

Token/Money: (Little understanding of money) but he needs to learn

5/88

Language Information:

Receptive: Understands basic directions. Acts as if he does not hear

Expressive: Speaks quickly and softly. Ask him to repeat and slow down.

Interfering Behaviors:

Behaviors: May scream, rock or bite his hand

Typical Correction: Tell him to calm down. Nick likes to take a brief walk when he is excited.

Prompt Sequence:
1. Begin with a demonstration of task.
2. Verbal prompt with a model
3. Verbal prompt with a gesture

DO NOT TRY PHYSICAL ASSISTANCE

General Comments:

Nick has a close relationship with Jean- a Coworker at EHR

5/88

CAREER PLANNING OUTCOMES

WORKER: ____________________ AGENCY: ____________________________

CAREER PLANNING TEAM MEMBERS:

____

____

____

____

IDENTIFIED QUALITY-OF-LIFE OUTCOMES:

Outcome: ____

Description/Standard: ______________________________

____

____

____

Outcome: ____

Description/Standard: ______________________________

____

____

____

5/88

Outcome: ______________________________

Description/Standard: ______________________________

____

____

____

Outcome: ______________________________

Description/Standard: ______________________________

____

____

____

Outcome: ______________________________

Description/Standard: ______________________________

____

____

____

Outcome: ______________________________

Description/Standard: ______________________________

____

____

____

*** Most Critical Outcome(s)**

5/88

CAREER PLANNING OUTCOMES

WORKER: Bob Smith AGENCY: EHR, Inc.

CAREER PLANNING TEAM MEMBERS:

Mary Jones, Jack Smith, Ernie Pancsofar,
Marsha Jenkins

IDENTIFIED QUALITY-OF-LIFE OUTCOMES:

Outcome: *Choice

Description/Standard: ① Choice in order of job duties
② Choice of purchases with earnings

Outcome: Relationships

Description/Standard: ① Daily interventions with Co-workers without disabilities
② One-two closer friends

5/88

Outcome: Competence

Description/Standard: ① Developing greater independence with current job activities
② Learning three new job skills
③ Learning work-related social skills

Outcome: ______

Description/Standard: ______

Outcome: ______

Description/Standard: ______

Outcome: ______

Description/Standard: ______

*** Most Critical Outcome(s)**

5/88

WORKER RESUME FORM

Worker: ______________________________

Agency: ______________________________

Address: ______________________________

____

Phone: ______________ Date of Birth: ______________

WORK EXPERIENCE:

1. Company: ______________________________

Dates: ______________________________

Job Title: ______________________________

Responsibilities: ______________________________

Supports: ______________________________

____

2. Company: ______________________________

Dates: ______________________________

Job Title: ______________________________

Responsibilities: ______________________________

Supports: ______________________________

____

3. Company: ______________________________

Dates: ______________________________

Job Title: ______________________________

Responsibilities: ______________________________

Supports: ______________________________

____

5/88

FORM 03

WORKER RESUME FORM

Worker: Randy Coors

Agency: C.A.A.C. Inc.

Address: 222 Main Street
Glastonbury, CT

Phone: 659-3333 Date of Birth: 4/10/53

WORK EXPERIENCE:

1. Company: Glastonbury Inn
   Dates: January 15, 1988 - Present
   Job Title: House Keeper
   Responsibilities: Cleaning rooms; vacuuming, dusting, making beds, mopping, and cleaning
   Supports: Transportation employment specialist assistance for work tasks and social interaction; assistance with managing finances

2. Company:
   Dates:
   Job Title:
   Responsibilities:
   Supports:

3. Company:
   Dates:
   Job Title:
   Responsibilities:
   Supports:

5/88

PARTICIPANT EMPLOYMENT SCREENING FORM

Type: Initial _____ Ongoing/Employed _____ Ongoing/Unemployed _______
# of Hours Participant Can Work Per Week ____________________
Months Participant Works Per Year ______ Hours Per Week __________
Current Hourly Rate __________
Participant's Name ____________________
Date of Screening __________ Evaluator ____________________

FACTOR	NOTES/DESCRIPTION

1.

2.

3.

4.

5.

Participant Employment Screening Form

FACTOR	NOTES/DESCRIPTION
6.	
7.	
8.	
9.	
10.	
11.	
12.	
13.	

Participant Employment Screening Form

FACTOR	NOTES/DESCRIPTION
14.	
15.	
16.	
17.	
18.	
19.	
20.	

5/88

PARTICIPANT EMPLOYMENT SCREENING FORM

Type: Initial ✓ Ongoing/Employed ____ Ongoing/Unemployed ____
\# of Hours Participant Can Work Per Week 25
Months Participant Works Per Year — Hours Per Week —
Current Hourly Rate —
Participant's Name Don Stone
Date of Screening 5/13/88 Evaluator Jill Martle

FACTOR	NOTES/DESCRIPTION
1. Availability	Day, M-F
2. Wages	Minimum wage or above
3. Travel skills	Requires assistance with bus travel
4. Site Orienting	Okay within small buildings. Has trouble finding way around large buildings
5. Mobility	No problems

Participant Employment Screening Form

FACTOR	NOTES/DESCRIPTION
6. Initiation	Requires verbal prompts to start new tasks
7. Tolerates Changes	Likes a consistent schedule Dislikes last-minute changes
8. Strength	Moderate
9. Endurance	Not used to standing for long periods
10. Rate/Pace	Moderate, for short periods
11. Attention to Task	Good; fine detail discrimination also
12. Communication	Uses manual signs plus verbalizations
13. Stress Tolerance	Low at this point

Participant Employment Screening Form

FACTOR	NOTES/DESCRIPTION
14. Need for Supervision	Needs systematic prompting
15. Math/Reading	Count items up to 25 A few sight words only
16. Interactions	Tends to keep to himself. Will interact if approached
17. Hygiene/Appearance	Excellent!
18. Interferring Behaviors	May become agitated if under excessive stress
19. Worker Attitude	Excellent Wants to work!
20. Time Management	Needs assistance

5/88

FORM 05

SINGLE FACTOR ANALYSIS

COMPATIBILITY FACTOR: ______________________________

WORKER VARIABLES	JOB SITE VARIABLES

MATCH:

_________ **EXCELLENT**

_________ **GOOD**

_________ **POOR**

_________ **UNDECIDED**

5/88

FORM 05

SINGLE FACTOR ANALYSIS

COMPATIBILITY FACTOR: Endurance

WORKER VARIABLES	JOB SITE VARIABLES
John McDaniels	A-B-C Corp.
• Needs frequent breaks • Works slowly • Prefers sitting • Takes Dilantin	• Breaks in midmorning, lunchtime, midafternoon • Standing required • Steady pace required

MATCH:

______ **EXCELLENT**

______ **GOOD**

✓ **POOR**

______ **UNDECIDED**

5/88

FORM 06

COMPATIBILITY ANALYSIS
SUMMARY PAGE

Participant: ____________________ **Company:** ____________________

Date: ____________________

CRITICAL FACTORS:	**MATCH**			**COMMENTS**
1. ____________________	**E**	**G**	**P**	
2. ____________________	**E**	**G**	**P**	
3. ____________________	**E**	**G**	**P**	
4. ____________________	**E**	**G**	**P**	
5. ____________________	**E**	**G**	**P**	
6. ____________________	**E**	**G**	**P**	
7. ____________________	**E**	**G**	**P**	
8. ____________________	**E**	**G**	**P**	
9. ____________________	**E**	**G**	**P**	
10. ____________________	**E**	**G**	**P**	

NUMBER OF **EXCELLENT** MATCHES: ________

NUMBER OF **GOOD** MATCHES: ________

NUMBER OF **POOR** MATCHES: ________

DECISION:

5/88

FORM 06

COMPATIBILITY ANALYSIS SUMMARY PAGE

Participant: Stedman **Company:** Stages, Inc.

Date: May 8, 1988

	CRITICAL FACTORS:	MATCH			COMMENTS
1.	Transportation	(E)	G	P	Public bus c̄ backups
2.	Schedule	E	(G)	P	Flexible on both sides
3.	Incentives	E	(G)	P	Need to monitor not a problem
4.	Conversations/Interactions	(E)	G	P	GREAT!!
5.	Rate	E	(G)	P	Goal setting procedure seems workable
6.	Interfering behaviors	E	(G)	P	
7.	Family supports	(E)	G	P	GREAT!!
8.	Managing time	E	(G)	P	
9.	Orienting	E	G	(P)	Needs close monitoring
10.	Appearance	E	(G)	P	

NUMBER OF **EXCELLENT** MATCHES: 3

NUMBER OF **GOOD** MATCHES: 6

NUMBER OF **POOR** MATCHES: 1

DECISION: Check this job c̄ respect to the outcome analysis factors from his career plan. This appears to be a good match and should be explored with Stedman.

5/88

FORM 07

WEEKLY SCHEDULE

TIME	MONDAY	TUESDAY	WEDNESDAY	THURSDAY	FRIDAY

5/88

FORM 07

WEEKLY SCHEDULE

FOR MARY

TIME	MONDAY	TUESDAY	WEDNESDAY	THURSDAY	FRIDAY
7:30	Copying, collating, and filing	→	→	→	→
10:15	BREAK	→	→	→	→
10:30	Continue work	→	→	→	→
11:30	LUNCH IN COMMUNITY	→	→	→	→
12:15	Deliver messages	→	→	→	→
1:15	Prepare packets	→	→	→	→
2:00	LEAVE FOR HOME	→	→	→	→

5/88

FORM 08

OBJECTIVES SUMMARY

Worker:	
Program:	
Job Site:	
Position:	

Objective Management

#	Date Added	Date Ended	Title

Employment Status

Date	Hours/wk	Wages/hr	Other status changes/comments

5/88

FORM 08

OBJECTIVES SUMMARY

Worker:	Don Stone
Program:	E.O.S.M.
Job Site:	Roger's Hardware
Position:	Assistant

Objective Management

#	Date Added	Date Ended	Title
1	3/1	5/1	Stocking materials
2	3/1	5/1	Cleaning back area
3	4/15		Conversing
4	5/1		Inventory

Employment Status

Date	Hours/wk	Wages/hr	Other status changes/comments
2/15/88	20	$4.00	

5/88

Instructional Plan

Worker: ____________________

Objective: ____________________

____

____

Criterion: ____________________

Instructional Sequence: ____________________

____

____

Reinforcement Procedure: ____________________

____

____

Data to be collected: ____________________

____

____

Location of Instruction: ____________________

Task Analysis Attached: ___ yes ___ no

Data Form Attached: ___ yes ___ no

Beginning Date: ____________ Ending Date: ____________

5/88

FORM 09

Instructional Plan

Worker: Theresa Mahoney

Objective: At the motel, Theresa will completely and correctly make a bed within 5 minutes without assistance.

Criterion: Completed without assistance for 5 consecutive sessions.

Instructional Sequence: Verbal prompt → verbal prompt plus model → verbal prompt plus physical guidance

Reinforcement Procedure: Social praise
Check sheet for recording completed beds

Data to be collected: Performance scoring

Location of Instruction: The American Hotel

Task Analysis Attached: ✓ yes ___ no
Data Form Attached: ✓ yes ___ no

Beginning Date: 5/15/88 Ending Date: ___________

5/88

5/88

FORM 10

Instructional Plan Type 2

Worker:

Employment Specialist:

Program:

Location of Instruction:

#

Objective:

Date	Current Skills/Data Summary	Instructional Sequence and Reinforcement Procedure	Comments	Who

Task Analysis Attached? ____ **Yes** ____ **No**

Data Form Attached? ____ **Yes** ____ **No**

FORM 10

Instructional Plan Type 2

Worker: Roger Smith **Program:** KLH.

Employment Specialist: Don Daniels **Location of Instruction:** Civic Center

4 **Objective:** Cleaning Restrooms

Date	Current Skills/Data Summary	Instructional Sequence and Reinforcement Procedure	Comments	Who
4/22	Requires gestural and physical prompts for all steps	Sequence: Verbal-gestural-physical R+ : Pat on back, "Great job!"	Should be able to fade prompts if sequence used consistently	Don

Task Analysis Attached? ✓ **Yes** ___ **No**

Data Form Attached? ✓ **Yes** ___ **No**

5/88

BEHAVIOR MANAGEMENT PLAN

Worker: ______________________ Today's Date: ________________

Employment Specialist: ____

Program: ________________________

Behavior to Reduce: ____

Behavior to Increase: ____

____

Date to Begin: ____________ Estimated Ending Date: ____________

Baseline Levels Summary: ______________________________________

____

____

Reviews Needed:

Worker/Guardian______ Supervisor______ Committee______

Procedures to Reduce Behavior: ________________________________

____

____

____

____

____

____

5/88

Behavior Management Plan

Estimated Frequency of Use: ______________ Review Dates: ________________

Criterion for Success: ____________________________

Criterion for Non-Success: ________________________

Persons Who Will Implement This Procedure: ________________________________

____

Data to be Collected: ____________________ Frequency: ______________________

Where Will Data Be Stored: ____

Who Will Supervise This Program: ____

Possible Side-Effects: ____

____

____

Anticipated Benefits: ____

____

____

____

- -

Worker/Guardian Permission

This behavior management plan has been explained to me by ________________ I understand that this plan was designed to teach social skills that will help now as well as in the future. I understand the possible benefits and side-effects of these procedures. I may review these procedures at any time. I may withdraw my permission at any time. I understand that staff members implementing these procedures will be properly trained and supervised.

________________ ____

Date Worker/Guardian's Signature

________________ ____

Date Worker/Guardian's Signature

5/88

BEHAVIOR MANAGEMENT PLAN

Worker: Jacob Jones Today's Date: 4-15-88
Employment Specialist: Dan Steere
Program: EHR, Inc. - Private business -

Behavior to Reduce: Screaming

Behavior to Increase: Verbalizing his anger or need for help

Date to Begin: 4-20-88 Estimated Ending Date: July 15, 1988

Baseline Levels Summary: Screaming occurs two times per day for the past 2 weeks (Average is 2.2 times per day)

Reviews Needed:

Worker/Guardian ✓ Supervisor ✓ Committee ____

Procedures to Reduce Behavior: Token economy and differential reinforcement of incompatible behaviors (DRI) - Each time Jacob verbalizes in regular tone of voice he will be R+ socially and receive a check mark on his work sheet Tokens (check marks) will be exchanged for opportunities to eat out after work (usually Friday with job coach and coworkers)

5/88

Behavior Management Plan

Estimated Frequency of Use: Daily Review Dates: 4 30; 5-7; 5-15; 6-15
Criterion for Success: Zero incidents for 10 consecutive days
Criterion for Non-Success: No reduction for 5 days
Persons Who Will Implement This Procedure: Dan Steere, Meg Story

Data to be Collected: Rate per day Frequency: Daily
Where Will Data Be Stored: Main office
Who Will Supervise This Program: John Butterworth
Possible Side-Effects: None

Anticipated Benefits: Increase benefit in communicating feelings. It will be nicer to be with Jacob

- -

Worker/Guardian Permission

This behavior management plan has been explained to me by Dan Steere
I understand that this plan was designed to teach social skills that will help now as well as in the future. I understand the possible benefits and side-effects of these procedures. I may review these procedures at any time. I may withdraw my permission at any time. I understand that staff members implementing these procedures will be properly trained and supervised.

4/16/88 Edith Jones
Date Worker/Guardian's Signature

4/19/88 [signature]
Date Worker/Guardian's Signature

5/88

Anecdotal Record

Worker: ____________________ **Job Coach:** ____________________

Target Behaviors: ____________________

____

Date Time	Antecedents (people, activity, place, etc.)	Behavior	Consequences	Comments	Observer

5/88

Anecdotal Record

Worker: Bill **Job Coach:** Paul

Target Behaviors: Stumbling - Bumping into things

Date Time	Antecedents (people, activity, place, etc.)	Behavior	Consequences	Comments	Observer
4/10/88	10 a.m. Working at Copy machine by self	Bumped into bookcase and Knocked over plants and board	Secretaries helped Bill. Call to Group home and Social Worker	Perhaps Bill is having a reaction to medication? Will mention to Social Worker	Paul

5/88

FORM 13

TASK ANALYSIS FORM

ACTIVITY: ______________________ **EMPLOYMENT SITE:** ____________________

STEPS:

1.
2.
3.
4.
5.
6.
7.
8.
9.
10.
11.
12.
13.
14.
15.
16.
17.
18.
19.
20.

COMMENTS: ____

____

____

5/88

FORM 13

TASK ANALYSIS FORM

ACTIVITY: Operating Copier EMPLOYMENT SITE: C.S.E.

STEPS:

1. Check paper tray
2. Load documents in self-feeder
3. Select number of copies
4. Push sort button to "sort"
5. Push start button
6. Remove originals
7. Remove copies
8.
9.
10.
11.
12.
13.
14.
15.
16.
17.
18.
19.
20.

COMMENTS: ______________________

5/88

INSTRUCTIONAL DATA SHEET
TYPE 1

Worker: ____________________ **Objective:** ____________________ **Employment Specialist:** ____________________

Legend:

STEP DATE																				
1.																				
2.																				
3.																				
4.																				
5.																				
6.																				
7.																				
8.																				
9.																				
10.																				
11.																				
12.																				
13.																				
14.																				
15.																				
16.																				
17.																				
18.																				
19.																				
20.																				
TOTAL SCORE (Possible)																				

5/88

INSTRUCTIONAL DATA SHEET.
TYPE 1

Worker: Stedman **Objective:** Hobart dishwasher **Employment Specialist:** Paul Harvey

Legend: 5= Independent 4= Verbal Prompt 3= Gesture 2= Model 1= Physical Prompt

STEP / DATE	4/10	4/11	4/14																	
1. Press switch on	4	5	5																	
2. Turn lever open	2	2	3																	
3. Watch drain (flow)	3	3	4																	
4. Turn drain lever	2	3	4																	
5. Open door	4	5	5																	
6. Inspect for debris	4	4	4																	
7. Remove strainers	1	1	2																	
8. Rinse strainers	5	5	5																	
9. Replace strainers	1	2	2																	
10. Close door	5	5	5																	
11. Turn water on	4	4	5																	
12. Watch drain (flow)	5	5	5																	
13. Turn water off	5	5	5																	
14. Open door	4	4	5																	
15. Press switch off	4	4	5																	
16.																				
17.																				
18.																				
19.																				
20.																				
TOTAL SCORE (Possible) (75)	53	57	63																	

5/88

FORM 15

5/88

INSTRUCTIONAL DATA SHEET

TYPE 2

Scoring Code:
/ = Steps Correct
— = Steps Incorrect
○ = Total Steps Right Per Trial

Worker: ____________________ **Job Coach:** ____________________

Task: ____

Comments: ____

Steps:	Date:																
12 ______	12	12	12	12	12	12	12	12	12	12	12	12	12	12	12	12	12
11 ______	11	11	11	11	11	11	11	11	11	11	11	11	11	11	11	11	11
10 ______	10	10	10	10	10	10	10	10	10	10	10	10	10	10	10	10	10
9 ______	9	9	9	9	9	9	9	9	9	9	9	9	9	9	9	9	9
8 ______	8	8	8	8	8	8	8	8	8	8	8	8	8	8	8	8	8
7 ______	7	7	7	7	7	7	7	7	7	7	7	7	7	7	7	7	7
6 ______	6	6	6	6	6	6	6	6	6	6	6	6	6	6	6	6	6
5 ______	5	5	5	5	5	5	5	5	5	5	5	5	5	5	5	5	5
4 ______	4	4	4	4	4	4	4	4	4	4	4	4	4	4	4	4	4
3 ______	3	3	3	3	3	3	3	3	3	3	3	3	3	3	3	3	3
2 ______	2	2	2	2	2	2	2	2	2	2	2	2	2	2	2	2	2
1 ______	1	1	1	1	1	1	1	1	1	1	1	1	1	1	1	1	1

Notes:

5/88

INSTRUCTIONAL DATA SHEET

TYPE 2

Scoring Code:
/ = Steps Correct
— = Steps Incorrect
O = Total Steps Right Per Trial

Worker: Dan Steere **Job Coach:** Tom Powell

Task: Operating Copier

Comments:

Steps:																	
Date:	5/1	5/2	5/6	5/8													
12	12	12	12	12	12	12	12	12	12	12	12	12	12	12	12	12	12
11	11	11	11	11	11	11	11	11	11	11	11	11	11	11	11	11	11
10	10	10	10	10	10	10	10	10	10	10	10	10	10	10	10	10	10
9	9	9	9	9	9	9	9	9	9	9	9	9	9	9	9	9	9
8	8	8	8	8	8	8	8	8	8	8	8	8	8	8	8	8	8
7 Remove copies	7	7	7	7	7	7	7	7	7	7	7	7	7	7	7	7	7
6 Remove originals	6	6	6	6	6	6	6	6	6	6	6	6	6	6	6	6	6
5 Push "on" button	5	5	5	5	5	5	5	5	5	5	5	5	5	5	5	5	5
4 Push "sort" button	4	4	4	4	4	4	4	4	4	4	4	4	4	4	4	4	4
3 Select # of copies	3	3	3	3	3	3	3	3	3	3	3	3	3	3	3	3	3
2 Load originals	2	2	2	2	2	2	2	2	2	2	2	2	2	2	2	2	2
1 Check paper tray	1	1	1	1	1	1	1	1	1	1	1	1	1	1	1	1	1

Notes:

FORM 15

INSTRUCTIONAL DATA SHEET TYPE 3

FORM 16

Worker ______________________ Activity ____________________

Legend:

TIME	M	T	W	T	F	M	T	W	T	F
Daily Totals										

5/88

INSTRUCTIONAL DATA SHEET TYPE 3

FORM 16

Worker Bill

Activity Frequency of Social Interaction with Coworkers (1 min or less · with break of 1 min)

Legend:

TIME	M	T	W	T	F	M	T	W	T	F
8-8:30	7	9								
8:30-9	15	3								
9:30-10	0	1								
10:30-11	0	0								
11-11:30	4	6								
11:30-12	9	2								
12-12:30	16	10								
Daily Totals	51	31								

5/88

FORM 17

5/88

INSTRUCTIONAL DATA SHEET
TYPE 4

Worker: ______________________ Agency: ______________________

Date Started: ____________ Job Site: ______________ Whole or Partial: ________

Legend:

			INTERVALS:																							
DATE	TIME	BEHAVIORS																								

5/88

INSTRUCTIONAL DATA SHEET
TYPE 4

Worker: James Trey **Agency:** KLH

Date Started: 5/1/88 **Job Site:** Marnet, Inc. **Whole or Partial:** Partial

Legend: + = Conversing w/ coworkers — = Not interacting

			INTERVALS:																							
DATE	TIME	BEHAVIORS	1'	2'	3'	4'	5'	6'	7'	8'	9	10'	11'	12'	13'	14'	15'									
5/1	10:15 - 10:30	Interaction at Break	—	—	—	—	—	+	—	+	+	—	—	—	+	—	—									

27%

FORM 17

INSTRUCTIONAL DATA SHEET TYPE 5

FORM 18

Name: ______________________

Work Site: ______________________

Dates: ____________ to ____________

	Mon	Tue	Wed	Thur	Fri	Comments

	Mon	Tue	Wed	Thur	Fri	Comments

	Mon	Tue	Wed	Thur	Fri	Comments

	Mon	Tues	Wed	Thur	Fri	Comments

5/88

INSTRUCTIONAL DATA SHEET TYPE 5

FORM 18

Name: Dave Steere

Work Site: Wellspring, Inc.

Dates: 3/15/88 to ______

	Mon	Tue	Wed	Thur	Fri	Comments
Collating	25 packets	30 packets	22 packets			
Filing	60 files	65 files	57 files			Not feeling well on Wednesday

	Mon	Tue	Wed	Thur	Fri	Comments

	Mon	Tue	Wed	Thur	Fri	Comments

	Mon	Tues	Wed	Thur	Fri	Comments

5/88

FORM 19

GENERALIZATION PLAN

Date: ____________________

Employee: ______________________________ Company: ______________________________

Activity: ____

____

Settings:	1. ____________________	2. ____________________
Persons:	1. ____________________	1. ____________________
	2. ____________________	2. ____________________
	3. ____________________	3. ____________________
Materials:	1. ____________________	1. ____________________
	2. ____________________	2. ____________________
	3. ____________________	3. ____________________

Prepared by: ______________________________

To Begin Implementation: ______________________

5/88

FORM 19

GENERALIZATION PLAN

Date: 4-10-88

Employee: Don Stone Company: A-B-C Corp.

Activity: Operating Copying Machine

Settings:	1. Mr. Beckwith's office	2. Mrs. Lewin's office
Persons:	1. Rob	1. Rob
	2. Mary	2. Mary
	3. Mr. Beckwith	3. Mrs. Lewin
Materials:	1. Single Copies	1. Single copies
	2. Double-sided copies	2. Double-sided copies
	3. Transparencies	3. Transparencies

Prepared by: Dereck Bruce

To Begin Implementation: 5/1/88

5/88

FORM 20

ONGOING SUPPORTS

NAME: ______________________________

DATE: From: ____________ To: ____________

TYPE OF SUPPORT	BY WHOM	HOW OFTEN	COMMENTS

5/88

FORM 20

ONGOING SUPPORTS

NAME: Nick Powell

DATE: From: 3-1-88 To: 7-31-88

TYPE OF SUPPORT	BY WHOM	HOW OFTEN	COMMENTS
Financial counseling with family	Steve	twice	Est. current benefit package
Afterwork Recreation Program	Theresa	weekly	Volleyball, Dancing Exercise Classes
Transportation - Bus Travel	Steve	daily	Focus on independent travel
Coworker reinforcement for helping Nick	Steve	monthly	provide monthly stipend to coworker
Update career planning outcomes	Ernie	6-1-88	involve 1 coworker

5/88

FORM 21

PERFORMANCE REVIEW

DATE Of REVIEW: ____________________

NAME: ________________________________ DAYS LATE: ____________________

JOB TITLE: ________________________________ DAYS MISSED: ____________________

SUPERVISOR: ________________________________ OVERTIME: ____________________

COMPANY: ________________________________ WAGES EARNED: ____________________

SCHEDULE CHANGES: ____

PLEASE CIRCLE THE RATING WHICH BEST FITS THE PERFORMANCE OF THE PARTICIPANT.

1=POOR	2=NEEDS IMPROVEMENT	3=AVERAGE	4=GOOD	5=EXCEPTIONAL	N/A NOT APPLIC.

I. WORK HABITS:

Arrives at work/returns from breaks on time ______	1	2	3	4	5	N/A
Dependable ______	1	2	3	4	5	N/A
Cooperates with others ______	1	2	3	4	5	N/A
Completes assigned tasks ______	1	2	3	4	5	N/A
Works alone ______	1	2	3	4	5	N/A
Maintains appropriate dress ______	1	2	3	4	5	N/A
Behavior toward supervisor ______	1	2	3	4	5	N/A
Behavior toward co-workers ______	1	2	3	4	5	N/A

II. RESPONSIBILITIES:

1. ______	1	2	3	4	5	N/A
2. ______	1	2	3	4	5	N/A
3. ______	1	2	3	4	5	N/A
4. ______	1	2	3	4	5	N/A
5. ______	1	2	3	4	5	N/A

III. ADDITIONAL COMMENTS AND RECOMMENDATIONS:

____

____

____

____

Employee Signature

5/88

FORM 21

PERFORMANCE REVIEW

DATE Of REVIEW: 4/15/88

NAME: John Marks

DAYS LATE: 0

JOB TITLE: Office Assistant

DAYS MISSED: 2

SUPERVISOR: James Robb

OVERTIME: —

COMPANY: A-B-C Corp.

WAGES EARNED: $4.50/hour

SCHEDULE CHANGES: None

PLEASE CIRCLE THE RATING WHICH BEST FITS THE PERFORMANCE OF THE PARTICIPANT.

1=POOR 2=NEEDS IMPROVEMENT 3=AVERAGE 4=GOOD 5=EXCEPTIONAL N/A NOT APPLIC.

I. WORK HABITS:

Arrives at work/returns from breaks on time	1	2	3	(4)	5	N/A
Dependable	1	2	3	(4)	5	N/A
Cooperates with others	1	2	(3)	4	5	N/A
Completes assigned tasks	1	2	3	(4)	5	N/A
Works alone	1	(2)	3	4	5	N/A
Maintains appropriate dress	1	2	(3)	4	5	N/A
Behavior toward supervisor	1	2	3	(4)	5	N/A
Behavior toward co-workers	1	2	(3)	4	5	N/A

II. RESPONSIBILITIES:

1. Copying collating	1	2	3	(4)	5	N/A
2. Delivering messages	1	2	3	4	(5)	N/A
3. Filing	1	2	(3)	4	5	N/A
4.	1	2	3	4	5	N/A
5.	1	2	3	4	5	N/A

III. ADDITIONAL COMMENTS AND RECOMMENDATIONS:

John Marks

Employee Signature

5/88

EMPLOYER CONTACT FORM

NAME OF BUSINESS: ______________________ PHONE: _____________

ADDRESS: ____

CONTACT PERSON: _______________________ PHONE: _____________

TITLE: ____________________________________

DATE of CONTACT: _____________ CONTACTED BY: _________________

RESPONSE TO CONTACT: ____

____

____

____

FOLLOW-UP PLAN: ____

____

____

____

COMMENTS: ____

____

____

5/88

EMPLOYER CONTACT FORM

NAME OF BUSINESS: Ernie's Emporium PHONE: 555-5525

ADDRESS: 234 Maine Boulevard, Portland

CONTACT PERSON: Terry Smith PHONE: Same

TITLE: Floor Supervisor

DATE of CONTACT: 5/1/88 CONTACTED BY: John Butterworth

RESPONSE TO CONTACT: Very positive. Would like to meet with us to discuss possibility of hiring one worker.

FOLLOW-UP PLAN: Steve and I have an appointment to meet with Mr. Smith on 5/6 @ 10:00

COMMENTS:

George Johnson

5/88

JOB ANALYSIS FORM

Type: Initial______Ongoing______Job Type______Analysis Date______________
Company______________________Position______________________
Evaluator____
Current Hourly Rate____ Hours Per Week____Months Per Year______________
Supervisor's Name______________________________________
Supervisor's Title______________Supervisor's Phone #______________

FACTOR	NOTES/DESCRIPTION

1.

2.

3.

4.

5.

JOB ANALYSIS FORM

FACTOR	NOTES/DESCRIPTION
6.	
7.	
8.	
9.	
10.	
11.	
12.	

JOB ANALYSIS FORM

FACTOR	NOTES/DESCRIPTION
13.	
14.	
15.	
16.	
17.	
18.	
19.	
20.	

5/88

JOB ANALYSIS FORM

Type: Initial ✓ Ongoing ____ Job Type Stocking Analysis Date 5/1/88
Company Dan's Market Position Stockroom Assistant
Evaluator Jim Gordon
Current Hourly Rate 4.00 Hours Per Week 20 Months Per Year 12
Supervisor's Name Dan Reed
Supervisor's Title Owner Supervisor's Phone # 444-4444

FACTOR	NOTES/DESCRIPTION
1. Schedule	Daytime 8:30–2:00 M–F
2. Wages	$4.00/Hour
3. Location	420 Broad Street On bus line
4. Site Orienting	Different areas in store
5. Mobility	Doors to back room (stock area) would present problems

FORM 23 Page 2

JOB ANALYSIS FORM

FACTOR	NOTES/DESCRIPTION
6. Initiation	Need to inform supervisor when certain items are running low
7. Task Changes	2-3 per day
8. Strength	Some lifting necessary under 30 pounds
9. Endurance	Standing most of day
10. Rate/Pace	Moderate; fast during deliveries in a.m.
11. Attention to Task	Close attention required
12. Communication	Only Key words required

JOB ANALYSIS FORM

FACTOR	NOTES/DESCRIPTION
13. Stress	Low-moderate; increases when deliveries arrive
14. Supervision	Daily contact; but fairly loose
15. Math/Reading	Counting/sight-reading helpful but, not critical
16. Interactions	Requires working cooperatively with coworkers
17. Hygiene/Appearance	Neat and Clean
18. Interfering Behaviors (Tolerance)	Stockroom area-somewhat tolerant. Customer area-not as tolerant
19. Employer Attitude	Excellent!
20. Time Management	Going to break/lunch

5/88

FORM 24

AGENCY WIDE ONGOING SUPPORTS

5/88

AGENCY WIDE ONGOING SUPPORTS

ADVOCACY	PUBLIC RELATIONS
CLINICAL	RECREATION
COMMUNITY	SOCIAL
COWORKER	TRANSPORTATION
EDUCATION SYSTEM	
EMPLOYER	
FAMILY	WORK DEVELOPMENT
FINANCIAL	
HOME / RESIDENCE	
INSTRUCTION	OFF WORK HOURS
MATERIALS MODIFICATION	

5/88

FORM 25

ONGOING SUPPORT ______________________

RANGE OF ACTIVITIES

- ______________________
- ______________________
- ______________________
- ______________________
- ______________________
- ______________________
- ______________________
- ______________________
- ______________________
- ______________________
- ______________________

5/88

FORM 25

ONGOING SUPPORT JOB COACH - PROFESSIONAL DEVELOPMENT

RANGE OF ACTIVITIES

- FORMAL COURSEWORK
- INSERVICE PRESENTATIONS
- PROFESSIONAL READING
- CAREER LADDER
- COMPETENCY PROTOCOL
- TEAM DECISION MAKING
- PERKS - INCENTIVES
- COMMUNICATION MECHANISMS
- RESOURCE SHARING WITH NEIGHBORING AGENCIES
-
-

5/88

IDENTIFIED SUPPORT: ______________________

MORE INTENSE TYPE

LESS INTENSE TYPE

5/88

FORM 26

IDENTIFIED SUPPORT: Coworker Involvement

MORE INTENSE TYPE

- Formally paying a coworker to assume supervisory duties with the worker.
- Asking coworkers for feedback about the worker.
- Fostering friendships by teaching initiating skills to the worker.
- Reinforcing naturally occuring friendships.
- Encouraging conversations by the worker to coworkers.
- Developing car pool with a co-worker.

LESS INTENSE TYPE

5/88

ONGOING SUPPORT: ____________________

ACTIVITY: ____________________

RANGE OF OPTIONS

MOST

LEVEL OF INTENSITY

LEAST

5/88

FORM 27

ONGOING SUPPORT: FINANCIAL

ACTIVITY: SSI - MEDICAID

RANGE OF OPTIONS

MOST

LEVEL OF INTENSITY

- Advocate for obtaining a job that contains necessary Health Insurance and benefit plans
- Meet with consumer and social security office to investigate details of incentives-disincentives
- Develop a current/future financial profile for the consumer
- Adjust consumer's work schedule to not jeopardize needed subsidy support
- Communicate with representatives from neighboring agencies about how They have dealt with SSI-Medicaid situation
- Attend workshops/conferences for update on social security policies
- Read current information from social Security office

LEAST

5/88

APPENDIX B

Quick Reference for Emergency First Aid Procedures

Emergency Numbers: **Ambulance:** ____________
Doctor: ____________
Poison Control: ____________

Symptom or Injury *(listed in alphabetical order)*	***Procedure***
Abdominal Pain	*1. Allow to rest.* *2. Do not administer laxative or medication.* *3. Refer to standing orders; notify doctor if becomes severe.*
Allergic Reactions to: **Bee sting**	*1. If person known to be allergic to bee stings, get **IMMEDIATE** medical attention. May have bee sting kit with nurse.*
Insect bites, skin contact or foods as indicated by itchiness, rash, weakness, or difficult breathing	*1. If person is in acute distress refer to standing orders for antidotal application. Seek medical attention.* *2. For minor skin reactions, administer cool applications and calamine lotion.*

Back and Neck Injuries	1. *Do not allow person to be moved.* 2. *Immoblize neck and spine in position in which injury occurred.* 3. *Handle as little as possible.* 4. *Get **IMMEDIATE** medical attention.*
Bites, animal and human	1. *Cleanse wound thoroughly to prevent infection.* 2. *Cover and seek medical attention.* 3. *If animal bite, note circumstance that might indicate if animal was rabid.*
Bleeding, severe, external	1. *Get **IMMEDIATE** medical attention.* 2. *Apply direct pressure with hand over a dressing covering the wound. Apply pressure bandage.* 3. *Attend to shock.*
Bleeding, internal as indicated by: cold, clammy skin, rapid breathing and pulse, pain in area of injury, blood in urine or feces	1. *Maintain open airway.* 2. *Do not give liquids.* 3. *Immobilize, transport in lying position.* 4. *Get **IMMEDIATE** medical attention.*
Bleeding, cuts and abrasions	1. *Clean wound.* 2. *Apply antibiotic and dressing if necessary.*
Nosebleeds	1. *Lie on back or tilt head backward.* 2. *Press nostril together against site of bleeding.*

Nosebleeds (continued)	*3. If nosebleed persists more than 15 minutes obtain medical help.*
Burns - **Major (3rd degree and 2nd degree)**	*1. Assess consciousness and respiratory status.* *2. Cool burned area in cold water to prevent further tissue damage.* *3. Cover lightly with clean cloth.* *4. Transfer to medical facility.*
- **Minor (1st degree)**	*1. Immerse in or apply cold water.* *2. Cover lightly with dressing.*
Cardiac Arrest (Heart Attack) indicated by complaints of chest pain, weakness, paleness, blueish tinge, loss of consciousness	*1. If person is unconscious, administer CPR, get* ***IMMEDIATE*** *medical assistance.* *2. If not unconscious, loosen clothing.* *3. Place in comfortable position.* *4. Get medical attention promptly.*
Chest Wounds	*1. Get* ***IMMEDIATE*** *medical attention.* *2. If puncturing item is in place, leave it undisturbed.* *3. Cover wound, if air is escaping, to make air tight seal.* *4. Give mouth to mouth resuscitation if necessary.* *5. Transport wound side down.*
Choking Asphyxia	*1. If person is breathing,* ***DO NOT INTERFERE.*** *2. If foreign object is blocking, bend victim over, facing outward, or lie sideways on floor, or across lap.* *3. Probe mouth with fingers to remove object.*

Choking (continued)	4. *If unsuccessful, do Heimlich maneuver:* - *stand behind victim with victim standing or sitting,* - *wrap arms around victim's abdomen slightly above navel and below rib cage,* - *grab your fist with opposite hand and press it into the victim's abdomen with a quick upward thrust - repeat if necessary.* 5. *If victim is not breathing, ensure air passage is open and administer mouth to mouth resuscitation.*
Dental Injuries	1. *Put lost tooth in milk.* 2. *Contact dentist immediately.*
Diabetic Reactions **Insulin reaction indicated by: dizziness, palor, sweaty skin, incoherent speech, headache**	1. *If able to react and swallow, give sugar solution, orange juice or candy.* 2. *Notify family members and medical personnel.*
Diabetic Shock indicated by: loss of consciousness	1. *Treat for shock.* 2. *Get **IMMEDIATE** medical attention.*
Drowning	1. *Do not try to get water out of victim.* 2. *Start artificial respiration **IMMEDIATELY.*** 3. *Continue until help arrives or victim begins breathing on his own.*

Electric Shock	1. *Treat for respiratory failure.* 2. *Clear air passageway.* 3. *Administer mouth to mouth resuscitation.* 4. *Get* ***IMMEDIATE*** *medical attention.*
Eye Injuries - **foreign body in eye**	1. *Wash eye with water.* 2. *If unsuccessful, cover with patch.* 3. *Get medical attention.*
- **penetrating injury**	1. *Do not attempt to remove object or wash eye.* 2. *Cover both eyes with clean dressing to prevent movement of affected eye.* 3. *Keep person quiet preferably on back.* 4. *Transport to emergency room.*
Fainting	1. *To prevent fainting, a person who feels weak or dizzy should lie down or bend over with his head on his knees.* 2. *If person faints, leave him lying down, loosen any tight clothing.* 3. *If he vomits, roll him to side and wipe out his mouth.* 4. *Maintain open airway, wipe face with cool cloth.* 5. *Note any injuries from fall, note subsequent behaviors in case fainting is indicative of further illness.*
Fever	1. *Notify guardian / home residence.* 2. *Allow person to rest.* 3. *If verified by guardian or physician, administer aspirin (appropriate dosage).*

Fractures (break or crack in bone)	1. *Attend to respiratory and bleeding problems.*
Dislocation (displacement of bone end at joint)	2. *Clear air passage.* 3. *Get medical attention promptly.*
Sprain (injury to ligament, muscle in region of joint)	4. *If sprain, apply ice packs, keep joint raised, do not allow person to put weight on joint.*
Head Injury (wound to scalp)	1. *Do not attempt to clean wound.* 2. *Wound will bleed profusely.* 3. *Place sterile dressing snugly on wound, do not use excessive pressure because of possibility of fracture.* 4. *When bleeding under control, apply bandage.* 5. *If severe or appears to need stitches, get medical attention.*
Itching	1. *Apply soothing lotions.* 2. *Determine cause of itching, report to physician or nurse for additional treatment.*
Nausea and Vomiting	1. *Assist victim maintaining clear air passage. If victim is lying down, turn on side to prevent aspiration.* 2. *Allow victim to rest if nauseous or after vomiting.* 3. *Note additional symptoms.* 4. *Report to medical personnel for additional input as to cause of illness.* 5. *Note: nausea and vomiting can be symptomatic of a variety of disorders, such as: toxic shock reactions or infections.*

Poisoning	1. *Call Connecticut Poison Information Center:* ***1-800-343-2722*** *Farmington, CT* 2. *Send victim and poison container to hospital.* 3. *If you do not know what poison the person has ingested:* - *dilute by administering water or milk* - *look for container or substance* - *get medical help* ***IMMEDIATELY*** 4. *If person has not swallowed a strong acid, alkali or petroleum product:* - *dilute by administering milk or water* - *induce vomiting* - *get* ***IMMEDIATE*** *medical attention*
Seizures: sudden loss of control of body movements, involuntary limb movements, lack of consciousness, may be total body involvement (grand mal), localized in one area of body or slight loss of awareness (petit mal). **Degree of seizures varies greatly**	1. *Administer mouth to mouth if victim not breathing. Get* ***IMMEDIATE*** *attention.* 2. *Clear area to prevent injury.* 3. *Do not restrain person.* 4. *Do not put anything in person's mouth.* 5. *Turn mouth to side to prevent aspiration.* 6. *Allow person to rest after seizure (will probably lose control of bladder).* 7. *Record occurrence and length of seizure for medical staff.*
Status seizures, (intense and grand mal) are *life threatening*, involves cessation of breathing	1. *Get* ***IMMEDIATE*** *attention.*

Splinters	*1. Remove if easily accessible, wipe with alcohol and bandage.* *2. If splinter cannot be removed, cover with bandage and get medical help.*

APPENDIX C

Checklist to Use to Determine Whether Buildings Are Accessible to People with Physical Disabilities

The following checklist can be used as a guide to complying with the American National Standards Institute (ANSI) standards for making your building accessible to people with physical disabilities.

Building Site

1. Does the grading of the building site allow the approaches to the building to be substantially level?
2. Is there parking within 200 feet of the building entrance?
3. Is any of the parking reserved for persons with disabilities?
4. Are any parking spaces open on one side to allow easy access for wheelchairs and for people who use braces to get in and out of the automobile?
5. Are the parking spaces on level ground?
6. Are there ramps or level spaces to allow people to enter the building without crossing a curb?

Walk Ways

1. Are walks at least 48 inches wide?
2. Is the gradient not greater than a one foot rise in 20 feet (5%)?

3. Are walks without interruption (i.e., steps or abrupt changes in level)?
4. If the walks cross a driveway, parking lot, or other walks, do they blend into a common level surface?
5. On elevated walks, is there at least a 5-foot by 5-foot platform if a door swings out onto the platform or 3-foot by 5-foot platform if the door swings in?
6. Do walks have nonslip surfaces?

Ramps

1. Do ramps have a slope no greater than a 1-foot rise in 12 feet (8.33%)?
2. If ramps are steeper than a 5% gradient rise, are handrails provided?
3. If there are handrails, are they at least 32 inches above ramp surface?
4. Are the ramp surfaces smooth?
5. Are the ramp surfaces nonslip?
6. Do ramps have a 6-foot clearance at the bottom?
7. Do ramps that have a gradient steeper than 5% have level spaces—a minimum of 3 feet in length—at 30-foot intervals?
8. Are these level rest areas at least 5 feet wide, to provide for turns?

Floors

1. Do floors have nonslip surfaces?
2. Are floors on each story at a common level or connected by a ramp?

Restrooms

1. Is there at least one men's room and one ladies' room on each floor with facilities for persons with physical handicaps?
2. Can persons with physical disabilities, particularly those in wheelchairs, enter the restroom?
3. Do restrooms have turning space 60 by 60 inches to allow traffic of individuals in wheelchairs?
4. Do restrooms have at least one toilet stall that
   a. Is 3 feet wide?
   b. Is at least 4 feet 8 inches deep?
   c. Has a door that is 32 inches wide and swings out?
   d. Has handrail on each side, 33 inches high and parallel to floor, 1 ½ inches in diameter, with 1 ½ inches clearance between rail and wall, fastened securely to wall at the ends and center?
5. Do restrooms have wash basins with narrow aprons, which when mounted at standard height are not greater than 34 inches at the top and which have a clearance underneath of 29 inches?
6. Are drain pipes and hot-water pipes covered or insulated?
7. Is one mirror as low as possible and no higher than 40 inches above the floor?
8. Is one shelf at a height as low as possible and no higher than 40 inches above the floor?
9. Do restrooms for men have wall-mounted urinals with the opening of the basin 19 inches from the floor, or have floor-mounted urinals that are level with the main floor of the restrooms?
10. Are towel dispensers mounted no higher than 40 inches from the floor?

11. Do restrooms have towel racks mounted no higher than 40 inches from the floor?
12. Are disposal units mounted no higher than 40 inches from the floor?
13. Are towel racks, towel dispensers, and other appropriate units located to the side rather than above the basins?

Water Fountains

1. Is there at least one drinking fountain on each floor for use by persons with physical disabilities?
2. Can persons in wheelchairs wheel up to fountains?
3. Do water fountains or coolers have up front spouts and controls?
4. Are they hand operated?
5. If coolers are wall mounted, are they hand operated, with basins 36 inches or less from the floor?

Public Telephones

1. Is there at least one public telephone in each "bank" accessible to persons who are physically handicapped?
2. Is the height of the dial 48 inches or less from the floor?
3. Is the coin slot located 48 inches or less from the floor?
4. Are these telephones equipped for persons with hearing disabilities? Are those telephones identified as such?

Entrances/Exits

1. Is at least one entrance to the building accessible to people who use wheelchairs?
2. Is at least one entrance accessible to wheelchairs on a level that would make the elevators accessible?

Doors and Doorways

1. Do doors have a clear opening at least 32 inches wide?
2. Can doors be opened by a single effort?
3. Is the floor of the doorway level within 5 feet from the door in the direction it swings?
4. Does this level space extend 1 foot beyond each side of the door?
5. Does it extend 3 feet in the direction opposite to the door swing?
6. Are sharp inclines and abrupt changes in levels avoided at doorsills?
7. Does the speed of door closers allow the use of doors by persons who are physically disabled?

Stairs and Steps

1. Do the steps avoid protruding lips on the edge of each step?
2. Do stairs have handrails at least 32 inches above step level?
3. Do stairs have at least one handrail that extends at least 18 inches beyond the top and bottom steps?
4. Do steps have risers 7 inches or less?

Elevators

1. If more than a one-story building, are elevators available to persons who are physically handicapped?
2. Can persons in wheelchairs enter elevators?
3. Are outside call buttons 48 inches or less from floor?
4. Are control buttons inside 48 inches or less from floor?
5. Are the buttons labeled with raised (or indented) letters beside them?

6. Are they touch sensitive and easy to push?
7. Is the elevator cab at least 5 feet by 5 feet wide?
8. Can a person in a wheelchair facing rear see floor numbers (by mirror or floor identification at rear of car)?
9. Are floors announced orally by recorded devices for the benefit of people with visual impairments?

Controls

1. Are light switches not more than 48 inches above the floor?
2. Are controls for heating, cooling, and ventilation not more than 48 inches above the floor?
3. Are controls for fire alarms and other warning devices not more than 48 inches from the floor?
4. Are other frequently used controls, such as drapery pulls, etc., not more than 48 inches from floor?

Warning Signals

1. Are audible warning signals accompanied by simultaneous visual signals for the benefit of those with hearing and sight disabilities?

Hazards

1. When hazards such as open manhole covers, panels, and excavation exist on the site, are barricades placed on all open sides at least 8 feet from hazard and warning devices installed?
2. Are there no low-hanging door closers that remain within opening of doorways or that protrude hazardously into regular corridors or traffic ways?
3. Are there no low-hanging signs, ceiling lights, fixtures, or similar objects that protrude into regular corridors or traffic ways?
4. Is lighting on ramps adequate?
5. Are exit signs easily identifiable to all persons with disabilities?

INDEX

Abdominal pain, 273
Abrasions, 274
Accessibility
  checklist to determine, 281–285
  need for, 164
Activities
  by level of intensity, 102–103
    forms for, 269–272
  range of, 101–102
    forms for, 267–268
Adult services, 178–179
Advocates
  adult service providers as, 178–179
  coworkers as, 119–122
  employment specialist as, 183
Agency representatives, 102
Agency-wide Ongoing Support Form (Form 24), 101, 265, 266
Allergic reactions, 273
Anderson, W., 176
Anecdotal Record Form (Form 12), 237–238
Animal bites, 274
Antecedent-behavior-consequence analysis, 168, 169
Antecedent change procedures
  explanation of, 48–49
  prompt sequences in, 51–54
  prompts involved in, 49
  types of prompts in, 49–51
Antecendents, 90
Applied behavior analysis, 82
Apprenticeships, 10
Asphyxia, 275–276
Assessment, 60
Assessment strategies, 60–61
  baseline assessment, 64–66
  data graphing, 75–80
  formative and summative assessment, 66–74
  natural cue identification, 61
  task analysis, 61–64
Austin, N., 13
Aversives, 97

Back and neck injury, 274
Backward chaining, 56–57
Baer, D., 138
Barcus, M., 29, 175
Barnes, E., 146
Baseline assessment, 61, 64–66
Beckett, C., 176
Behavior, 87–90
Behavioral contracting. *See* Behavior interventions
Behavior intervention process, 86–91
Behavior interventions
  behavior contracting, 95
  differential reinforcement of incompatible behavior, 92
  differential reinforcement of low rates of behavior, 93
  differential reinforcement of other behaviors, 92–93
  extinction/ignoring, 93–94
  gentle teaching, 94
  physical restraint and aversives, 97
  positive reinforcement, 91–92
  response cost, 96
  time-out activity, 95
  time-out contingent observation, 96
  token economy, 95
  use of, 97–98
  verbal reprimand, 96
Behavior management plan, 90–91
Behavior management principles, 83–86
Behavior management programs, 85, 86
Behavior problems
  explanation of, 82–83
  factors influencing, 88, 89
  formal plan to deal with, 90–91
  implementation of management plan for, 91
  monitoring, 91
  prevention of, 90
  skills needed to deal with, 83
  strategies for generalization and maintenance, 91
  strategies for prevention, 90
Bellamy, G. T., 50, 55, 116
Benefits, 6
Berrigan, C., 146
Biken, D., 146
Billingsley, F. F., 40
Bites, 274
Blackwell, R., 48
Blatt, Burton, 66
Bleeding, 274
Body mechanics, 162–163

Boredom, 88
Brainstorming games, 170
Breen, C., 121
Brown, L., 139, 140
Bruininks, R. H., 1
Buckley, J., 117
Building site, 282
Burns, 275

Cardiac arrest, 275
Career planning
  goals, 20
  process, 8, 9
  role players in, 21
Career Planning Outcomes Form (Form 2), 209–212
Career planning process, 21
  action plans, 27–28
  compatibility analysis, 25–27
  employment outcomes analysis, 24–26
  job experiences as part of, 178
  optimal employment challenges, 27, 28
  orientation, 21–22
  personal profile development, 22–24
Cerebral palsy, 153–154
Chaining procedures, 56–57
Challenging behaviors, 82
Chest wounds, 275
Chitwood, S., 176
Choices, 17
Choking, 275–276
Color coding, 57
Communication between transdisciplinary team members, 45–46
Community members, 16
Compatibility analysis
  definition of, 30
  forms, 215–220, 259–264
  myths regarding, 30–31
  as steps in career planning process, 25–27
Compatibility Analysis Form (Form 6), 38, 223, 224
Compatibility analysis steps
  decision making, 39
  developing matches, 36–38
  employment observation, 33–36
  initial screening, 38
  job retention, 32–33
  participant observation, 36
  proactive planning, 31–32
  single factor analysis, 38–39
Competitive work, 4
Consequences, 90
Consequent change procedures
  error correction, 55–56
  positive reinforcement, 54–55
Contingent observation, 96
Continuum approach, 30–31
Controls accessibility, 285
Corporal punishment, 84, 97
Coworkers/supervisors
  as allies, 17
  as friends or advocates, 119–122
  as instructors, 123–125
  involvement in supervision and training of workers, 117
  as observers, 122–123
  ongoing support from, 101–103
  as partner, 125
  roles and functions of, 119
Creed, development of supported employment, 14–18
Crowding, 88
Cue identification, 61
Cuts, 274

Data collection procedures, 67
  for behavioral program, 89–90
  graphing, 75–80
Decision making regarding compatibility, 39
Dental injury, 276
Department of Labor
  volunteer regulations, 192, 193
  wage regulations, 10, 11
Developmental Disabilities Act of 1984, 4
Diabetic reactions, 276
Differential reinforcement
  of alternative behavior, 92
  of competing behavior, 92
  of incompatible behavior, 92
  of low rates of behavior, 93
  of other behavior, 92–93
Dignity, 16
Dineen, J., 117
Direct participation strategies, 125
Dislocation, bone, 278
Documentation
  of behavior problems, 84–85
  of behavior program implementation and effectiveness, 86
Donnellan, A. M., 92
Doors and doorways, 285
Dressing physically handicapped employees, 164
Drowning, 276
Duration recording, 71

Eating, 164
Educators, 43
Electric shock, 277
Elevators, 284–285
Emergency first aid, 273–280
Employee safety, 152
Employer Contact Form (Form 22), 257–258
Employers
  as allies, 17
  incentives for, 194–195
Employment matches, 36–38
Employment observation, 33–36
Employment outcomes analysis, 24–26

Employment screening
forms, 215–220, 223–224
initial, 38
Employment specialists
as allies, 17
career development for, 184
coworker/supervisor relationships and, 118–125
functions of, 11–12, 43, 182–183
job description, 183
relationship with family, 135–137
roles of, 184
sources of support for, 184–188
training and orientation of, 183–184
Enclaves in industry, 10–11
Entrances, 284
Environment
factors influencing behavior, 87–88
modification of, 57–58
Equipment for physically disabled employees, 156–159. *See also* Wheelchairs
Error correction procedures, 55–56
Evans, I. M., 166
Exits, 284
Extinction, 93–94, 97
Eye injury, 277

Fainting, 277
Fair Labor Standards Act, 192
Families
desired outcomes for disabled members of, 134–135
functions of, 129, 130
interaction, 129
involvement in supported employment process, 17
life cycle of, 129, 130
needs of, 130–131
resources, 129
role in transition from school to employment, 176
role of transdisciplinary team, 44
supported employment and, 11, 131–133
as team members, 134
Family systems theory, 128–130
Fear, 88
Fever, 277
Financial planning, 101
Financial resources, 179
First aid procedures, 152–153
Floors, 283
Ford, L., 117
Formative and summative assessment, 61
duration recording, 71
frequency recording, 68, 69
interval recording, 71–73
overview of, 66–68
percentage recording, 69–70
performance scoring, 74
rate recording, 69, 70
Forms
individual worker records, 203–204
samples of varied, 205–258
worker documentation, 203
Forward chaining, 56
Fractures, 278
Frequency recording, 68, 69
Friendship with coworkers, 119–122
Frustration, 88
Full physical prompts, 51
Functional activity, 66

Gaylord-Ross, R., 121
General case programming
explanation of, 142–143
implementation of, 144–145
Generalization, 139–140, 145
Generalization map, 140–142
Generalization Plan Form (Form 19), 251–252
Generic services, 175
Gentle teaching method, 94
Gestural prompts, 50–51
Goal setting
example of, 108–114
need for, 106
steps, 106–108, 114–115
Gold, Marc, 47, 67
Gordon, L., 174
Governmental/regulatory issues, 190
employer incentives, 194–195
PASS, 192
SSDI, 191
SSI, 190–101
subminimum wage, 193–194
volunteer work, 192–193
Graphing data, 75–80
Guiding principles, 14–18

Hagner, D., 124
Hall, J., 117
Hamre-Nietupski, S., 139
Haring, N., 40
Haring, T., 121
Hasazi, S., 174
Hayden, S., 176
Hazards, 285
Head injury, 278
Heart attack, 277
Horner, R. H., 50, 55, 124, 144
Human bites, 274
Human rights, 84
Human service programs, 2–3
Hunger, 88

Ignoring as method of behavior intervention, 93–94
Independence, 175
Individual jobs, 9–10
Industry enclaves, 10–11
Inman, D. P., 50, 55
Institute for Human Resource Development (Connecticut), 15
Instruction, 1, 6, 8, 9
Instructional Data Sheets (Forms 14–18), 241–250

Instructional Plan Forms (Forms 9–11), 229–236
Instructional strategies
antecedent changes, 48–54
consequent changes, 54–56
modification of task, 56–58
Instructors, coworkers as, 123–125
Insulin reaction, 276
Integrated work setting, 4
Integration
as characteristic of supported employment, 5
levels of, 117
Interaction with coworkers, 121–122. *See also* Coworkers/supervisors
Interval recording, 71–73
Intervention strategies, 124–125
Interviews to determine employment compatibility, 34–35
Itching, 278

Job Analysis Form (Form 23), 33, 35–36, 259–264
Job development, 171
forms, 215–224
as phase of supported employment, 8, 9
Job placement, 6, 36–38
Job retention, 32–33
Job training, 6, 8, 9. *See also* Instructional strategies
Job-sharing model, 125

Kennedy, John F., 81, 97
Kiernan, W. E., 1
Kneeling position, 156–157
Kregel, J., 175

Latency of response, 71
LaVigna, G. W., 92
Least prompting sequence, 52
Legal guardian consent, 86
Legal rights, 84
Level of intensity
activities by, 102–103
forms for, 269–272
Life cycle, family, 129, 130
Lifting physically handicapped employees, 160–163
Lowering physically handicapped employees, 163
Luckasson, R. 173
Ludlow, B. L., 173

Mank, D. M., 117, 124
Mechanical lift, 160
Medicaid benefits, 190, 191
Medical conditions, 147–149
Medical needs, 147
Medical problems, 88
Medicare coverage, 191
Medications
list of common, 150–151
supervision of, 147, 151
Menchetti, B., 124
Meyer, L. H., 166
Minimum wage, 193, 194. *See also* Wages
Mobile work crews, 10
Modeling, 51
Momentary time sampling, 72, 73
Monthly profile, 103
form for, 253–254
Mooslin, M., 189
Moseley, C. R., 20
Mount, Beth, 20

Natural cues, 61
Nausea, 278
Neck injury, 274
Nietupski, J., 139
Nisbet J., 125
Noise, 88
Nominal group process, 170
Nosebleeds, 274–275

Objectives Summary Form (Form 8), 227–228
O'Brian, J., 20, 186
Observer, coworker as, 122–123
Occupational therapists, 43
Occupational therapy goals, 154
Off-work hours contact, 102
Ongoing services, 175
Ongoing supports
agency-wide, 100
benefits and challenges of, 103–104
definition of, 100
forms for, 100, 253–254, 265–266
level of activity by intensity, 102–103
listing of, 100–101
monthly profile, 103
range of activities for, 101–102
Ongoing support services, 5
Ongoing Supports Form (Form 20), 103, 253–254
On-the-job training, 194–195
Orientation as step in career planning, 21–22
Overt support strategies, 123–125

Pacing prompts, 50
Pancsofar, E. L., 48, 59
Parental consent, 86
Partial interval recording, 72, 73
Partial physical prompts, 51
Participant Employment Screening Form (Form 4), 33, 35, 215–220
Participant observation, 36
Participation in community life, 16
PASS (Plan for Achieving Self-Support), 194

Patterson, Joe, 20
Percentage recording, 69–70
Performance Review Form (Form 21), 255–256
Performance scoring, 74
Perske, R., 105, 133, 171
Personal profile development, 22–24
Peters, T., 13
Peterson, C., 45
Physical integration, 117
Physical restraint, 84, 97
Physical therapists, 43
Physical therapy goals, 154
Physically disabled employees
  accessibility for, 164
  assistance for, 153–154
  body mechanics of, 162–163
  equipment for, 159–160
  guidelines for working with, 103–104
  positioning procedures for, 154–159
  transferring, 160–161
Physicians, 44
Pictorial prompts, 50
Pitts-Conway, V., 121
Poisoning, 279
Positioning procedures, 154–155
  guidelines, 163
  kneeling, 156–157
  prone-standing, 157–158
  sitting, 155–156
  supine-standing, 158–159
Positive programming, 82
Positive reinforcement
  as behavior intervention method, 91–92
  as consequent change procedure, 54–55
Posture, 154
Potential, 16
Powell, T. H., 186
Praise, 91–92
Principles, guiding, 14–18
Proactive planning, 31–32
Problem solving
  steps for, 166–172
  strategy for, 166
Prompts
  definition of, 49
  full physical, 51
  gestural, 50–51
  modeling, 51
  nonspecific verbal, 49–50
  pacing, 50
  partial physical, 51
  pictorial, 50
  sequences of, 51–54
  specific verbal, 50
Prone-standing position, 157–158
Protection in behavioral intervention process, 87
Provencal, G., 180, 187
Psychologists, 43–44
Public telephones, 284
Punishment. *See also* Behavior interventions
  corporal, 84
  use of, 97

Quality of life, 67
Quality of life outcomes, 24, 25

Ramps, 184
Ramsing, K. D., 116
Range of activities, 101–102
Range of Activities Form (Form 25), 101, 267, 268
Range of Options Form (Form 27), 102, 271–272
Rate recording, 69, 70
Regulatory issues. *See* Governmental/regulatory issues
Rehabilitation Act of 1973, 164
Rehabilitation Act of 1984—Amendments, 4
Reinforcement
  differential, of incompatible behavior, 92
  negative, 97
  positive, 91–92
Reinforcer, 106
Relationships, 117
  development of, 120–121
Reprimand, verbal, 96
Respect, 16
Response cost method, 96, 97
Restraint, physical, 84, 97
Restrooms, 283–284
Rhodes, L., 116
Roe, C., 174
Role release, 41–42
Rusch, F., 99, 124

Safety, employee, 152–153
School
  preparation received in, 176–178
  transition process. *See* Transition process
Schutz, R., 124
Seizures, 279
Self-esteem, 16
Shaping procedure, 57
Sheltered employment, 67
Single factor analysis, 38–39
Single Factor Analysis Form (Form 5), 221–222
Sitting positions, 155–156
Skill development, 30
Small enterprise, 10
Social integration, 117
Social networks, 117
Social Security Act, 191
Social validation strategies, 122–123
Social workers, 44
Society, benefits of supported employment for, 11

Sprains, 278
Specific verbal prompts, 50
Speech/language pathologists, 43
Splinters, 280
Sprague, J., 144
SSDI (Social Security Disability Insurance), 191
SSI (Supplemental Security Income), 190–191
Staff, training, 88
Stairs, 284
Status seizures, 279
Steps, 284
Stings, insect, 273
Stokes, T., 138
Subminimum wage, 193–194
Summative assessment, 61. *See also* Formative and summative assessment
Supervisors. *See* Coworkers/supervisors
Supine-standing position, 158–159
Support
  lack of sufficient, 88
  need for flexible, 6–7
  ongoing, 7, 9 (*see also* Ongoing supports)
Supported employment
  access to, 17
  benefits of, 133
  as a concept, 5–8
  definition of, 2, 4–5, 131
  families and, 131–133
  goals, 118
  individuals intended for, 2, 6
  persons benefited by, 11
  phases of, 8–9
Supported employment models, 9
  apprenticeships, 10
  enclaves in industry, 10–11
  individual jobs, 9–10
  mobile work crews, 10
  small enterprise, 10
Supported employment team, 41–42. *See also* Transdisciplinary team

Targeted Jobs Tax Credit (TJTC), 195
Task analysis
  explanation of, 61
  guidelines for developing, 62–64
Task analysis branching, 58
Task Analysis Form (Form 13), 239–240
Task modification procedures
  chaining, 56–57
  color coding, 57
  modifying the environment or complexity of the task, 57–58
  shaping, 57
Telephone, public, 284
Temperature, 88
Therapeutic handling, 154
Thirst, 88
Time delay prompts, 52–54
Time-limiting services, 175
Time out
  activity, 95
  contingent observation, 96
  use of, 97
Toileting, 164
Token economy, 95
Traditionally time-limited post-employment services, 5
Training-consultant model, 125
Transdisciplinary team
  description of, 41–42
  facilitating communication among members of, 45–46
  identifying, 44–45
  implementing, 42–44
Transfer of physically disabled employees, 160–161
Transitional employment for individuals with chronic mental illness, 5
Transition process
  adult services and, 178–179
  explanation of, 174–175
  individualized planning for, 178
  principles of, 175–176
  role of family in, 176
  school preparation and, 176–178
Turnbull, A. P., 129, 173
Turnbull, H. R., 129

Verbal abuse, 84
Verbal prompts, 50
Verbal reprimand, 96
Vocational assessment instruments, 31
Vocational needs
  for disabled persons, 3–4
  preparation, 177–178
Vocational rehabilitation counselors, 43
Volunteering services, 192–193
Vomiting, 278
von Oech, R., 165

Wages, 6
  apprenticeship, 10
  Department of Labor regulations regarding, 10, 11, 193
  need for fair, 17
  subminimum, 193–194
Walkways, 282–293
Warning signals, 285
Water fountains, 284
Weekly Schedule Form (Form 7), 225–226
Wehman, P. 175
Weithers, J., 124
Wheelchairs
  adapted, 156, 157
  guidelines for use of, 164
  transfer from, 162, 163
Whole interval recording, 72
Wilcox, B., 144

Will, M., 175
Work crews, mobile, 10
Worker documentation, 203
Worker Information Form (Form 1), 205–208
Worker notebook, 203–204
Worker record system, 203–204
Worker Resume Form (Form 3), 213–214
Work settings, 16
Work team support for employment specialist, 185

Zero degree inference strategy, 139